MW00882696

CROSSROADS

CONFLICTED JOURNEY OF A NEW JERSEY STATE
TROOPER

To: David
Thank you for
your support.

Dr. Brian Droydes

1/17/19

CROSSROADS

CONFLICTED JOURNEY
OF A NEW JERSEY STATE
TROOPER

DR. VINCENT LUCAS MARTIN

To order additional copies of this book, contact:
Xlibris
1-888-795-4274
www.Xlibris.com
Orders@Xlibris.com
778669

CONTENTS

Dedication vii

Acknowledgments ix

Introduction xi

Disclaimer xvii

Chapter 1   Rooted 1

Chapter 2   A Change of Scenery 10

Chapter 3   Decisions 19

Chapter 4   Perpetual Motion 27

Chapter 5   Building Blocks 35

Chapter 6   Venturing Out 43

Chapter 7   Rerouting 48

Chapter 8   What's in a Number? 53

Chapter 9   Sphere of Indoctrination 60

Chapter 10 The Weeding-Out Process 66

Chapter 11 The Culture 77

Chapter 12 On-the-Job Realities 89

Chapter 13 Model of Diversity 98

Chapter 14 Outside the Lines 110

Chapter 15 Rules Need Not Apply 116

Chapter 16 Contrasting Treatment 121

Chapter 17 Serendipity 124

Chapter 18 Getting Out of My Way 127

Chapter 19 No Boundaries 135

Chapter 20 Divergence 141

Chapter 21 Life's Realisms 148

Chapter 22 Peter Principle.. 151

Chapter 23 Heightened Alert 155

Chapter 24 Revelations 158

Chapter 25 Recycled Newcomer 162

Chapter 26 Adulterated Process...................................... 167

Chapter 27 Presumption of Compliance........................... 171

Chapter 28 The Unveiling... 177

Chapter 29 Federal Training Academy 182

Chapter 30 Now What? 188

Chapter 31 Endless Nonsense 193

Chapter 32 Deprived... 198

Chapter 33 Coalition of Dishonesty 203

Chapter 34 Fraudulent Supremacy 206

Chapter 35 Medical Awakening...................................... 214

Chapter 36 Under Siege 220

Chapter 37 Unsympathetic 226

Chapter 38 The Redeemer 230

Chapter 39 Tested Supervision 235

Chapter 40 Manipulated Outcomes 237

Chapter 41 Rendered Invisible 244

Chapter 42 Deconstructing the Hype 251

Chapter 43 Decolorized Gatekeepers...............................254

Chapter 44 Resilience..262

Chapter 45 Day of Reckoning..268

Chapter 46 The Final Judgment......................................280

Dedication

I dedicate this book to the memory of my loving family members and close friends who have made their transitions. I miss you all tremendously.

Professionally, I dedicate this book to my former colleague Bobby. Words will never express what our friendship meant to me. Rest in peace, my friend.

Acknowledgments

Seek acceptance from yourself because you matter.

Venturing into unchartered terrain is never easy, especially if you are traveling alone. I realized this truism before attempting to take on the monumental task of writing this book. However, along the way, I encountered extraordinary individuals who agreed to read several drafts of my manuscript. I made only one request: "Please do not spare my feelings." Some of their criticisms made me think about whether I had been fair in my depictions of specific situations and made me dig deeper into my subconscious for clarity. I cannot say enough about their honesty and profound thoughtful insight.

Over the course of my life, I have had the pleasure of meeting some remarkable young ladies who became my surrogate daughters. They will never know the full extent that their presence has meant to me. To my princesses Damary, Nellabella, and Babygirl—thank you for making me feel like a dad when I didn't have biological kids. To my godchildren Jakeem, Anamae, and Selena—your presence in this universe has made me a better person.

No one knows when he or she will meet people who will change their life's course. I want to thank the Spinola family and the Rusolina family for being there when a young fifteen-year-old kid needed advice and a surrogate family. There is no way I could've accomplished all that I have if it were not for all your support.

My story wouldn't have been worthy of repeating if not for my students, who have played a significant role in my intellectual development. I have had the opportunity to instruct some phenomenal critical thinkers, and collectively, we've helped one another to view life from different perspectives. Many have gone on to become law enforcement officers and military personnel, attained graduate and law degrees, or became productive citizens in their respective fields. I wish them all success in their future endeavors. I would hope that my fingerprint appears at the scene of some of their phenomenal achievements.

I would also like to thank "all" the state troopers who undertook the gargantuan task of sacrificing their careers to expose the internal wrongdoing. Moreover, for those state troopers who stood by me, you know who you are, and I thank you more than you'll ever know.

My sincerest appreciation goes to my former professors "Alfred" and "Janet" for enhancing my interest in higher education.

This book was made possible because my former criminal justice professor, "Bill," suggested that I write about my whistle-blowing experience. Although I did not appreciate it at the time, I believe that our discourse was probably the catalyst for me becoming an author.

To my immediate family, I love you all dearly. And lastly, to my partner, you have made my life complete with the addition of our children.

Introduction

Don't spend your future trying to clean up your past.

One of the most significant possessions a person can leave is a book that provides information for others to educate themselves. *Crossroads: Conflicted Journey of a New Jersey State Trooper* is a gift to my ancestors, who were forced to come to this country on the bottom of vessels, stripped of everything—and yet they still persevered. They made it possible for me to be able to tell this story. It is also for my friends, colleagues, students, and those interested in the criminal justice system.

This book recounts my trek through the streets of the City of Elkanda, New Jersey, where crime, riots, drugs, murder, police brutality, and political corruption were all commonplace.

During my youth, I endured the mental anguish of my father's verbal abuse against my mother and our ultimate abandonment. His absence caused her to look for comfort in the company of a violent second husband, who subjected my family to the despicable reality of domestic violence.

While trying to figure out how to become a young man, without any proper direction, I made many unwise decisions. My stupidity could've landed me as a likely participant in the criminal justice system if it weren't for three caring men who gave me an opportunity to work at their local pizzeria. Ultimately, it was their fatherly instruction that showed me how to be responsible and saved me from the perils of the inner-city streets, which had taken the lives of so many of my close childhood friends.

This book also details how—after struggling with what is the typical teenager confusion about future life plans—I proudly enlisted in the US Army Reserve and subsequently became a New Jersey state trooper (the latter coming at a significant mental and physical cost).

The New Jersey State Police (NJSP) is one of the premier law enforcement agencies in the United States. Unlike most police academies that try to keep as many candidates as possible, they went out of their way to get rid of those they deemed unworthy. What I observed early on was that predetermined factors played a role in retaining only a manageable number of minorities and women.

After graduating, I learned that I had joined an organization that had a history cloaked in racial and gender inequity. I tried to reconcile how they believed their exploits had been ethical. Their backstory had no moral justification, but what disturbed me more was how I quickly allowed them to enslave my persona and make me a mindless cog in their wheel.

Early on, I believed that I was a member of the "family," but my expectations vanished as I soon experienced several bouts of racial intolerance. Mistakenly, I always overlooked them because the incidents were often isolated.

As I progressed in my career, I worked in several high-profile units and completed many supervisory-level courses. I also attained what only a handful of state troopers could say they had earned: a doctorate. To put it mildly, they considered me for promotional elevation, which would seat me at the table where they made institutional and promotional decisions. As such, I took advantage of an opportunity to work with investigators in the Work Intervention Unit. I earnestly wanted to ferret out discrimination, and ostensibly, this was the unit responsible for investigating these matters. Nonetheless, my rude awakening came after six months, when I noticed many inconsistencies in how they conducted and resolved investigations.

During my assignment, I witnessed the pattern and practice of intentionally stalling investigations, which enabled highly ranked commissioned officers to retire without being disciplined, all while punishing lower-ranking members to the fullest extent. I also witnessed that discrimination—based on different sanctions meted out to African-American state troopers compared to their Caucasian counterparts—had been prevalent. I wasn't going to be risk-averse and allow this behavior to go uncontested. Consciously, I'd never cosigned these blatant violations and fall prey to the "bystander effect." Ironically, while serving in this unit, I noted numerous workplace violations.

I reported my allegations directly to those in charge. They led me to believe that they were going to weed out the rotten apples, but there wasn't a modicum of truth in any of their corresponding actions. It seemed as though corruption held a figurative gun to the heads of anyone who attempted to expose it. In due course, my persistent vocalization against their biased policies caused my career to take a precipitous plunge.

Instead of making institutional changes, they retaliated against me, transferred me, forced me to work for some of my adversaries, denied me promotions, and stripped me of supervisory duties.

After filing numerous complaints, which were routinely unsubstantiated, I reluctantly filed a civil lawsuit. I understood that going forward, I'd be treading alone by becoming an official whistle-blower, but I wasn't going to turn back and live in my fears. The world had transformed, and the mantra of "see something, say something" should've resonated. However, that same sentiment fell on deaf ears as it related to the corrupt and contemptible "trooper wall of silence."

In a matter of a few months, they had placed an irrevocable lien on my career. For me, I knew that the commissioned officer rank was like a door with no knob or lock to open—I'd never be able to join that club. I couldn't control what they did, but my whistle-blowing actions spurred the decrease in the backlog of complaints that languished in file cabinets; and for that, it was worth it.

Over the years, the wheels of justice within the New Jersey civil court system moved predictably slow. My litigation would span more than a decade. In that course of time, the country elected two presidents—one that made history and another that made a mockery of the office. Also, I welcomed the birth of my two children. Moreover, I sadly said goodbye to several close friends, colleagues, and my beloved mother.

Throughout my career, I realized that some of my minority colleagues got entangled in the web of controversy and had their false consciousness sequestered in the assimilation of their state police identity. Instead of reaching back and assisting others, some pulled up the ladder when they made it to the top. My observations weren't benign because many of them sold out to the establishment and sought acceptance over self-worth. In echoing my feelings regarding their actions, Martin Luther King Jr. said it best, "In the end, we will remember not the words of our enemies, but the silence of our friends." Even though I acknowledged their zest for upward mobility, what concerned me the most was that a group of reliably vetted minorities and female state troopers, when placed in leadership roles, exhibited immoral conduct mirroring their white male superior's cult of egotistic personalities.

After coping with occasional instances of ostracism, an autoimmune medical condition, and a few bouts of extreme unhappiness, I took inventory of who I had become. I didn't want to be the iconic figure in this fight, but I wasn't going to stand on the sidelines and complain. I had earned the right to praise and also to level the harshest criticisms against our organization because I genuinely care about its well-being.

As they ignored the metaphoric mirror that I held up to expose our problems, I questioned whether our core values were meaningful or just pointless words included in our mission statement. As such, over the latter part of my twenty-five years of employment, I conscientiously discarded the devoted lens in which I had viewed them.

What I observed in the era of promoting the fool's paradise of diversity was that a select group of state troopers expressed—in their words and actions—that minorities and women needed to know their place. Conversations about a fair promotional system had utilized too much oxygen in the equality dialogue. I could no longer bear working with men and women who pined for the old ways of doing things. Familial legacy over qualified leadership is a failed experience that has continually plagued the organization.

Our organization definitively needs transparency like human beings need air. However, I intended to help improve and leave the outfit in a better condition than it was when I enlisted in the mid-1980s. I tried my best, along with other litigants, to dismantle the structural racism and discrimination. My problem was that in the concluding years, I held our leaders to a moral standard that they would not uphold.

For those contemplating employment as a police officer, please research the particular department that you want to join. Doing so might save you from having to play the internal games (which have absolutely no rules for guidance) and help you make an informed choice on whether or not to pursue this vocation.

To my former colleagues who have not retired—if you aren't a whistleblower already, why not? The problems still exist. I implore you not to let the internal injustice go unchallenged.

For those who maintain a romanticized view of the organization, just know that there are a lot of state troopers that they targeted whose perspective could be a bit skewed. Also, some of you may have strong opinions about what I've expressed in this book. I suggest you don't judge me or levy rude comments about my character. One day, you may find yourself in a situation, and those you once considered colleagues might subject you to similar scrutiny. Moreover, the outfit that you pledged your allegiance may, in fact, abandon you as it consistently does to those who challenge them. Remember, everyone is replaceable.

Finally, here is the cautionary tale of one man who refused to be bound by the world of unethical behavior and didn't filter any of his ethical decisions through a police value system. I declared my independence from their authoritarian rule and became a crusader. Racial discrimination, sexual harassment, and disparate treatment against anyone is reprehensible and needs to end. It is my ambition that my story will become a part of the broader conversation in policing and that it helps to rebuild the squandered currency of trust.

Disclaimer

This book is based on a true story. I will share with the reader my inner city upbring to becoming a New Jersey State Trooper and ultimately a whistleblower. Along the way, I discuss some of my trials and tribulations, including being mistreated based on the American with Disabilities Act, sexual harassment and racial discrimination. More important, I outline what led me to report internal corruption and detail the subsequent retaliation that followed. After serious consideration, I reluctantly filed a civil lawsuit against several individuals, who I deemed responsible for retaliating against me. Lastly, I discuss the trial process that led to my victory in the New Jersey Supreme Court and the eventual settling of my case.

In an attempt to be fair and unbiased, I conferred with several disinterested individuals to make sure my emotions didn't distort my view of some events. Also, my infuriation needed an object to attach itself to; therefore, I strongly emphasize that my dissatisfaction is solely directed toward the particular persons depicted in this book between the years 2002 to 2011 and isn't a condemnation of all the fine men and women who wore our uniform.

The New Jersey State Police is referred to throughout this book as "the division," "the outfit," "the organization," and "the NJSP." All these terms are used interchangeably.

Chapter 1

Rooted

A nurtured beginning enhances future outcomes.

Never underestimate the resilience of a child's ability to withstand the pressures of living in an inner city. My coming of age on the mean streets of Elkanda, New Jersey, taught me some valuable lessons related to my station in life.

In 1956, at the age of nineteen, my mother departed from the South to escape country life. She settled in the City of Elkanda because her former classmates had convinced her to come live with them.

After three years of trying to find her way, she became involved in a relationship with a man and ultimately gave birth to my oldest sister, Faith. However, their romance did not last, and she became a single parent. I never asked my mother about the identity of this man because Faith is my sister—even though we don't have the same biological father.

My father, who was fifteen years older than my mom, hailed from the Deep South, which, during his time, had been a bastion of white supremacy and racial discrimination. His life had always been extremely secretive. According to my mom, she didn't question him about his early life. I believed it had something to do with their age difference. Nevertheless, she had learned that when he was sixteen years old, he changed his name, illegally increased his age to eighteen, and joined the US Army. He served two years and was honorably discharged; but after that, not much is known about what he did or how he came to live in Elkanda.

My mother worked at a local restaurant, and my father worked as a laborer at a nearby produce market. They eventually met, and he pursued her because, as she claimed, "He liked the way I looked in my uniform." I've seen pictures of my mother during this time, and I could see why he was attracted to her.

In the early 1950s and 1960s, the American-born institutional racism was rampant, and change didn't appear to be on the horizon. A large number of African-Americans traveled north as a part of the Great Migration, to get away from racial segregation and discrimination. For many, working the fields in the South lessened their prospects of upward mobility. They believed the Northern states would provide greater opportunities.

Elkanda's bustling metropolis and nightlife captivated my mother, even with the rampant political corruption that landed many of its politicians in federal prison. She spent some of her time with friends going to the renowned Apollo Theater in New York City and local clubs when she was able to find a babysitter. My father didn't approve, but he realized that she needed to experience life on her terms. After dating for less than a year, they married and started our family.

They had three children born in Elkanda's hospital: my sister Andrea; my twin brother, Kenan; and me. However, according to my mom, I wasn't expected. During her pregnancy, she thought she had only one child in her womb. The medical profession wasn't as advanced in the early 1960s, so the doctors, for whatever reason, didn't know I was in there. It wasn't until she was lying on the table giving birth to my brother that the doctors realized that I had been hiding out. I want to think that I am my mother's miracle baby.

At the time, it must've been financially overwhelming for my parents to support a family of six; but we survived. Nevertheless, monetary issues weren't the only problems they had to experience.

In 1967, with a strong reaction to white oppression and civil rights chaos, riots erupted in many inner cities around the country, and

Elkanda was no exception. The controversial events surrounding the arrest of a black cabdriver by two white Elkanda police officers made living in the city problematic. The local military and another police department were called in to assist in quieting things down.

My mother told me (years later) that during that summer, she had asked her sister to take us to our maternal grandmother's. Together with her three sons, we hopped on a bus headed back to their little Podunk town. I have no personal recollection of any of the purported mayhem, which speaks volumes about my mother's resolve to shield us from danger. While relaying this story, she never mentioned my father's whereabouts.

Throughout this time, parts of the South were still untouched by modernization. A fast-paced city environment replete with streetlights, loud noises, trash strewn in the streets, and paved sidewalks were my norm. However, large open fields, poorly constructed homes, dusty roadways, and drinking liquids out of mason jars became new thrills for me. Also, back then, many Southern dwellings still had outhouses and no running water. I didn't have a clue what an outhouse was until that summer. Reality set in when I asked about the location of the bathroom, and my grandmother pointed to an old flimsy shed outside.

Curiosity set in as I walked toward the old rickety wooden structure. As I opened the door, the squeaking hinges sent a chill down my spine, and I prayed it wouldn't collapse. There was no light to turn on, just a glimmer of the sunset that seeped through a large crevice. Buzzing flies, a lingering stench of poop, and sweltering heat shortened my stay. I held my breath, did my business in the white steel pot, and I was out of there. While this had been my least favorite memory, other things left a favorable impression upon me.

My grandmother's cooking stood out as one of my most unforgettable experiences. Her selection of foods included grits, molasses, fried apples, angel biscuits, homemade preserves, and a heavenly tasting pound cake that always kept me coming back for more. The smell of her kitchen made my mouth water.

Country life was a learning experience, but it had also been challenging. My cousins and I often played made-up games outside in the front yard to occupy our time. We stood toward the end of my grandma's gravel driveway and threw rocks into the densely populated bushes and thickets. Danger accompanied this adventure because of the ever-present unfriendly snakes, bugs, and animals.

The calmness of the South made trying to decipher the chorus of sounds emanating from the woods fun. We could tell when one of us had come upon something because we'd hightail it out screaming for our lives. By our actions, I am sure the vermin were more afraid of us than we were of them.

The family's several acres of land served as a bonding place for all my cousins. There were times when we'd lie out on the grass at night, counting stars and telling stories. Although I knew nothing about astronomy, I formed several imaginary figures by connecting the bright speckles. Most evenings were spent sitting on the front porch listening to my grandmother talk about our family's history. I sat spellbound and saddened as she told stories about the South.

My grandmother had cleaned homes for white families since the early 1940s and reared their kids. She also recounted her experiences living under and surviving the homegrown terrorism of Jim Crow laws, which legitimized racial segregation in the South. It depressed me knowing my family had lived through segregation, but they never used it as a crutch. On one occasion, she said that some white kids, while riding on an all-white school bus, maliciously chanted to my mother and her schoolmates, "Nigger, nigger, black as tar, stick your head in a jelly jar," as they rode by laughing. Some years later, I asked my mother about the teasing, and she confirmed it; but she said she didn't let it bother her because they were just kids. I think this was her way of teaching me to have thick skin.

The tales that my grandmother shared transferred our family history to another generation. It was priceless! My family's beautiful piece of property served as the centerpiece for our bonding; but through all the storytelling, there had been no mention of my maternal grandfather.

It wasn't until decades later that I met him and learned that he was a World War II veteran and a retired school principal with a master's degree. But I needed to know more and had so many questions to ask him about his life. The most pressing question would've been "Where have you been?" However, I never asked because I didn't know him, but I wished that he'd played a bigger role in my mom's life; all little girls need their daddy. My mother was fortunate that they had reconnected because he passed away several years later.

We eventually returned to Elkanda at the end of the summer. Although the street violence and destruction of property due to allegations of police brutality had subsided, I was not prepared for what new challenges awaited me.

Not long afterward, I started to see a change in my parents. They argued relentlessly, and in a year, my father's presence at home slowly decreased. I was five years old, but I can still visualize the last day I spoke to him.

It was early in the morning, and my father's loud voice had awakened everyone. He stood more than six feet tall and always seemed like a gentle giant to me, so I couldn't explain his behavior. He picked up my brother and me and sat us on the kitchen table. My feet dangled off the edge while I stared into his eyes. As he spoke, I heard my mother crying in another room. I thought, *Daddies aren't supposed to make mommies cry.* He then grabbed and pulled us closer to him. The scruff of his beard against my face gave me a false sense of security.

The conversation lasted for about fifteen minutes, but it seemed never-ending. My father said they were having problems, and he would no longer be around. I thought our relationship was special.

My brother and I are fraternal twins. We are both Geminis and were born on the third Sunday in June—which, in 1966, President Lyndon B. Johnson officially recognized, in a presidential proclamation, as Father's Day. He hit the trifecta and treated us like his pride and joy, so why was he leaving? Also, what I couldn't grasp was how two people who argued and physically fought still claimed they loved each other. I can't measure the total effect that his departure had on my life, but when I got older, my mother explained to me why their union had ended.

He faked her signature on bank checks and had stolen her money. She told me that this was a part of his controlling personality, which made her life unbearable. She also said that my father was semi-illiterate. I suspected that this might've caused him to have low self-esteem and become violent. Regardless, I find his actions unforgivable because a real man wouldn't do this to his children. I resent him for treating her poorly and not being there to teach my brother and me about manhood. I wished he could've shared his experiences about the segregated South and guided me in navigating a society that, I later learned, still had problems divorcing itself from its past.

Many families grow up without fathers, therefore leaving mothers to take on the role of fathers as well. I give my mom credit for being responsible and providing for us.

There is nothing like the love of a doting mother, and mine always made me feel truly special. I didn't know how she was able to share that much affection with her four children, given the stress she lived through with my father. Still and all, she moved on with her life and did the best she could.

In later years, my mother said that my father's desertion left us in a financial bind because her salary didn't suffice. For less than a year, she had accepted a Welfare benefit but wasn't proud of it. The fact that we had received public assistance is the reason why I now have empathy and a greater sense of understanding of those struggling to survive.

Like most youngsters, I enjoyed having fun during the summer and often spent time with my brother and three cousins. We played in the neighborhood or went to the community Boys and Girls Club. On numerous occasions, I came home with scarred knees or a bloody busted lip from playing too rough. I ran home crying to my mother, and within minutes, she had kissed away the hurt and sent me on my way. Since there were five of us, we consistently found ways of getting into trouble. My cousins, too, were fatherless, so our bonding helped diminish thoughts of being abandoned. Most of the kids in the neighborhood didn't live with their fathers either, so we weren't alone. Nonetheless, my dad's departure contributed to some of my poor decisions as a six-year-old.

One summer's day, a group of kids asked me to go to the sweet cake factory located not too far from my home. Although I knew they were going to be doing something wrong, I agreed. We ran a few blocks and were there in a matter of minutes, but the steel doors were locked. A few kids stood around while an older boy broke the cheaply designed front latch, which allowed our entry.

Once inside, the factory looked like it could span a city block, and the ceilings appeared butted up against the sky. A well-functioning air-conditioning system chilled me as I walked around and gawked at all the goodies. The smell of pure sugar permeated the air, and all those damn sweets called out to me.

I tore open boxes and placed as many wrapped coffee cakes and apple pies that I could fit in my T-shirt. It was wrong, but I was caught up in the moment. Afterward, I sprinted home while darting past several friends, who had quizzical expressions on their faces. When I got in the house, I made sure that my mom wasn't home and then stashed the goods in my bedroom dresser drawers and returned. Along the way, I wanted to stop and brag to my friends, but I was too excited to slow down. I made three return trips before quitting.

When I got back to our bedroom, my brother had seen all the pastries and asked, "Where did you get all this stuff?" I didn't want him to know that I had been stealing, so I told him, "A friend gave them to me." He wanted to know the name of the friend, but I immediately interjected, "Don't say anything to anyone, and I will share them with you." His eyes lit up when he realized that he, too, would be partaking in the sweets.

We hid boxes everywhere I thought my mother wouldn't find them. In the coming weeks, collectively, we probably put on about ten pounds. I couldn't have imagined that I would be a juvenile delinquent at such a young age, but the thrill of doing something illegal was overwhelming. Fortunately, I was never caught.

During the summer months, the heat in our house had been oppressive. I am unsure if home air conditioners were around back then; but even if they were, we probably couldn't afford it. Late one evening, I cried to my mother to keep my windows open because I couldn't sleep. My bedsheets were soaked with sweat, and a cool breeze was what I needed.

Several hours later, I thought I was dreaming when a dark silhouette of a man appeared at my window. "Who the heck is this guy?" I pondered. I sat up in my bed, wiped my eyes, and stared as he climbed in, walked past me, and headed toward the front room where my mother slept. He must've seen me, but I didn't think much of it because, again, I thought it was a dream. I figured he would go to the refrigerator and get a cold glass of water because he too was hot. A few minutes later, I heard a bloodcurdling scream coming from the front room.

The moonlit-illuminated room allowed me to see what was happening. I watched as a man ran past me and jumped out of the window. I should've tripped him. My mother then ran in and slammed it shut. I hurried to her, thrust my arms around her waist, and squeezed tightly. I then asked, "What happened, Ma?" She was breathing heavily, but the expression on her face had been more of a concerned parent making sure her babies were safe than someone who was afraid.

She said the man placed a knife to her neck and attempted to rape her. She also stated that he tried to steal her pocketbook, but she fought back. At that moment, my mom's status was elevated to "Superwoman." While my father was no longer around, the security of our home remained. After that, I got used to the heat and never again asked for the window to be opened.

My mother has always been an exceptionally caring woman. I observed her kindness when she interacted with people and often wondered why my father had taken advantage of her. I want to think that some of the character qualities I have today I learned from her. I also wondered what traits I would've gleaned from my father if he had decided to stay. I needed for him to tell me the story about his side of the family, to share with future generations. He factored into giving me life; but other than that, I got nothing from him. Sorrowfully, there will always be many unanswered questions.

My parents eventually divorced, and Mom began dating a new man. What a big mistake! He subsequently moved into our home shortly after the near-rape incident.

As crime got worse, I assumed my mom had had enough. She packed up our belongings, and we moved to the historic section of

Elkanda, a primarily white middle-class and Jewish neighborhood. She said the new home was going to be in a safer area—which, before the Elkanda riots, didn't allow African-Americans. As a seven-year-old, I didn't know what that meant, but I looked forward to my new surroundings.

Chapter 2

A Change of Scenery

Believing in yourself accentuates your virtue.

The new neighborhood was lined with tall trees and well-maintained grassy center islands. Each home had a long extended driveway, which could accommodate three or four cars. We were living the lives of the Jeffersons, characters from a television sitcom that aired in the mid-1970s. The show was about a black family that moved out of the ghetto to the Upper East Side of New York. However, this time, it was the Martins, and we had moved to a more beautiful section of Elkanda.

Our new house, while not turnkey, had an unfinished basement, fireplace, attic, three bedrooms, three bathrooms, a decent front lawn, a two-car garage, and a sizeable backyard with a beautiful cherry tree.

The neighbors seemed pleasant, and for the first time in my life, we lived near white people. Watching their children playing in the streets made me wonder if we played the same games. However, in no time, that mystique was removed, and I played with most of the kids on the block. I couldn't understand how we could afford this new home, but my mother realized the importance of our family growing up in a diverse community.

After a month of being settled, my siblings and I prepared to attend the local elementary school. As I entered the classroom for the first time, I sensed the eyes of my classmates piercing through me as they critiqued my every move. Even though I was outgoing, I stayed reserved until they got to know me. I soon learned that this new neighborhood had different challenges.

From my earliest recollection, I fought with the resident bullies to protect my family's name. One day, while playing outside our house, I saw two boys walking up the street. I suspected we were about the same age, but they were a little taller and bigger. My imaginary danger antennas were on high alert because they looked mean as they approached me. I sensed something was going to happen when one of them asked me, "Do you think you're a tough guy?" My heart started to beat a little faster as I prepared to stand my ground. One of the kids bumped into me, and we faced off. He then brutishly asked me, "What the hell are you looking at?" I quickly responded, "You!" Talking back wasn't the smartest thing, but I planted my feet and readied myself, just in case they decided to hit me.

We began pushing each other to see who was going to be the area's alpha male. I wasn't going to back down, but when he punched me in my chest, I lost my breath instantly. I gasped for air and took a step backward to gather myself. They laughed at me as I clutched my chest, but I didn't allow their enjoyment to last. When I saw him smile, I quickly punched him back. I then grabbed him, and we tussled each other to the ground. After a minute or so of wrestling, we got to our feet, breathing heavily. We looked at each other, and for some odd reason, we knew the fight was over. Strangely enough, the three of us then stood around talking as if there was a newfound respect for one another. I survived the first fight, but there were more to come.

My brother (who was several inches shorter than me at the time) often got into physical confrontations because of his propensity to speak his mind. One afternoon, I had a terrible headache and was lying down on my bed when I heard him crying as he ran up the stairs and into our bedroom. I was about to tell him to shut up when he told me whom he had just fought. As I sat up in my bed, I looked out the window and saw several kids muddling about in the street. It was a sunny day, and I thought they were playing, but little did I know that they had followed him home. I intently put on my sneakers and quickly ran downstairs.

Once outside, I had expected to see the tough guy in the group, but everyone yelled, "He's down the street!" I then knew it was my archrival. Even though we were friends, we had had two previous fights. The first one I won; but in the last one, he gave me a black eye that took about two weeks to heal. I can still feel his knees pinning my arms down while he pounded my face. The embarrassment of having to go to school and showing my bruised face pissed me off. I didn't need any other motivation; I wanted to get his ass back. I took off running, followed by a cheering crowd.

I found him in the alleyway of an apartment building. From the startled look on his face, I could tell he was not expecting me. He was physically bigger, but I owed him an ass-kicking.

"Yo, what did you do to my brother?" I yelled.

"Fuck you and him," he replied.

"Why did you have to hit him?" I angrily asked.

"He keeps running his damn mouth," he responded.

I then ran straight at him and punched him in his face. He stumbled backward slightly and returned the favor. We swung wildly at each other; some punches landed while most missed. I then resorted to kicking him. My days of watching Bruce Lee karate movies paid off. He attempted to kick me, but he lost his balance and fell to the ground— just like I had done when we last fought. Payback is a bitch. I then stomped on his chest and arms. Unexpectedly, an unknown adult came from inside the building and screamed, "Get the hell out of here!"

I still wanted to fight and angrily told him, "Let's finish this out front!"

I guess he had had enough, and he ran inside while the group of cheering spectators continually yelled my name, "Vincent! Vincent! Vincent!" I didn't receive any bruises to my face, so I didn't have to explain anything to my mother about why I was fighting—again.

As with many kids, juvenile delinquency is just a part of finding your way. I tried to stay out of trouble, but some of my friends had a tendency to cut class; and because I wanted to be cool like them, I played hooky too.

We'd often meet older kids down by the train tracks in Eeway Park. The park had a seedy history of dead bodies floating in its lake. Regardless, I enjoyed playing there because I liked digging up harmless garter snakes.

One day, the older kids claimed that the trains contained radios and televisions, which we could steal. I wasn't afraid of being caught because I had been down this road before. My friend pried opened the train doors, and we climbed into the cabin and ripped several boxes open, but there were only kitchen appliances and other useless items. Suddenly, a voice screamed out, "Run! The cops are coming!"

I jumped out of the train and immediately spotted two Conrail police officers running toward us. I then darted up the hill and ran to an apartment building down the street from my house, where I rejoined my friends. They were laughing, but I knew that I had almost gotten into trouble again. I wanted nothing else to do with stealing and decided to find new friends because if I continued on this path, before long, I would've probably been locked up in a juvenile facility. My fear wasn't of going to jail—instead, it was the reality of having to deal with my mother. She was no joke when it came to discipline. Her methods of whupping ass were passed down from previous generations. I guess it is a Southern thing. However, she improved the art form and graduated to having a black belt, literally and figuratively.

The lashings from the leather belt, extension cord, and plastic orange Hot Wheels racing track still resonate in my memories. Of course, you'd never talk back to her because you'd run the risk of getting popped in the mouth. In later years, I guess my behavior got out of hand, and she broke a broomstick handle across my back. Damn, it stung like hell! After she had hit me, I looked at her, and for some odd reason, tears streamed down her face. I asked, "Why are you crying? I'm the one who got hit." She said, "I feel like I am losing control of you."

I couldn't stand myself for hurting her feelings. I knew that she did everything in her power to keep me from going astray, even enrolling my brother and me in the Boy Scouts to keep us out of trouble. Looking back, today her actions might be considered child abuse. But then again, she was raised in the South, and this type of discipline was the norm. It may not have been right, but it was right for me. I learned many lessons, and I sincerely thank her for turning me into the man I am today.

Over the coming years, I noticed many different things about my neighborhood. My reclusive Jewish neighbors—with their dark suits, little black hats, and dangling curly hair—walked up the street to their synagogue. They were different than the other white people, so as a young boy, I didn't consider them white. They didn't speak much, but it was fascinating to watch them. I wanted to learn more, but I couldn't get them to talk to me. Their little kids always appeared to be deep in thought and intent on getting to their place of worship. However, in the blink of an eye, they soon vanished. Our shared living arrangements were a positive experience, and they should've cherished the diversity. Their mass exodus allowed other African-American families to upgrade their status and also move into a better section.

My working-class Irish and Italian neighbors also disappeared. Their departure affected me the most because I was sad to see my friends taken away. Back then, I didn't know what "white flight" meant. However, it became apparent that race played a distinct role in their decision to leave because they were all gone.

My mother told me that in the early 1960s, black people weren't allowed to live in our neighborhood. This historic section—which housed synagogues, Jewish restaurants, and a sprinkling of white ethnics—had come to an end. The abundance of city resources afforded to my former neighbors had also ceased.

As the face of the community changed, a new family had moved onto the block. They were a married couple with three boys and twin girls, which meant more play friends.

On the surface, they looked like average people; however, they were Muslims and members of the Nation of Islam. Initially, none of this meant anything; but after immersing myself in their customs, I understood our differences.

Their presence in the community had been particularly influential to many of my friends. I couldn't explain the impact that they had on me. They had unfamiliar names, which made them unique, unlike the all-too-common names that most black people inherited over the years.

I wanted to be like them so much that I considered changing my name to Basil. I have no recollection of why I chose that name, nor did I know the name's derivation; but it was different.

In time, my brother and I were invited to attend their place of worship—the mosque. The Muslim prayer ceremony differed from what I had experienced in my family's Baptist faith. There were no people yelling, screaming, and catching the "Holy Ghost." As a child, it was uncomfortable watching smartly dressed women act possessed while running up and down the aisles, but I eventually came to understand what religion meant to them and was glad they had their faith to get them through the rough times. We went to church on special occasions, but my mother didn't force religion on us.

Conversely, in the mosque, I witnessed a more deliberate and ritualistic style of worship. Everyone appeared intent on receiving the word from the spiritual leader, the Imam. Years later, I recognized the benefits of this religion, particularly in providing discipline to wayward males needing to turn their lives around. The only downside was their strict adherence to not eating pork. My mother didn't conform to this rigid belief system. She allowed us to attend the mosque, but we ate all of her cooking—including the pork. My exposure to different cultures and religions at an early age opened my eyes to diverse lifestyles.

My new friends and I enjoyed spending time together. We played baseball, basketball, and football and often rounded up potential rivals for games. The thought of going to the park never dawned on us; it was easier to play in the streets. Our neighbors constantly warned against it because they were fearful that we'd cause damage to their homes. As snot-nosed little boys, we ignored their pleas, and the inevitable occurred. I can't recount the number of times we scattered like roaches when someone turned on a light because a baseball smashed through a window. They knew we did it, but we weren't asked to pay for any damages. Even if they did, I knew we couldn't pay for our mischief, which made it even worse.

As a young male reared on the streets of Elkanda, I knew my actions had the potential to affect my family financially. We didn't have the luxury of having inherited wealth. Everyone struggled, so I needed to find a hustle.

My mother couldn't afford to give us money, but I wasn't upset. I remembered her working long hours at a psychiatric hospital, as a nursing assistant caring for mentally ill patients. I didn't understand what she did because she never spoke about her work. On two separate occasions, however, she brought home two little white women—Connie and then Mary—to stay with our family. They had been released from the mental facility and had no one to look after them.

They were noticeably quirky when they didn't take their medications. Connie was the more outgoing of the two. She had a little plastic contraption that allowed her to roll cigarettes. I thought it was cool, and I begged her to let me try it. After a while, I rolled all of her "fags" (as she called them).

Mary, on the other hand, was frail and always talked to herself. When I engaged her in conversation, she acted normal, which baffled me. I thought she was messing with my head. I didn't understand the depth of their mental health illness, but I learned to accept it.

Although money was tight for the time (almost a year) that they stayed with us, we treated them like family. As a result of our financial status, I, unbeknownst to my mom, became an errand boy for a few of my neighbors. I went to the store, cleaned up yards, and did anything else that they needed. Most of the people I worked for were normal, but there were a few strange characters as well.

A middle-aged female client, on several occasions, paraded around her apartment with her massive breasts exposed. I didn't know what to make of her behavior, but I was too young to be excited by this. I guessed she was just a free spirit or didn't care who saw them.

The same woman asked me to purchase a box of sanitary napkins. Thinking that this was an easy request, I ran to the store and kindly told the attendant, "I need a package of napkins." He asked, "Any particular brand?" I said, "Not really. I'll take the light-blue ones." I paid for them and ran back.

I rang her buzzer, and when she opened the door, I proudly handed her the brown paper bag. She looked inside and started laughing uncontrollably. I stood there wondering, "Did I do something wrong?" After she composed herself, she kindly explained that she wanted a package of Kotex. I asked, "What is that?" She walked into her bathroom and returned with a sample. I blushed and said, "Oh! I know what they are, but I didn't know what they were called."

I quickly ran back to the store and returned them. I embarrassingly told the attendant that I had bought the wrong item. He smiled pleasantly and took the bag. He then replaced the napkins with the sanitary things. Note to self: next time, ask questions.

My reputation for being reliable spread, and my client base grew. I was well-mannered and had been available whenever they needed my services. However, during this time, one person had an irreparable impact on my life.

Sandy was new to the neighborhood; she had moved into one of the nearby apartment buildings. She became friendly with many of the tenants that I had worked for running errands. She spoke to me often and, from first impressions, seemed like a nice person. On a few occasions, she asked me to go to the store and buy her some groceries.

One fateful day, she told me to run to the store and pick up a newspaper. As I stood outside her front door listening to her request, I didn't give a second thought as to any unfavorable behavior on her part. Within a few minutes, I returned to her apartment, and she asked me to come in so that she could pay me. I stepped inside, and she quickly closed the door behind me.

A few moments passed, and when she returned, I noticed her waving two dollars in her hand, which was more than she had ever paid me before. It seemed odd because the paper only cost a quarter. Suddenly, I recognized that she had huge hands and a lot of facial hair for a woman. I had never been that close to her, so her appearance petrified me.

As I stood in front of her, something didn't seem right. I was backed up against the door with nowhere to go. Like a calculating predator, she walked toward me, extended her massive hands, and slowly pulled my zipper down. I wanted it to be a bad nightmare, but she didn't go away. She then forced her right hand into my pants, pulled down my underwear, and fondled my penis. My heart thumped around in my chest as I had just finished running a one-hundred-yard dash, but I literally couldn't move. Shocked and petrified, I thought that I was going to pass out and die. I was eleven years old.

After a minute or so of her fondling me, she zipped my pants up and calmly handed me the money. I stood there motionlessly, hoping and praying that she wasn't going to kill me. Before allowing me to leave, she menacingly said, "Don't say anything to anyone!" The stern look on her face and piercing eyes relayed she wasn't joking. I emphatically reassured her that I would keep my mouth shut.

I left her apartment, relieved to be alive. I ran up the street to our house, quickly went to my bedroom, and closed the door. It took me a while to calm down and catch my breath. With my mind still reeling, I wondered if a lot of women liked touching a little boy's penis.

Some days later, my friends informed me that Sandy was a man. After thinking about it for a while, it began to make sense. When I first met him, I thought he was butt-ugly for a woman. His awkwardly fitting wig, razor-stubble face covered in mounds of makeup, and disheveled clothes should've raised warning flags; but I was just a kid. Undoubtedly, he had groomed me before he took advantage of me. I didn't tell anyone about what he had done because I knew that I would've been the laughingstock of the block.

After decades of being abandoned, the dilapidated old building where he molested me had been given a face-lift and converted to luxury condominiums. On certain days when I drove by it, a queasy sensation engulfed my stomach.

Molestation is a silent plague that arrests the soul and innocence of its victims. Although I kept my secret for more than thirty-plus years, I neither blamed myself nor needed anyone's sympathy because it was a one-off. I just hoped that I was his only victim. I have forgiven Sandy or whatever his real name is, but I've often wondered, "Why me?"

Chapter 3

Decisions

Personal problems do not exempt inexcusable actions.

Like many kids have to experience in their lives, my friends often teased my brother and me for wearing knockoff designer clothes and footwear. We always had the essentials, but I wanted Converse sneakers and Swedish Knit buckle pants. Even so, my mother did her best to accommodate us. She traveled to a popular flea market in Central Jersey and bought everything in bulk. I didn't just get one pair of knockoff pants—I got five, one for each day of the school week. She bought what she could afford because prices for items at the flea market were reasonable. Her efforts to shield us were commendable, but I had to do something to be able to dress more fashionably.

My friend told me that his parents needed kids to work as office custodians. I figured a real job would occupy my time, and I could make some money. My mother gave me permission, and they hired me.

I worked hard at wiping off desks, cabinets, and vacuuming floors. We cleaned four buildings in an office complex and typically finished within two hours. I can't remember how much they paid me, but the job kept me out of trouble. However, a few months later, they lost their contract, and I became unemployed again. I didn't want to surrender to idleness. I needed another job, but who would hire a thirteen-year-old kid?

My mother suggested that I work weekends at a family member's car wash located in an adjoining city. It had been the winter season, and the temperatures dipped below the freezing level, but the prospect of getting another job excited me.

On Friday evenings, I took a bus downtown and then hopped on a path train, which was home to many homeless people who lined the exterior walls with their makeshift sleeping materials. I didn't know how society could condone people not having a regular place to live. They looked lost and in need of assistance, but I was just a kid with no money or means to help them.

Traveling on my own, I'd often have silly conversations with myself about my coolness. As I rode in the musty-smelling and overcrowded path train, I watched various people going about their daily lives. I was intrigued by the speed at which the train moved underground and fascinated by the colorful graffiti sprawled on the train's interior compartments. Nevertheless, what I most appreciated was the casual interactions of other passengers. I tried reading their lips because I wondered if they also thought they were cool. I couldn't wait to make this a part of my routine.

During the first couple of weeks, I learned a lot about the car-washing process. At times, the work was fast-paced and exhausting. I washed cars by hand because they couldn't afford to modernize their business. I filled sizeable recycled Spackle buckets with soap powder and hot water until the lather overflowed. The cars pulled into the boomerang-shaped building, where we washed them with oversize yellow sponges. Once we rinsed them off, they were parked on the sidewalk and dried by the outside workers, who braved the freezing temperatures.

I thought they would've had a dryer for the towels we used, but a white open-top washing machine with an attached electrical wringer served in its place. The contraption should've been in a museum because it was so old. Concrete walls gave the building an unfriendly appearance, and consistent dampness produced a stale smell; but it was family-owned, and I soon became hugely fond of it.

The cold weather didn't make my job any easier, but I wasn't deterred and worked hard to prove that I was capable of handling myself. I became well versed in my chores and eventually graduated to drying cars.

When the business slowed down, we gravitated toward the back, where an old gray steel barrel served as a wood-burning stove that briefly defrosted our frozen bones.

We made a lot of money because customers wanted to get rid of the road salt on their vehicles. They frequently left a nice tip if we did an excellent job. On a good weekend, I earned about fifty dollars. I was rich! Having money relieved some of the financial stress on my mom. I bought my school clothes and saved as much as I could. I believe this set the stage for me learning to be a responsible person. My mother never asked me for a dime, but I wasn't comfortable making that much money, so I always gave her half.

In the middle of the week, my brother and I spent time with our friends; and as always, there were numerous opportunities to get into trouble. My mother worked evenings. Her new boyfriend—whom she later, unfortunately, married—was never around, and my sisters did their own thing. The only rule that all of us had was to be home before the streetlights came on.

One Friday evening, my friends brought over a bottle of Seagram's Seven whiskey. I had no idea where they got it. While sitting in my living room debating about what to do with it, we decided the person who drank the most was the toughest. Oh, what a big mistake! Of course, like macho juveniles, we all took the challenge and passed the bottle around. When they handed it to me, I looked at the light-brown liquid and said, "Bottoms up!" The nasty taste burned my throat, and after a few seconds, I passed it to my brother. After about twenty minutes, my slurred speech was a clear sign that I was wasted. Before long, four drunken teenage boys sat on the floor laughing hysterically about stuff that wasn't even funny.

An hour or so later, my friends staggered out the front door and went home. My brother and I dragged our stumbling butts upstairs and collapsed on our respective beds. We tried to have a simple conversation, but it soon turned to laughing and hearing who could fart the loudest. I had forgotten about catching the path train the next morning.

My mother came home from work that evening and found the empty bottle on the living room floor. I can only imagine what she must've thought; but within moments, she barged into our room and yelled at us. I couldn't make out a damn word she said, but it was evident that I had to get up soon and go to work.

Six o'clock in the morning came, and my mother's shouting and loud knocking startled me. "Get up and get your ass ready for work!" I stumbled to my feet, and the room started to spin. Fortunately for my brother, he hadn't been hired at the car wash, and he rolled over and went back to sleep. Lucky bastard.

I went to the bathroom and washed my face with cold water. I glanced in the mirror and noted that my eyes were bloodshot. I also had a disgusting aftertaste in my mouth and a throbbing headache. I went to my mother's room to plead my case. "Ma, please, I don't feel well. Can I stay home?" She didn't want to hear it and screamed, "You shouldn't have been drinking!" She then raised her hand as if to pop me upside my noggin, but I ran away.

Several minutes later, I knew that I just had to deal with being hungover and tough it out. I got dressed, and we were out the door. She drove me to make sure that I made it on time. I tried to catch a little shut-eye in the back seat, but she intentionally kept talking and annoyed the heck out of me.

This particular day, I was scheduled to dry cars. I thought it would help because I'd be outside in the brisk air. A few of the workers commented, "You look like shit," which was followed by happy laughter. I had a few choice words for them, but I didn't have the energy to defend myself, so I let it be.

After about an hour, someone recommended that I eat something to combat the hangover. My head was still pounding, and I didn't think food would hurt, so I agreed. I ate eggs, sausages, grits, and toast. It went down well; and after burping on a few occasions and smelling a disgusting mixture of eggs and alcohol emanating from my breath, I eventually returned to my duties.

I hopped into a light-blue Cadillac that belonged to the lead singer of a famous R&B group, whose soulful music probably increased the American population beginning in the early 1960s. He was a frequent customer and was known for leaving a good tip. I wiped down the car's interior and was in the process of vacuuming when a grumbling in the pit of my belly, followed by an uncontrollable urge to spew, told me to get out fast. As I placed my foot on the ground to step out of the car, I violently gagged and threw up everything that was in my stomach. My throat was on fire! The stinking puke had steam coming off it as it simmered on the sidewalk. I looked to see if my intestines needed to be doused with a water hose. I kept my head down because my eyes were watery, and I had a glob of snot running down my upper lip. I took a dirty towel and wiped my face before I glanced up and observed a relieved look on the owner's face. I dodged a bullet that time.

After a year of working at the car wash, my uncle had given me the responsibility of collecting money. I was fourteen years old and well-liked by many of the workers; however, there was a level of envy among some of them. While they never expressed any problems with me, I knew a few believed I didn't deserve to be promoted.

Periodically, I brought cash into the office and kept just enough to give customers their change. On one occasion, just before dropping off some money, I walked into the bathroom and attempted to close the door behind me, but the lock was broken. As I stood relieving myself, I eerily sensed someone standing behind me. I turned my head slightly and suddenly felt a sharp object around my throat. A man's baritone voice then whispered, "Don't fucking move!" My urine flow immediately ceased as I stood there dazed while he dug into my front pocket, snatched the money, and ran out. I should've peed on his hand. The door slammed against its frame and caused me to snap out of my state of shock.

No longer needing to relieve myself, I nervously fastened my pants and stepped outside the bathroom. The robbery had taken all of thirty seconds. I asked some of my coworkers if they saw who had robbed me, and everyone said no. From their deceitful expressions, I knew that I had been set up. I then ran inside, and as I attempted to tell my uncle what had happened, my body trembled uncontrollably.

I stayed at the car wash for a few more months as I looked for another job. I didn't want to be robbed again because the violence unsettled me. More importantly, I wanted to be closer to my mom because there had been a lot of drama going on at home.

During this time, her second husband had been physically and verbally abusing my family. He'd often yell at all of us, and on several occasions, he would hit my mother in her face. He would also beat my sisters who came to my mom's defense. His actions were more violent than what I could remember about my father. I made a conscious decision never to view him as a role model because he didn't deserve it.

Over the years that he tormented us, not once did I say anything disrespectful. My mother taught us to be respectful of all adults. More importantly, I didn't want to upset him and have my mom be the recipient of his brutality. Her occasional busted lip and black eyes always reminded me that he was a volatile person. It only fueled my anger and disgust toward him.

One day, while he and I were home alone, he asked me to get a shovel from the garage. I guess I didn't move quickly enough because when he came downstairs and didn't see it in my hand, he became noticeably infuriated.

He yelled, "Didn't I tell you to get me a shovel!" His body language was awkward, and he had a scowl on his face. I responded, "I was about to go get it." He then walked toward me with a closed fist and punched me in my jaw. What the hell! I was just a kid. There were no stars or blacking out, so I knew I had survived. I didn't know what to say, but I didn't want to give him the benefit of seeing me cry, so I just stood there. When another punch didn't come, I went and retrieved that damn shovel. Afterward, I ran to my room and closed the door.

The left side of my face throbbed and swelled slightly. I thought my jaw was fractured. I didn't go back downstairs to put ice on it because I didn't know if he'd hit me again. I didn't tell my mother what he did. However, right then, I knew I would fight back when I got older.

On another occasion, a year or so later, my mom and I had stayed overnight at my uncle's home. The next morning, we stopped at a grocery store before returning home. We pulled into the driveway, and I grabbed the bags out of the trunk of the car. I walked toward the front door with the bags in my hands as she trailed behind. I waited in the hallway for her to bring the key when, unexpectedly, her second husband snatched open the door and stood in front of me, breathing heavily like a wild animal. What the heck was his problem? My mother stood behind me as they exchanged a few heated words. I guess she didn't tell him why we had stayed out.

At that moment, everything happened in slow motion. As I tried to walk into the house, he swung at her. Instinctively, I dropped the bags and grabbed him under his arms, and the force of my moving body caused us to fall backward. The next thing I heard was a loud thump as the back of his head hit a metal corner of the living room table. A physical confrontation was what I had been waiting for, and adrenaline was my backup.

He was about 6'2" tall and weighed about 240 lbs. I was about 5'9" tall and weighed about 160 lbs. I knew I couldn't physically match his strength; however, he needed to know that from this day on, it was only going to get worse for him, and I would never back down.

Just as I struggled to get up, warm blood oozed out of the back of his head and ran down the side of his neck onto my hands. Having his fluids on my skin disgusted me.

We wrestled until he positioned himself on top of me, and he was about to punch me when I heard a resounding thud. My mother then yelled, "Get off my damn son!" I looked up and witnessed her hitting him on the back of his head with a baseball bat. I forgot she played sports as a teenager.

She struck him several times, and he eventually rolled off me and ran to the bathroom. The jackass deserved it. I wasn't hurt, just jolted from what had happened.

My siblings ran downstairs to investigate the commotion. The splattering of blood puddles on the floor shocked my sister Faith as she gasped and then ran to check on my mother. For whatever reason, his punk ass didn't seek medical attention. I gathered that if he did, an official report might've been filled out, and the police would've eventually shown up, and he'd go to jail. I knew that I couldn't allow him to continue with his brutality. He no longer frightened me.

Growing up, I routinely lifted weights. I became extremely muscular and grew a few more inches. I eagerly awaited any future confrontation because I wanted to hurt him in the worst way. However, he had also observed how much I had grown and never again attempted to hit, yell at, or menace any one of us again.

Victims of domestic violence carry mental scars well past the mended bruises. It isn't easy trying to erase the horrible memories of my mother getting beaten by him; however, I believe that coming to terms with my past was part of the healing process. Still, in all, there's no doubt that today, my intense dislike of bullies stems from his punkish actions.

Chapter 4

Perpetual Motion

Let your actions be a prelude to the road of success.

In the latter part of December 1979, by chance, I walked into Italian Pizzeria—which was located on a busy street corner a short distance from my home—and politely asked the owner, Sal, for a job. He looked at me and said, "Bambino, how old are you?"

What the heck is a bambino? I quickly said, "Fifteen!"

He responded, "Okay, you come next week, and I'll think about it."

I turned around and walked out of the store with a big-ass smile on my face. For the next couple of days, I couldn't think about anything else.

I returned after the New Year's festivities and met with him. He told me that he was in the process of selling the business, and I needed to meet with the new owners: Listano, Giano, and Nicholi. Listano and Giano were brothers, and Nicholi had married their sister, Marla. They were a close-knit family from Italy. I walked up to them and nervously said, "Hi, I'm Vincent."

Ignoring all salutations, Nicholi said, "Okay, kid, your first job will be washing pizza dough pans. Follow me!"

Damn, hello to you too!

Entering the kitchen, about two hundred aluminum pans, soiled in oil and flour, were stacked on the countertop and all but smacked me in the face. Nicholi said, "If you can finish this job, I'll give you a chance." He then walked out of the kitchen and left me to contemplate my plan of action.

I looked at the pans and mouthed, "No way in the friggin' world am I going to be able to clean these filthy things." It looked like they had been used for years and were never washed.

I filled the two deep stainless steel sinks with steaming-hot water, hoping that it would loosen up the caked-on grit. After several moments, I started scrubbing them with an industrial-strength Brillo pad, which tore into my fingertips. Ouch! I begged Nicholi to give me gloves. I couldn't have imagined how difficult it would be, but I was going to get it done. I worked my ass off and sweated like a pig because of the steam coming from the sink.

Several days later, the dough pans sparkled like new. No one was going to tell me that I didn't do a great job. For my performance, they gave me four red T-shirts adorned with the name "Italian Pizzeria" stenciled in white across the front. At that moment, it was the proudest day of my life. I had gotten this job on my own.

They hired me for a meager salary of fifty dollars a week. Even though this was far less than I had made at the car wash on the weekend, I was closer to home.

I did everything they asked of me. I washed dishes, sliced cold cuts, mixed pizza dough, made pizza sauce, grated mozzarella cheese, and cleaned. Most evenings, I went home and bragged to my mother about what they had said regarding my efforts. The smile on her face conveyed that she was pleased.

Months passed, and we had developed a closer relationship. Their kids looked up to me as an older brother, and they were my younger siblings. On the days they came to help out (when it was slow), we played *Asteroids*, *Galaxy*, and *Pac-Man* video games. My bosses owned the machines, so when each game was over, I opened the front door and just added more free credits.

When not serving customers, the bosses often spoke Italian and taught me several phrases. Albeit, they were mostly cursing words; nevertheless, I became proficient at understanding them. They soon stopped calling me Vincent and started calling me Cornuto. Thinking it was a term of affection, I soon learned it meant "a husband whose wife had been unfaithful." What the hell that had to do with me, I had no idea, but the name stuck.

I quickly familiarized myself with other job functions and became adept at making cheeseburgers, hot dogs, and a variety of hoagies. My ultimate challenge was to make a pizza. It seemed fascinating—throwing dough in the air and spinning it on your hands. I studied their every move because I wanted to be a pizza maker.

After nearly a year and a half, I got up the nerve and asked them to teach me. I was met with resistance because they were concerned with the customer's perception of a black man making pizza. I am unsure if they thought that making pizza was only for white people, but up to that point, I, too, had only seen white men making pizza. My position was that it would be cool to allow me to do it. Having gotten nowhere with them, I played upon the compassion of their spouses. It was endearing as I watched all three wives, on separate occasions, playfully threaten their respective husbands into allowing me to make a pizza. It must've aggravated my bosses looking at me sulk and listening to their wives say, "You see what you are doing to him!" Fortunately, after weeks of badgering, they agreed.

When Nicholi told me the good news, I ran up to him and gave him a big hug. I smothered him because I was about half a foot taller. I then went to the back and gave his wife, Marla, a big kiss on her cheek. Her caring smile warmed my soul because she always treated me like her son.

I knew the basics of making a pizza from watching them. I grabbed the pans from the refrigerator and gently removed the dough. I doused it in flour to suck up the moisture. I threw a little flour on the large pizza board to keep the dough from sticking. I then placed it on the marble countertop and manipulated it into a spherical shape. Afterward, I maneuvered it onto the backside of my hands while flipping it clockwise, stretching it to fit the outer portions of the pizza board. Once large enough, I made a few adjustments to make sure it was perfectly round. I grabbed the stainless steel dipper, scooped up some pizza sauce, and spread it evenly across the dough. The final step was generously dispersing mozzarella cheese over the sauce.

The repetitiveness of making pizzas would be the only way that I was going to perfect it. I wanted to be able to say that I taught myself, but they provided guidance when I got frustrated. My first few pizzas looked oblong because while putting them into the oven, they slammed against the back wall. I also put several holes in the dough, and I had to start from scratch. They laughed at me as I struggled; however, there was no way I was going to fail. Their wives were my biggest fans and encouraged me when I may have appeared to be flustered. After three weeks of practicing, I got the opportunity to showcase what I had learned.

I came to work one Monday morning knowing that my skills were going to be on display. Marla told me not to be nervous and reassured me that I would do well. After going through the ritual preparation of heating up the ovens and getting out the saucepan and cheese bucket, I made the first couple of counter pies. They came out round and bubbling hot, and my initial nervousness subsided. I then went and opened the doors for business.

Throughout the day, I stood in front of the window and made pizzas while observing daily commuters standing at the bus stop. Occasionally, one would glance in and give me an acknowledging smile. I don't believe any of my friends or customers had ever seen a young black man make pizza. I received numerous compliments and generous tips. My bosses were pleased with their decision. Over time, our relationship progressed to more than just employee and employer; I had indeed become an integral part of their family.

They gave me an opportunity to supervise newly hired workers, and my weekly salary periodically increased to $250, which allowed me to give my mother more money. However, one of the requirements was that I completed all my homework or the deal was off.

The added responsibility also required more hours of work. Ultimately, I signed up for a work-study program at school and went to class from eight o'clock until eleven thirty in the morning. Afterward, I walked to the pizzeria and worked eleven hours. I didn't know of any other high school student who worked more than sixty hours a week. There was no doubt that some child labor laws were broken; but back then, no one cared. I know I didn't because I was getting paid.

My bosses also hired a lot of the neighborhood kids, who were able to keep money in their pockets and stay off the streets as well.

Unfortunately, working at the pizzeria had its pitfalls. I worked many hours and was unable to develop a close relationship with my siblings, and I often wondered what my brother was doing. I couldn't hang out with friends, court high school girls, or get involved in any extracurricular sports. In addition to my depressing social life, the store closed at 11:00 p.m., which left us vulnerable to the potential antics of hoodlums.

One evening, two men stormed in wearing ski masks and brandishing shotguns. One of them stuck their shotgun in my face and demanded I open the cash register. Looking down the shotgun's barrel gave me a new perspective on wanting to live. I didn't have any time to be scared as he hurriedly jumped over the counter and pushed me out of his way. As he stood in front of me fumbling with the register, it would've been very easy for me to choke the shit out of him.

I looked around and noticed Giano's shocked facial expression. I had been robbed before at the car wash, but I believed this was probably his first time. After taking what was in the cash drawer, the robbers jumped back over the counter and ran out. Fortunately, there weren't any customers present, and no one got hurt. We contacted the police, but nothing was ever resolved.

On a different occasion, I was in the rear making sandwiches when an acquaintance staggered through the front door and shoved a handgun in Listano's face. His hand was unsteady as he tried to keep the gun elevated. There was no doubt in my mind that he was high as hell. I had seen similar behavior displayed by other drug addicts, who had an incredible sense of balance—they swayed back and forth but never fell. Listano reluctantly gave him the money, and the dope fiend stumbled out the door.

We immediately reported the robbery to the Elkanda Police, and two officers responded. After providing them with a detailed description,

I wanted to know their next move. They said they'd follow up on the case; and if they caught him, I might have to testify in court. I wasn't concerned with ratting on him because if I ever saw him again—sober or high—I was going to kick his ass.

The store robberies wouldn't be my only interaction with the Elkanda Police. I grew up in the Southwin section, which had an abundance of drug users and drug dealers. We were fortunate enough to have had adequate police protection because the city's mayor lived in the area, but crime was still prevalent.

I realized the cops had a tough job trying to protect people in poor neighborhoods. Back in the day, I enjoyed watching them on television because they always seemed to show up and save the day. Frequently in real life, I couldn't tell the good from the bad.

Some of the police officers used foul language and displayed a rude demeanor while interacting with citizens. I didn't think their behavior was befitting those in law enforcement because taxpayers paid their salaries. My disdain doesn't place the blame on the entire department because I've known many who were consummate professionals. My criticism is solely directed at the unprofessional officers that I had routinely encountered when I was younger. For whatever reason though, their presence didn't deter the local criminals.

The location of the pizzeria was a prime spot for selling drugs. Unfortunately, I saw many former acquaintances get caught up in this activity and knew that if it weren't curtailed, some would end up in jail, prison, or dead.

The tsunami of drugs filtered into inner cities has routinely destroyed neighborhoods and families. The poison of choice for many drug users back in the 1980s was the highly addictive crack cocaine. While at the pizzeria, I had spoken with several drug addicts to get their perspective on getting high. They told me about the euphoric sensation they experienced. Once the feeling subsided, they claimed that they yearned to get high again, and this caused some to commit crimes to support their dependency.

Due to peer pressure and curiosity, I, too, had messed around with illegal substances. I was lucky because I wasn't one of the many people with an addictive personality, who dabbled in it and couldn't get that humongous monkey off their backs. It was the worst decision I had made up to that point in my life. I'm glad I quickly got it out of my system because I didn't want my future self to regret it.

The Elkanda Police Department had "special" police officers that attended an alternate-route police academy but had full police authority. My bosses hired them as security due to the increasing violence. The accumulating filth on the streets and the growing problems of drug gangs marking their turf with hideous graffiti were indicative of the problem. Nonetheless, some of the things the police officers did, while at the pizzeria, disturbed me.

One evening, a rather large man—nearly 6'6" tall and weighing about 350 lbs.—came into the pizzeria and began arguing with the not quite 6'2" tall police officer. The man didn't physically touch the officer, but his yelling and cursing in the presence of other customers needed to be addressed. I was quite amazed that anyone would disrespect a uniformed cop, so I stood by to see what would happen next.

The officer sternly told the man several times to keep his fucking mouth shut or leave the store. Unfortunately, the man didn't heed his warnings and took up an aggressive stance, as if to throw down a challenge. The officer then agitatedly walked toward him, removed his silver-and-black .357 Magnum from his holster, gripped it in his right hand, and struck him across the left side of his face. The corner of the man's eyebrow immediately split open and bled profusely. I cringed at the sound of the metal striking his orbital socket and yelled out, "Damn!" Some of the customers, like rubberneckers at an accident scene, gathered around to gawk. The injured man impulsively clutched his face and ran out of the pizzeria. A streak of bloody drops followed him out the door.

At the time, it was the most violent act with a weapon that I had ever witnessed. It even trumped my mother busting open her second husband's head with a baseball bat. While the man may have been disrespectful, I didn't think the officer's brute force was necessary. Later on, the officer laughed and bragged about his performance. He acted a bit psychotic because he showed no remorse. My boss was thoroughly satisfied, possibly believing it would send a message to anyone else seeking to cause a problem. I guess the cop did what he needed to do.

A lot of action took place at the pizzeria, which was located on a busy commuter's corner. Just down the street was Jackson's liquor store, the meeting spot for many troublemakers who got their attitudes and muscles after getting drunk. I earned a PhD in street life watching everything and everybody, and I would put my savvy street skill set to work later in my life.

Some of my friends hung out on the corner drinking Olde English 800 forties and smoking joints. They were having the time of their lives, but I had to engage the responsibility of getting paid. Fortunately, I was never a beer drinker or pot smoker, so I didn't miss out on much.

The streets had its way of getting the news out, and I was privy to a lot of the gossip. A few police officers were rumored to have protected some of the local drug dealers. On numerous occasions, I saw cops meeting with shady individuals outside the store. Their conversations were unusually lengthy, which led me to believe that it was more than just casual.

These observations later became a determining factor in my decision not to seek employment with the Elkanda Police Department. I suspected that there might have been an underlying problem of misconduct and corruption within the force, but I had no proof. Nonetheless, having police officers around meant my days of being robbed were over—or so I thought.

Chapter 5

Building Blocks

Conviction is paramount for erecting a foundation.

Working in the pizzeria was extremely monotonous. The sandwich orders never changed, and a slice of pizza was just that—a slice of pizza. To break up the monotony, I'd often bring along my boom box for entertainment. The radio was massive and took ten D-size batteries to make it work. I'm glad I was able to plug it into an electrical socket at work, or I would've gone broke trying to entertain myself.

While at the back of the store, I intentionally danced while making sandwiches, to entice the young women who came to order food. My goal was to get them interested so they'd come back to keep me company. Let's say that I was never without a smiling face sitting at the counter ordering a sandwich.

At the end of the evening, I'd lug that huge radio home and listen to Queen's "We Are the Champions" on my cassette tape before going to bed. Back then, it was a catchy tune.

One night, after work, I walked home with my friend Steve, whom they had recently hired. As we talked and strolled toward our street, a man in a dark-colored car waved us down and asked for directions. "Can you tell me where Princess Street is?" I knew the area because my bosses had another store located across town. As I approached the car, the driver shoved a silver handgun in my face and yelled, "Give me the fucking radio!" The barrel of his gun looked like a damn cannon.

Without thinking, I ducked down, tucked my radio under my arm, and ran like the comic book character the Flash. I didn't look back until I was halfway down my street. I had expected Steve to be by my side; however, when I turned around, I noticed he hadn't moved. Breathing heavily, I screamed, "Steve, what the hell are you doing?" When he didn't answer, I sensed something was wrong. I placed the radio on the sidewalk, ran back, and pulled him to safety. The driver then put his car in reverse, screeched his tires, and sped away. I wanted to kick Steve's ass for not running, but he looked noticeably shaken. It shocked me seeing what behavioral changes a victim of crime goes through. I settled him down and walked him home.

It later dawned on me that I wasn't afraid during the entire ordeal. It had to have been the frequent robberies at the pizzeria that desensitized me to danger and made me tougher. After this incident, I always paid attention to my surroundings and left that hefty radio at home. For whatever reason, crime and danger seemed to follow me.

On another occasion, I came home from school to drop off my books before heading to work. As I got closer, I noticed the side door was damaged. My mother was working, so I walked in and called out to my siblings, but no one answered. I immediately went to my room and noticed that a bag, which had contained my new shoes, was missing. I ran downstairs, grabbed a baseball bat, and went looking for the asshole that had stolen my shit.

My instincts told me to run up the street and cut over one block. As I turned the corner, I saw a person walking with a bag in his hand that resembled the one taken from my closet. As I got closer to him, I yelled, "Yo, hold up! I wanna talk to you!" He then took off running. I chased him until I got close enough to hit him in his leg. His punk ass then dropped the bag, and he fled. I wanted to kick his ass, but fate was with both of us that day. Fortunately, I had to go to work, or I would've hunted him down.

I can't express how much going to school and working kept me out of trouble. The downside was that I never really had many opportunities to socialize. My only enjoyment came after work, when I went to a club called Zanzee, which was a gathering spot for an incredibly diverse group of people.

Situated in the downtown shopping district within the Linklin Motel, Zanzee had been to the City of Elkanda what Studio 54 and Paradise Garage had been to New York City. Many marquee singers were frequent headliners. Due to the drinking age, they only catered to an older clientele. Although only seventeen years old, my muscular build and facial hair made me appear of age, and they never questioned me.

Zanzee had two humongous floors for dancing and mingling. The subdued lighting enhanced the ambiance, and the remarkably loud music allowed us to dance freely without any judgment. The crowd's exuberance was normally an indication of whether the night was going to be sensational or not.

Most mornings, after leaving the club, my friends and I would go to a local diner and pig out after several hours of dancing. We'd reminisce about people we danced with and when they played certain songs. The NYC Peechboys' "Don't Make Me Wait" and "Life Is Something Special" were the consensus favorite. The club fellowship made many of us inseparable.

Partying at Zanzee also enhanced my personal life and reputation as a ladies' man who was thought to be popular. I had lots of "friendships" with high school girls because they knew that I was a part of the club scene. I became obsessed with this new lifestyle, but going to school, work, and the club scene became challenging. Several mishaps with mass transportation caused me to come home late and almost miss school. My mother had given me the liberty to hang out because I had worked hard, and my grades, though not stellar, were passing. I rectified this situation by applying for my driver's license so that I could drive back and forth to the club.

I took advantage of my mother's available car keys because she usually carpooled to work with friends. Of course, I stole them without her knowledge. She would've kicked my ass if she'd known what I had done. I practiced for several weeks and received strange looks from my friends as I cruised around our neighborhood. Before the test, I had a few minor collisions, but I wasn't going to tell since there was no damage to the car or the side of our house.

My mother drove me to the Department of Motor Vehicles to take my driving test, which I passed. Interestingly though, she never asked me how I learned to drive. Nevertheless, as we were driving back home, she said, "If you want to drive, you'd better get your own damn car and insurance." As a result, I saved my money knowing that I wanted a beautiful set of wheels.

Within two months, I purchased my first car: a brown 1974 Buick Regal. It was eight years old and had rust spots everywhere. The white interior was tattered; but to me, it was my brand-new baby. More importantly, I could get to the club with no problems—or so I had expected.

After several months, it continually stalled and emitted ridiculously large clouds of black smoke. It was embarrassing, especially when I was trying to woo the women. I didn't know you had to put oil in the damn thing. The motor eventually seized like a bounced check, so I scrapped it. I learned my lesson, but it was a good four-hundred-dollar investment.

In a matter of a few months, I purchased my second car: a white 1978 Pontiac Firebird with T-tops. A sizeable multicolored eagle painting adorned the hood. The interior was periwinkle blue, and it had a loud sound system, mainly when the T-tops were off. I just knew that the ladies would notice me now. Unluckily, within two months, it was stolen, stripped, and torched.

As time passed, I continued working at the pizzeria, but I was frustrated because I needed to reinvent myself. A lot of my days had been spent making sandwiches and pizzas. I had many conversations with my bosses, and they fully understood my desire to branch out. I had been a little reckless, and discipline was something that I desperately needed in my life. I knew that if I continued with my irresponsible behavior, there could be dire consequences.

Like a lot of growing boys, I played with GI Joe military action figures and often fantasized about one day becoming a soldier. These thoughts originated when I was in the Boy Scouts because everything had been so regimented. The military seemed like a good idea, so I visited a US Army Recruiting Office to learn more.

After speaking with a recruiter, I viewed a motivational video titled "Standing Tall." Watching young men and women train hard inspired me. It didn't take much more for me to decide that this could be the change I sought. In the video, they looked like they had a great time, and I pictured myself traveling around the world in a drab camouflage army uniform. It was the perfect brainwashing tool for those who, like me, were lost and needed direction.

Going to the military would be a significant decision, so I discussed it with my mother. She told me that our family had a rich history of military service, and she supported my choice. She'd later add that as a young black male, I had to be twice as good as the next person.

As a result and out of respect for my family's military veterans who fought in World War II, the Korean War, and the Vietnam War, I proudly enlisted in the United States Army Reserves.

My bosses were also in my corner. Everyone is replaceable, but they allowed me to take time off and attend basic training. I cannot say enough about the surrogate-father roles they played in my life.

In the summer of 1981, after completing an uneventful junior year of high school, I attended an eight-week basic training course at an army base located in Central New Jersey. The base was huge, and sand was everywhere. Any thoughts of falling back on the comforts of home were over. Survival was my mission because my family and community looked up to me.

Most of my fellow soldiers were approximately the same age. On several occasions, some of them expressed a similar feeling of being homesick. We were young and had been accustomed to our respective neighborhoods, but the base became our new home.

Basic training consisted of many aspects of military life. We learned combat techniques and proper courtesy in addressing a superior officer. We also underwent rigorous mental and physical conditioning. Every morning, we were awakened by a bugler playing reveille and ordered out of our bunks. With just minutes to put our clothes on and get into formation, we looked like a bunch of idiots bumping into each other.

It was difficult to collect my thoughts while someone was yelling at me. No one wanted to be the last person coming out of the door because that person would have to do hundreds of push-ups. After being screamed at, we marched to the chow hall for breakfast. There was no time to be particular. We grabbed what we could and ate just as fast. I often chose gooey oatmeal because I was used to my mother making it at home. It was very bland, but a little milk and sugar gave it flavor. Of course, we dared not talk to one another because that would've resulted in us doing exercises late into the evening.

As part of our training, we were taught how to make a bunk bed properly so that a quarter could bounce off the sheets. We also mastered the use of Kiwi shoe polish to spit-shine our leather gear. For those unfamiliar with military protocol, we spit on our leather gear while rubbing in shoe polish. We were expected to be able to see our reflection on our equipment; if not, you didn't do a good job. We also got down on our hands and knees and cleaned bathrooms with a toothbrush and Brasso metal polish. Everything had to pass the white glove test. There was no excuse for having dirt under our bunks or water stains in the bathrooms. What had been most nerve-racking was standing beside my bunk bed while the instructor inspected my gear. I didn't know if I had paid enough attention to all the details. Fortunately, my roommates and I always did well and passed. I started to view myself as a disciplined soldier rather than a teenager.

I learned to shoot an M-16 rifle and, within weeks, routinely pierced the surface of a three-hundred-meter target. It was also surreal having thrown hand grenades that blew stationary objects to smithereens. One of my comrades froze up when it was his turn and almost killed himself. Our drill sergeant knocked him upside his head, which caused him to drop the grenade, and the drill sergeant then picked it up and threw it downrange. Talk about a close call.

The most exhilarating contraption was the M-72 light anti-tank weapon (LAW). I jacked opened the drab green cylindrical tube and positioned it firmly on my shoulder. As I pressed down on the trigger, I marveled at how the projectile pierced the steel-armored target. I never believed that I'd be capable of handling such sophisticated weaponry.

Next up was the infamous gas chamber. Our drill sergeant warned us that it was probably going to be the absolute worst thing about boot camp. Everyone had to don a gas mask and go through a staged indoor maze before having to remove the mask and run out of the building. There was only one catch. Once we took off the mask, we had to say our name, loud and clear, and repeat our social security number before running out. If we didn't say it explicitly, they would make us repeat it until we had done so correctly. The drill sergeant couldn't care less because he kept his mask on while he watched. The one thing that they stressed was that once we ran out, we had to make a hard left and avoid the big-ass oak tree that was about fifteen feet from the door.

When my turn came, I did as I was instructed and yelled out my name. Well, the playful drill sergeant made everyone repeat it so that we'd experience the pain of the gas fumes, which made us cough violently, and our skin burned like hell. As I ran out, I made the hard left, but a few of the soldiers behind me ran straight into the tree and almost knocked themselves out. A lot of indentations became permanent fixtures from the collisions over the years.

They trained me to be a fighting machine, and together with a group of soldiers from Charlie Company (C-2-5), we made it through. This experience exceeded the limits I had set for myself.

At the end of the eight weeks, we had a lavish graduation ceremony. The day was perfect as the sun beamed overhead, and the army band played music in the background. Family and friends of my comrades reveled in the pomp and circumstance of watching their loved ones shake hands with the commanding officers. I sat among my fellow soldiers thinking how much happier I would've been if my family had also been there. However, I had become accustomed to doing things on my own.

Later that afternoon, I lugged my duffel bag to the center of town and boarded a bus back to Elkanda. The ride home took about an hour and a half, but it gave me some time to reflect on what I had just accomplished.

When I arrived at the terminal, there was no one to pick me up, so I waited for a local bus. The filthy garbage scattered around the terminal and downtown area confirmed that I was home. A few unknown passersby greeted me with what was equivalent to "Nice uniform. Welcome home, soldier." I nodded and kept it moving. I didn't outwardly express any sorrow for not having a more elaborate ceremony, but my pride was hurt because this was a special occasion for me.

Chapter 6

Venturing Out

Enrich your character by your surroundings.

Returning home with a more disciplined approach to life and a confident personality, I knew that I had changed—but I didn't know to what extent. Some of my friends were curious about my ventures, so I painted the best picture of the army lifestyle. From their nonchalant expressions and indifferent comments, I sensed that my overzealousness lost them in translation.

My high school senior year was rather humdrum. While I believed that I was regimented, I didn't take a real interest in my schoolwork. Walking through the hallways showed me that I had been oblivious to books and teachers. I don't recall interacting with most of my classmates because I was partying and working long hours. I didn't attend my senior prom because I hung out with an older crowd, but I regret missing it. Nonetheless, somehow I was able to graduate in the summer of 1982.

Several days after graduation, I hopped on a plane and flew to an army base in the South. This additional commitment comprised of ten weeks of Advanced Individual Training. I had taken the Armed Services Vocational Aptitude Battery Test to measure what I'd be best suited to do because I didn't have a clue. No one had ever asked me about future aspirations. In the back of my mind, I didn't want to go to jail. I ultimately chose "36 Kilo" as my military occupation specialty, which is a tactical wire operations specialist responsible for maintaining a unit's radio communication.

The training intensified because I had to decipher technical manuals and climb a sixty-foot telephone pole with tree gaffs. For the latter, *nervous* was not the right word to express my thoughts. The mounds of sand at the bottom of the pole couldn't help reconcile my aversion to what I needed to accomplish. Every scenario about falling and busting my ass ran through my mind.

The first few attempts were futile. The damn gaffs wouldn't stick, and I inevitably slid halfway down the pole. Fortunately, I had on thick gloves, or my hands would've been shredded. After the third attempt, I finally made it to the top and breathed a sigh of relief. However, a comrade who was on a pole next to me wasn't as lucky.

She was a feisty little soldier whom I'd befriended while in one of our classes. She expressed to me that she wasn't sure that she'd make it to the top. I thought she was primed to do well because she had rather strong-looking legs, and that was half the battle. However, her first try would be her last.

As I thought, she was able to make it up the pole with relative ease, but a misplaced step caused her to lose her balance and slide down at breakneck speed. A resounding thump, followed by a shrieking cry when she hit the ground, shocked us all. I looked over at her and cringed because she had large wood chips protruding from her pants and shirtsleeves. From the constant moaning, I knew she had severely injured her arms and legs. The instructors ran to her side and immediately called for medical personnel. They subsequently transported her to the hospital, and a few weeks later, they sent her home because she could no longer physically continue.

I also trained with soldiers who came from different parts of the country (i.e., Tennessee, Missouri, Kentucky, and California). Some spoke with a thick Southern drawl that made it difficult to understand them. Their composed mannerisms and slow speech patterns were funny, but I made sure not to offend them by deliberately laughing in their presence.

This new environment mentally confused me because it contrasted with my inner-city experiences. My family members had shared some disturbing stories regarding Southern racism. The thoughts of black folks being hanged and terrorized by ignorant white men who had nothing better to do just seemed preposterous. How could people be so uncaring? Even though I was in the military, I never lost sight of the fact that I was stationed in the South; but that didn't stop me from crossing some dangerous taboo boundary lines.

During this time, I met a white female soldier from Michigan. She was short, cute, and had a tough facade, which was why I liked her. Her spunky attitude intrigued me, and she had a very shapely body in that ugly uniform. As this was the South, I didn't know what white people expected of me regarding pursuing an interracial relationship, but I took a chance.

We dated and spent a lot of time together on and off the base. I had anticipated plenty of stares because of the potential for controversy. I had never been with anyone outside my race, but surprisingly, no one said anything. We had a great time together, and to this day, we are still in contact via social media. My perception about the South was slowly changing.

The advanced training was more intense than I had envisioned. Along with the associated technical training, we stood guard duty and conducted military drills, which seemed to last an eternity. Who knew that some people had trouble distinguishing their left foot from their right foot? What was so hard about "left, right, left, right, left"? Their ignorance caused us to march damn near all day until we got it correct.

Additional training required that I dig a six-foot ditch called a foxhole, which served as cover and concealment in a combat situation. It also provided a place to stand guard when it was my turn for the night watch. Staying awake had been difficult, but it was important because, in a real war scenario, sleeping could get a soldier killed.

The last demanding activity was a twenty-mile march. We set out on our journey during an oppressively hot day. Temperatures peaked at around 105°, making the cotton-nylon cloth uniforms extremely unbearable. Drinking water was my remedy to avoid heatstroke. I tried to keep up with the group, but hovering black spots blurred my vision. The forty-pound backpack, which we were required to carry, didn't make it any easier. About fifteen miles into the trek, several soldiers (including me) experienced heat exhaustion. I threw up on several occasions and collapsed. A pickup truck traveled behind us to transport those needing a ride back to the base—which, ultimately, included me.

As I got situated on the bed liner, I noticed some of the other sickly looking soldiers sitting next to me. Instead of the standard drab green, their uniforms were a shade of brown from all the intense perspiration. I sat next to a deranged-looking guy from Kentucky, who rambled on about some indecipherable gibberish. Concerned about his mental status, I asked him if he was all right. When he tried to respond, he vomited all over me.

The tannish milky substance smelled horrible, and chunks of undigested food remained stationary on my lap. I sat staring at the pile of puke and forced myself not to regurgitate as well. The country boy then looked up at me and said, "I'm sorry, buddy." His Southern drawl tickled me as I laughingly replied, "It's okay, but I wasn't hungry." My remark brought a shy smile to his face, which probably assured him I wasn't too upset. I was just happy that we'd eventually recover.

As time progressed, some of my fellow soldiers and I went out drinking at a few of the local spots to socialize and wind down. They referred to the bars as a "hole in the wall" because of the unsteady wooden chairs, a few vintage cigarette-memorabilia posters, and plumes of smoke that filled the air. Interestingly, I had discovered two important things from my colleagues from the South. I had learned how to stack Budweiser beer cans, and I had acquired a fondness for rock music—specifically Lynyrd Skynyrd's "Free Bird" and "Sweet Home Alabama."

On many evenings, I made a fool of myself attempting to sing a karaoke version of old songs. Afterward, we sat around in a drunken stupor, smoking cigarettes and telling jokes about our respective states. I had the time of my life, and to this day, I still maintain an appreciation for Southern rock music.

We eventually completed our training and had an elaborate graduation ceremony. Stadium seating was sprawled on two sides of an open field to accommodate family, friends, and dignitaries. We looked sharp in our formal green uniforms as we marched in proper cadence, and then we were commanded to stand at parade rest in front of the crowd. Several commissioned officers came to the podium and spoke about what a disciplined group we were and what our future roles meant to the military.

As I stood there admiring the smiles in the audience, I wished that some of the praises had been for me. My family didn't attend because I was hundreds of miles away. Curiously, it had been around this time I recognized that I harbored father abandonment issues. I longed to see my dad's smile and hear him say, "I am so proud of you, son." My graduation should've been one of those bonding moments that we'd cherish; but I never saw him again, and I am only left with two pictures of the man I used to call Daddy.

Following the graduation, most of us returned to our respective reserve units, but they sent a few of my good friends to South Korea for active duty. There hadn't been any wars going on, but I had mixed feelings because I wanted to go with them.

The training was fulfilling, and my perception of Southern folks dramatically changed thanks to my firsthand experience. Days before my journey back north, to my amazement, I received a letter of commendation for the military bearing I had displayed during our formal inspection.

While I knew it was a standard form letter, it meant a lot to me because many of my comrades were outstanding as well. But they chose me. It was a privilege to wear the US Army uniform.

Chapter 7

Rerouting

A proper perspective involves manipulation.

After completing the training, I became a weekend warrior. Mandatory military drills were held one weekend a month and two weeks during the summer. Soldiering made my life a little bit more interesting; however, returning to work at the pizzeria left me feeling a bit empty. The pizza parlor routine couldn't withstand my eagerness to do something else with my life.

One evening while watching television, a commercial about a truck driving school caught my attention. The slick-talking pitchman convinced me that I needed a change. I wrote down the particulars and eventually talked it over with my bosses and they, again, allowed me the time off to chart a new path for my future.

Within a month, I enrolled in an eight-week course. The training wasn't free, so I took out a twenty-five-hundred-dollar government student loan. How the hell was I going to pay this back?

My days were long, but I was excited and sad at the same time. If I succeeded, I'd be moving on to a new stage in my life. If I failed, I'd be stagnant—again.

The first day of class, interesting glances met me at the front door. Initially, I speculated that I had something dangling out of my nose. Afterward, I thought it was because I was the only black student;

however, I later found out it was because I rolled up in my recently purchased, sexy-ass brown Chevy Camaro.

Eventually, I sat at the front of the room and sparked up a few conversations with my classmates. We had a lot in common and were all there to make a better life for ourselves. The instructor soon walked to the front of the class and gave us his "welcome aboard" speech. Soon after, he went over the course content and commented on how demanding it would be for some of us. I doubted that I'd be able to complete it, but I took it seriously because it cost a lot of money, and my future depended on me.

I studied the manuals at home and paid particular attention while I drove in the courtyard. First gear up, second gear down. Don't forget to pull the T-bar. Why did it have to have so many movements? The hard grinding noise must've damaged the engine. Several glaring mistakes, while shifting the truck's gears, brought penetrating stares; but my instructor was very patient as I struggled to make sense of it all. My classmates also calmed me down when I became noticeably frustrated and wanted to quit.

After two long and arduous months, I passed the written portion, but the driving test loomed as my biggest obstacle. Parking within the designated lines, driving in reverse, and distinguishing objects in the rearview mirrors complicated matters even more. Upon reflection, I must've looked like a damn fool. How in the hell could they have thought I was ready? I should've just given up.

The day of my road test, I had arrived early and watched several classmates pass and celebrate. When my turn came, I hopped into the truck's cabin and positioned myself behind the oversized steering wheel. Music from the movie *Smokey and the Bandit* echoed in my head as I got caught up in the moment, trying not to psyche myself out. The instructor cleared his throat and said, "Hey! Are you ready?"

I snapped out of it, smiled, and quipped, "Yes, I am."

I pulled out of the parking lot grinding the truck's gears. The instructor looked at me with a condescending sneer. Not a good way to start. I then drove onto Route 47 and avoided speeding cars, which seemed to be conspiring against me. I mumbled under my breath, "Get out of my way. I'm trying to impress this guy!" Periodically, I glanced over and watched the instructor jot down notes on his clipboard, and I thought, *What the hell are you writing?*

Except for a few slipped gears and slamming on the breaks, I thought I did okay. We eventually returned, and I impatiently waited for him to grade my performance. There were red check marks all over that damn score sheet. He then unapologetically looked up and said, "You didn't alley dock properly and failed to keep to the right while driving on the highway, so you've failed."

I responded, "You should've instructed me better!"

With no discernible look of sympathy, he replied, "It's not my job to instruct you. I'm just here to observe." His decision was final, but by no means did I accept it.

I climbed out of the truck and sulked like a little spoiled kid who didn't get his way. I walked over to my school instructor and told him the bad news. He put his arm around my shoulder and said, "Martin, I could see that you were nervous, but you'll do better the next time."

As fate would have it, several weeks later, I retook the driving test with the same instructor and got the exact same results. I didn't let my failure deter me because it was a learning experience, but it took several years to repay that damn student loan.

While exploring different career prospects after the truck-driving debacle, my high school best friend and I discussed opening a dance club. We'd partied at a few clubs and knew enough about the business to attempt to open our own. I had no clue how we were going to pull it off. Friends that trained with us in martial arts assisted with logistical matters, and with a little financial support from my bosses, we had our sights set high on becoming entrepreneurs.

We searched the neighborhood and found the ideal location: an old dank and cluttered car garage located across the street from a middle school. At no point did we ever consider getting an occupancy permit— wrong decision.

It wasn't visually appealing, but it attracted the local kids. Our closest friends gave us a hand, and we gutted the place within days. We hosed down the cement floor and washed it with a special detergent that removed oil from its surface. Next, we scraped the walls and painted them black to simulate a rugged ambiance. After a lengthy discussion, we settled on the name Club Hardware, which we painted, in white, on the walls so that it glowed under ultraviolet light. Newly acquired track lights and a reflective disco ball glamorized the club's decor. If we would've had more money, an illuminating floor similar to the one in the movie *Saturday Night Fever* with John Travolta would've been our next investment, but someone else would've worn the white suit.

My brother and I owned two Technic 1200 turntables and a Gemini mixer, but we didn't have an adequate sound system. With the money loaned to us from my bosses, we bought Cerwin Vega speakers, which were the industry standard to accommodate the size of the club. Strategically placed old rubber car tires along the walls served as a veiled attempt at soundproofing.

Printed fliers were distributed throughout the neighborhood and at Club Zanzee and other sites in New York City. Our karate teacher (who was the deejay) trained our security personnel during the week for potential problems.

After weeks of preparation, we had our grand opening. The club had a capacity of about 150 people, but we estimated that about 250 would attend our first night. We charged four dollars for entrance and one dollar for coat check. Although four dollars may have been steep for some, we didn't turn away those who didn't have enough money. Many of our friends who had initially thought we were a bit peculiar because we went to clubs came to our spot to party.

Standing in the middle of the dance floor, watching people dance—I was awestruck. The aromatic smell of weed permeated the air. My slight contact high made me move to the beat of the music's deep bass and caused the walls to vibrate. I couldn't stop smiling as I looked up and noticed how elegantly the words *Club Hardware* illuminated the wall. After snapping out of it, I grabbed the first young lady who wanted to dance and partied for the rest of the evening.

Club Hardware opened on Friday and Saturday nights. It became so popular that we had to open on Thursday as well. Our ability to make money exceeded expectations. After paying the deejay, rent, concession staff, and personal security, we cleared about four hundred dollars each per week. Not too shabby for two inner-city teenagers. However, numerous residential "loud noise" complaints brought some unwelcomed guests.

One morning, around two o'clock, a swarm of Elkanda police officers in riot gear raided the club. They came in with such force, it shocked everyone. Officers yelled and screamed, but their voices were drowned out by the deafening music. Several individuals discarded drugs and weapons on the floor and took off. Since we knew that these items entered our establishment, we weren't in a position to check everyone. Maybe we should've charged an illegal contraband fee as well.

Eventually, the deejay turned the music off, and it became apparent whom they wanted. An officer approached me and asked, "Do you know where the club owners are?"

I stuttered, "I-I-I . . . just saw them run toward the back door." As soon as he turned around, I ran out of the front door wondering what I had done.

In the following days, we held a staff meeting and discussed the feasibility of remaining open or relocating to another part of the city. The residents were tired of the loud noise, and there had been a serious potential for violence. While it provided a great business adventure, we decided that it wasn't worth the trouble, so we sadly closed Club Hardware's doors.

Chapter 8

What's in a Number?

Careful planning negates burning bridges.

As time passed, I couldn't picture myself working at the pizzeria much longer. Even though my salary had increased to $325 per week, which was indeed significant, I was getting older and had to do something more meaningful.

By luck, one of the police officers that had worked security in the pizzeria came by to say hello. Standing 6'5" tall, I immediately noticed that he looked fit and had dropped about forty pounds. He told me that he was training at the New Jersey State Police (NJSP) Academy. I asked him about the process, and he provided me with information regarding an upcoming special test. The thought of pursuing law enforcement had never entered my mind. Nevertheless, I had to try it.

State police representatives administered the test in an auditorium at South Community College located in downtown Elkanda. The line of applicants extended outside onto the sidewalk, which shattered my confidence. Just the same, I took the test with my brother and a friend.

About three hundred of us filed into the building and sat in the close-quartered chairs. An African-American first officer proctored the examination and explained the process in detail. His tailored french-blue blouse (coat), light-blue shirt, and dark-blue pants with gold stripes extending the length outside of both legs, coupled with his broad shoulders and tapered waistline, gave him the appearance of a disciplined drill sergeant.

As I sat daydreaming, he shocked me back to reality when he loudly barked, "When I tell you to pick up your pencils, do it. And there will be no talking! Do you understand?" His voice echoed and sounded like there were four of him.

Some of us responded, "Yes, sir!" I then snapped out of it and observed a contemptuous frown on his face. I surmised that the response wasn't to his satisfaction. He again screamed, "Do you understand?"

We yelled thunderously in unison, "Yes, sir!" My body vibrated, and a big smile came to my face because it brought back memories of my time in the military.

I opened the test package and started answering the questions. Occasionally, I looked up to see what others were doing. Unexpectedly, most—if not all—of the participants were African-American, Hispanic, or women.

The entire exam took about two hours to complete. The first officer, along with two uniformed state troopers, walked around and monitored our actions. The reading comprehension portion of the test didn't appear to be too complicated; however, the math section, now that's another issue. I didn't know most of the answers, so I guessed and darkened the circles. I should've paid more attention in school.

At the conclusion, I put my pencil down, closed my booklet, walked to the front of the room, and handed in my test. I then waited outside for my brother and friend to finish. When they came out, the blank looks on their faces told me that they probably did as poorly as I thought I had done.

In the coming weeks, I took the civil service exam, which is for all law enforcement positions (e.g., local police, county police, and corrections). I did not expect to get into the NJSP, so this gave me more options. At that moment, the possibility of me being a cop began to materialize, and any job in law enforcement would've sufficed.

Within a couple of months, I received the results from both exams. I had scored a 61 out of 100 for the NJSP exam and had, therefore, passed! Huh? If it were up to me, I wouldn't have welcomed such a low score, and I wondered why they had accepted me.

On the contrary, I had scored a 93 on the Civil Servant Council exam, which placed me in the top 5 percent and gave me a better chance of employment. However, joining the Elkanda Police Department wasn't an option because it would've been awkward and probably dangerous locking up people I knew. Furthermore, working with prisoners in the Department of Corrections was not part of my future because I didn't want to be locked down with inmates and probably a lot of my friends, so my decision was easy.

The fact that I had done so poorly and passed the NJSP test plagued me. I later found out that there were two standards for acceptance: a minimum score of 80 out of 100 for white males and a minimum score of 60 out of 100 for everyone else, including white females. Initially, it didn't bother me because I got into the academy, but it later dawned on me that having the two standards left an indelible mark on nonwhite male applicants who scored lower than 80.

Afterward, I learned that they accepted me under a 1975 federal consent decree, which was imposed upon the NJSP due to their discriminatory hiring practices. Before the consent decree, they had a paltry 1.7 percent minority representation; and as a result, they were required to increase the minority population to approximately 14 percent. The policy seemed reasonable because it afforded assistance to minorities and women, thus leveling the playing field in an arena historically fraught with discrimination. Although this social service allowed me a spectacular opportunity, it also weighed heavily on my insecurities.

Years later, I found out that over the years, a slew of white recruits had intentionally received the test. Hypocritically, some of them espoused meritocracy, but having the test is no different than the handout given to some minorities. Now I don't want to discount the individuals who scored high on the test, but they failed to accept that many white males have access to the "my buddy" inner circle that gives them a leg up in the hiring process. It is somewhat ironic that at one point in history, black people had to abandon their seats on buses for white people—and now, a white person had to relinquish their spot in the academy for me. I hoped things would change and that no other minority state trooper had to carry around this same race burden.

After I had completed the exam, the background investigation was the next phase. My investigator, an African-American, was an academy instructor with eight years of experience. He, too, was from the City of Elkanda and a graduate of our local high school. I believed it was important to have minorities and women involved in the background investigative process, to ensure that minorities had a fair chance of getting into the academy. Not that a minority would automatically give another minority a pass; instead they would be empathetic to some of the difficulties they overcame.

The investigator came to my home dressed in a tight-fitting blue suit, and he looked like the black version of the Incredible Hulk. I thought that I had huge biceps, but damn!

He was a consummate professional but stern when he felt it was needed. He demanded, "I expect you to get all the documents to me ASAP!" My first reaction was to say, "Who do you think you're talking to?" However, from the firm and mechanical tone of his voice, I knew he was serious, and I didn't challenge him.

While conducting my background investigation, he uncovered that I hadn't filed any paperwork for Club Hardware. He showed me a document, which claimed I owed the State of New Jersey upward of three thousand dollars in back taxes. He then asked, "Do you know anything about this?"

With a confused expression, I said, "Sir, I have no idea what you are talking about."

According to the tax record, the landlord (who, ironically, was a Baptist reverend) claimed that he had worked for me and that I laid him off. After looking into this matter, he told me that the landlord had a record of filing false unemployment claims and that I was just his stooge. I was relieved. But if he knew this already, why was he bringing it up? I guess this was the start of the head games.

After several weeks, he ultimately signed off on the report. In our last meeting, he wished me luck and said, "If all goes well, I should see you shortly." His words jolted my senses because the reality of becoming a state trooper seemed within my grasp.

With my background investigation completed, I eventually appeared before a three-person interview board at their headquarters. The voyage to the headquarters fueled my excitement and uncertainty. I had never been to this part of the state, so heading down the Black Dragon toll road gave me an indication of what my new job might possibly entail. It also provided me an opportunity to reflect on things that had happened in my life that put me on this path.

As I pulled into the parking lot, several large visibly numbered buildings overwhelmed the scenery. I noticed a few uniformed state troopers standing in front of the doors. I gathered they had been assigned to direct incoming applicants of where to go. As I approached one of them, he asked, "What is your last name?"

I promptly responded, "Martin, sir."

He barked, "Building 15!"

I then quickly walked to my destination.

When I entered the room to meet the interview panel—two state troopers and a civilian—it shocked me to see an African-American male sitting at the table. He was a squadron officer and only the third African American that I had encountered. I then sat down and waited for the interview to start.

The squadron officer asked me questions about Club Hardware and the back taxes issue. I immediately told him, "Sir, the landlord's accusation was untrue." He and I went back and forth until, I guess, he was satisfied with my answers.

The other trooper on the panel then asked the unexpected. "Mr. Martin, have you ever experimented with drugs?"

As I watched the last word slowly leave his lips, my heart sank into the pit of my stomach. *Wow, please not that question*, I said over and over in my mind. In a split second, I had a big decision to make. I could lie or tell the truth and see what happened.

I replied, "Yes, but I grew out of it."

I sat back and waited for him to ask follow-up questions, but he didn't. I didn't know if they were going to hold it against me, but I told the truth. What did they expect from a young kid from Elkanda or any young person for that matter?

Once I had completed the interview, I walked outside the room and breathed a sigh of relief. I couldn't gauge if I had done well or not. As I was about to leave, the door abruptly opened, and the squadron officer sauntered out. He walked up to me and said, "Son, I am impressed with your honesty, but my only concern is the tax matter." I gave him my word that I wasn't involved in the landlord's scheme, and he said that he believed me. His words were fatherly and lifted my spirits.

Afterward, I went to another building and took a five hundred–question psychological test, which I thought was rather strange. It asked a series of repeated questions, some worded differently but which meant the same thing. I could see how someone could mess up if they weren't paying attention.

Lastly, I went to another building and was given a full medical examination by a battery of physicians. It was extremely thorough. Why that doctor wanted to touch my testicles and hear me cough was foreign to me. Nonetheless, I drove home later that afternoon thinking it would be great to work for them.

About a month later, they sent me a letter. I ripped it open, and it read that I had passed all the exams. The entire process had taken about seven months, and my life was about to change.

Upon reflection, I realize that everything I had endured set the stage for my future career. One of the greatest lessons I learned came from failing the truck-driving course and being bullied at a young age. Those experiences showed me that no adversity was insurmountable; and later in my life, I used them as motivation.

Working at the car wash and at the pizzeria provided me with a strong work ethic and kept me grounded. If I had been on the streets, I would've suffered a fate like many of my friends—in jail, strung out on drugs, or dead.

My military experience oriented me to the concepts of mental discipline and teamwork. Embarking upon a business venture showed me that I could be successful. I had friends looking up to me for guidance, which made me realize I could also be a leader. It meant a lot to know that others saw something special in me at a time when I questioned my capabilities.

Finally, being a poster child for affirmative action helped me realize that it wasn't my fault. The generational head starts given to some in society needed to be corrected to make the race fair for all.

Chapter 9

Sphere of Indoctrination

Know your limitations, but don't let them know you.

In September 1985, like abandoned children dropped off on the steps of a house of salvation, 250 recruits and I reported to the academy. A paramilitary organization with a rank structure similar to that of the US Army, the academy had a reputation for being academically and physically challenging. We stayed during the week and came home on weekends—unlike most police academies, which trained Monday through Friday from 9:00 a.m. to 5:00 p.m.

Driving up to the front gate screamed out that hell would eventually commence. I parked my car and then stepped out sporting a fresh haircut and a well-fitted blue suit. I looked around and observed worried expressions on the other recruits' faces. I approached one person and asked him about his concerns, and he responded, "I have no idea what they are going to do to us."

I took his words for what they were worth and removed my stuff from my car. I then placed my green elongated duffel bag on the ground. When I turned around to grab my suitcase, I sensed someone's hot breath on the back of my neck. I slowly looked over my right shoulder, praying that I was imagining it, and noticed a tall white state trooper standing directly behind me. He scornfully asked, "Is there a reason why you are taking your time?"

I anxiously turned and jumped to attention. Not daring to look at him, I screamed out, "No, sir. I was getting my bags out of the car, sir!"

He then started yelling at me. "Grab your gear and get in that formation! Now! Do you hear me? Move it. I said move it!"

What the hell? I snatched up both items and ran to the formation. I dropped them on the ground and waited for the next order. My knees almost buckled, and beads of sweat slowly ran down my back as my body temperature immediately surged. I thought, *Now I realize what the other recruit meant. What did I get myself into this time?*

While my eyes were positioned on the back of the head of the recruit in front of me, another academy instructor approached and yelled, "What the hell is that above your lip?"

Please, not another ballbuster. I nervously responded, "A mustache, sir!"

"Who told you that you could have it?" he angrily asked.

"No one, sir!" I said.

He screamed, "Are you trying to piss me off?"

I yelled, "No, sir!" Although we weren't previously told to shave, we recruits who had facial hair were ordered to retrieve a razor from our luggage and return to the formation.

There was a mad dash back to our bags, and a few recruits tripped and scuffed their pants. We immediately returned and resumed our places. The other recruits looked at us, trying their best not to laugh.

The instructor called out, "Now take that crap off of your faces!"

We did so without uttering a word. I had never shaved without a mirror, which made it even tougher. My facial hair had been prominent for years, and I looked weird without it.

After we had followed their instructions, I looked to my left and noticed that a recruit had mistakenly cut the bottom of his nose and bled all over his suit and white shirt.

The instructor sarcastically said to him, "What are you, stupid? Don't answer me. Get out of my face and go clean yourself up now!"

The injured recruit ran to one of the academy buildings and disappeared inside its doors. In the military and law enforcement, they used humiliation to build character; but if not kept in check, it could mentally devastate weak-minded individuals.

While watching the instructors harass other recruits, I surveyed the academy's landscape, which was also a training facility for the military. Due to our large class size, they divided us into two groups or what the military calls platoons. It didn't make a difference where they placed me because I didn't know anyone.

Numerous white buildings served as dorm rooms for the first platoon. They were arranged alphabetically, so the recruits whose last names began with A through M slept there. The main building housed the second platoon, whose last names started with N through Z. There was also an adjoining beach we'd become well acquainted with, but not for recreational purposes.

The grueling orientation process kept us in suspense for about half an hour as they told us what to expect for the next twenty-six weeks. The one thing that stood out in my mind was when an instructor coldly stared at us and said, "Look to your left, now look to your right. One of you will not be here in the end."

Those words shook me to my core. How did he know?

The academy was structured to break us down and then build us up. We knew when to eat, sleep, crap, shower, and shave. It appeared that this process also served to get rid of weaker recruits. Many of us were in our early twenties and hadn't been away from home, so the yelling and screaming were thorny for some.

In the first week, one recruit jumped over the fence and never returned; and subsequently, ten more recruits dropped out. It was difficult building friendships early on; however, they taught us the concept of teamwork, which they reiterated daily.

From the outset, the test scores of minority recruits were always a topic of conversation. Embarrassed by my low score, I kept my information private; but it didn't make a difference. One white recruit said, "They lowered the scores so more minorities could get in, and now my friend has to wait for the next test."

From the tone of his disagreement, it became evident that to be accepted, African-American and Hispanic males had to appear less threatening and make the white recruits feel psychologically comfortable. Since I had made it to the academy, I thought they'd accept me regardless of my test score. Whatever happened to teamwork?

The competitiveness of the process had been astounding. Approximately five thousand individuals applied to take the test for my class. After getting over the initial self-inflicted mental pressure of being viewed as a "special case," I prepared myself for what was to come.

The academic classes consisted of Arrest, Search, and Seizure; 2C Criminal Law; Title 39; Psychology; and English Composition. Every recruit was afforded two opportunities to pass each test. The minimum score was a 70 out of a possible 100. Passing the first couple of tests increased my confidence. My classmates said that the most challenging course was 2C Criminal Law. I had surrounded myself with a few smarter recruits because they appeared to be knowledgeable. Some of them had already gone through other police academies but left to become a state trooper. I also prepared myself by setting aside additional studying time when we went home on the weekends.

On the day of the test, we marched into the classroom, and the makeshift cardboard nameplates directed us where to sit. An instructor passed out the test and said, "You have an hour to complete it." He then yelled, "Anyone caught cheating will be automatically dismissed. Now pick up your pencils and begin!"

As I skimmed over it, the answers appeared to jump out at me. After about forty-five minutes, I put my pencil down, wiped the slight trickles of sweat from my forehead, and turned in my score sheet to the instructor, who was sitting at the back of the room. He looked at me cross-eyed because most of the class was still taking the test. I asked whether I had done something wrong. He smirked and asked me, "Recruit Martin, how do you think you did?"

I replied, "I don't know, sir."

He then jumped to his feet and mockingly blurted out, "Wrong answer. Now get out of my face!"

I immediately double-timed it out of there and ran back to my dorm room.

Later that evening, one of my roommates scolded me. "Martin, what the hell is wrong with you? You will only bring attention to yourself if you are the first one done, you bonehead!"

I didn't know what to think.

The next day, as we entered the classroom, the instructors told us to look at the information board to verify our test results. I stood in line while everyone checked his or her respective score. When my turn came, I looked up and read that I had failed with a score of 68. Damn it! If I didn't pass the makeup test, I would be sent home.

I turned around and saw the instructor shaking his head. He arrogantly said, "Recruit Martin, it appears your speed failed you, right?"

I replied, "Yes, sir. I believe so."

He then asked, "Now what are you going to do about it?"

I dejectedly replied, "Study harder, sir."

There was no doubt that some of the recruits and instructors wanted the likes of me out. I maintained a false sense of inferiority because I belonged at the back of the line when things mattered. I didn't belong, and the failed test proved it. It would've been easier for me to just quit.

Going home that weekend was stressful. I knew that the following week, my journey could be over. However, my roommates rallied around a few other classmates who had also failed, including me. I met with a few of my classmates, and we studied feverishly. The teamwork our instructors consistently drilled into us had finally surfaced.

We returned on Monday, and for some of us, it was probably going to be our last day. It was the most stressful period that I had experienced while at the academy. I noticed a few serious looks on my classmate's faces. The presumption may have been that my time was coming to an end.

Physical training occupied the entire morning. We made our way down to the scenic beach and ran several wind sprints in the sand. It was exhausting, but they then had us walk for about a hundred yards with a classmate on our backs. I blocked out the pain because I still had a test to take.

Later that afternoon, about twenty-four of us returned to the classroom. From what I can recall, I was the only African-American recruit. The concerned facial expressions made the atmosphere tense. My stride hadn't been as deliberate as I walked to my seat and sat down. The instructor strutted to the front of the class, looked at us, and yelled, "Listen up. If any of you don't pass this test, you will automatically be dismissed! Do you understand?"

We all screamed, "Yes, sir!"

He then distributed the test papers and told us to begin.

I closed my eyes briefly, looked down, and told myself, "You can't screw this up . . . you just can't." I then opened my eyes, wiped my sweaty hands, and started. This time, I intentionally read each question.

After about an hour, the instructor yelled out, "Time's up!"

I put my pencil down, picked up my test, and walked to the back of the room. The instructors scored them immediately. I impatiently waited with the other recruits until I heard my name called. "Recruit Martin."

I ran over to him and stood at attention. He looked at me and said, "You scored an 85."

My heart skipped a few beats. I gasped excitedly and said, "Thank you, sir."

I left the classroom with a huge cheesy smile and ran to share the good news with my roommates. I thanked them for their support and assured them that I would do better. My most challenging moment was in the past; but for some, it would only get worse.

Chapter 10

The Weeding-Out Process

Don't let giving up be the precursor to your failure.

Next up was the swimming portion of the training, which I believed had been used by some instructors to retaliate against minority recruits for being permitted into the academy. The minimum standard of swimming fifty yards and treading water for approximately five minutes should've been used to teach non-swimmers to swim. However, the mental terror of possibly drowning before the test was what forced some recruits out.

Growing up, my cousins taught me how to swim at the community pool, where all the inner-city kids flocked to during the summer. As a result, my thoughts about this portion of the academy weren't as frightening as it may have been for others.

They transported us in a large yellow bus, which sounded like the transmission would fall out at any moment. Everyone instinctively remained quiet, fearing that any extraneous chatter would get us punished. The silence was nerve-racking because I wanted to hear how others were coping. Looking around, I noticed many panicked faces and hoped that the nonswimmers had adequately prepared themselves.

When the bus stopped, we exited and went to the locker room to change into our bathing suits. Another black male recruit approached me and told me that he didn't know how to swim. I tried to console him, but in the back of my mind, I knew that if he didn't know how to swim by now, he'd be going home.

The facility had an Olympic-size pool; but for the weaker swimmers, it may as well have been an ocean. We lined up on the edge and were told to jump into the eight feet of water. I can't imagine the amount of water they had swallowed. The recruits with large muscles had a difficult time staying afloat. I gathered that body mass made them less buoyant. A few recruits flopped around like they were drowning and scrambled to get to the side of the pool to survive, but the instructors immediately ordered them back to the middle. Some of the white recruits (who were excellent swimmers), entertained themselves by pulling some of the nonswimmers underwater so they'd panic. I was afraid that someone was going to die if they continued this outrageous behavior. Putting it mildly, they were assholes!

After completing the practice session, an instructor then explained what would happen if we failed the minimum standards. He said, "I know there are some of you who are going to have problems. You'd better practice! Do I make myself clear?"

We screamed, "Yes, sir!"

The test finally came and, as expected, several minority recruits failed. Even though I knew how to swim, I failed. I had psyched myself into believing that I wasn't going to make it and had become exhausted. They gave us one chance to retake it or do it the next day. Several recruits and I opted to try again. I didn't want to go back to my room and think about being sent home. Three black recruits, including me, passed the retest. However, one white recruit, who had been pressured by his wife to come home, adamantly refused and was sent packing.

The following day, several black recruits failed and were also dismissed. At that point, we were about a quarter of the way into the training, and I thought it was fiscally irresponsible to release someone because of noncompliance. One of my classmates referred to it as a pseudo-ethnic cleansing, but I realized we had to perform twice as well for us to remain in the academy.

As we progressed, some of the black recruits socialized on the weekends. We often talked about our collective experience, which was that it wasn't comfortable being in the academy. I can't recall the exact number; however, after a few weeks, mainly due to swimming, our numbers had significantly dwindled. I said goodbye to a few good friends who—if not for the swimming—would've probably graduated. Their departure mirrored the adage, "Last to hire, first to fire." However, it didn't deter us because there was one activity that we could pursue with utter confidence.

A lot of the minorities anxiously waited for the boxing portion to commence; I know I did. It could've been surviving the streets of an inner city that made some of us such capable fighters. I had an advantage because I had trained in martial arts and boxing with a lot of my neighborhood friends. Nonetheless, I knew there were other exceptional pugilists in the class because some of us often bragged about knocking each other out once we were in the boxing ring. Their boasting made me believe that they could back up their words. However, I couldn't wait to test my fighting skills against someone.

The instructors weren't looking for the next boxing champion. Instead, they wanted to see if we had the heart to fight, even if we were getting our ass kicked. They had a strange way of selecting participants for our four fights. We sat on the floor mats in a circle with our backs to each other. Stenciled last names on the front of our T-shirts and the rear of our shorts made us easily identifiable. The intense expectation of waiting made me need to use the bathroom before each fight.

In a moment's notice, the instructor called out the names of the participants. We couldn't prepare for any particular fighter. Nevertheless, I wanted to fight the biggest person. I needed to experience being hit hard to gauge my response. This behavior might've appeared to be a bit strange; but if I couldn't take an ass whipping in the ring, I didn't want to get my ass kicked while I had a gun on my side. Ultimately, my first fight strengthened my reputation—a reputation that my instructors wouldn't forget.

The first recruit called up was a stocky guy with broad shoulders, massive biceps, and tree-trunk legs, who appeared capable of knocking someone's head off. After his selection, an instructor yelled, "Martin, put the gear on!"

I thought, *This should be fun.* After securing the headgear, gloves, and mouth guard, the instructor motioned for us to fight.

During the first minute, I needed to feel his power to assess my risks. I pressed the action after he had hit me and didn't knock me down. After punching him in the nose several times, he unexpectedly bled like a gutted pig. The canvas and our T-shirts were heavily soiled and resembled a crime scene. I continued the onslaught until the instructor yelled, "Time!" As we left the ring, I was exhausted from all the punches I had thrown and the numerous times that he had hit me. We didn't want to quit; but in the minds of the instructors, we had passed.

My next fight troubled me because it was against my roommate. I didn't want to fight anyone I considered a friend, but it wasn't my decision; they planned it.

Over the course of several weeks, my roommate complained that women shouldn't be allowed into the academy. A few of the instructors had found out about his comments, and in their minds, he needed to go.

They called us to the ring, and I put my gear on and got mentally prepared. My classmate—who was very muscular and about twenty pounds heavier—stood in the opposite corner. The ring instructor then calmly walked to my corner and told me very sternly, "You'd better knock him out. If you don't, I am going to find someone to knock you out! Understood?"

With my mouth guard in place and the instructions received, I replied in a muffled tone, "Yes, sir!"

The bell rang, and I charged him. I threw punches to knock his head off like the old Rock'em Sock'em toy robots. After striking him about five times as hard as I could, he fell to his knees. The instructors, who stood on the outside of the ring, repeatedly yelled at him to get up and fight. About thirty seconds had passed before he got to his feet, and we were told to fight again. We threw punches at each other, and his power assured me that I'd need smelling salts to wake my ass up if he connected with my jaw. Every time he punched me, my body violently trembled; even so, I didn't realize how hard I hit.

After approximately ten minutes of fighting, I had knocked him down numerous times. I thought they proved their point, but they wanted him out. As I approached him to continue, he hit me with a punch I didn't see coming and damn near broke my jaw. In an instant, I lost my vision. As darkness crept in, I believed that I was about to cross over and pass through the pearly gates. Fortunately, I heard voices, so I knew I wasn't dead. I had never been walloped that hard before.

Surprisingly, I stumbled to the corner and raised my hands to protect myself in anticipation of my probable ass kicking. I stood trying to get my sight back as the instructors yelled, "Hit him! Hit him! What are you waiting for?"

I was confused; I thought they wanted me to kick his ass. Was I being duped? Nevertheless, his lack of killer instinct was going to cost him dearly.

Once I regained my bearings, I observed him cowering in the corner. It's on now. I ran toward him and unleashed a barrage of punches. He couldn't cover up quickly enough before I dropped him. The instructor screamed, "Martin, get to a neutral corner!"

Blood poured from his crooked nose. The instructor was unsympathetic and yelled for him to "get up and fight!" He lifted himself from the canvas and walked around the ring. When he was ready, the instructor looked at me and winked. I then unleashed an avalanche on his ass because I didn't want him to hit me again. This time, he was out for good.

Breathing heavily, I waited in my corner for further instructions while he lay on the mat for about ten minutes before they assisted him out of the ring. Unfortunately, if I hadn't done it to him, the beating most certainly would've been done to me. I believe they wanted to maintain control over who stayed in their academy.

Later that evening, after eating dinner, we returned to our rooms to complete homework and wind down. As I walked in, I noticed my roommate, whom I had boxed earlier, sitting at the end of his bed with his head down. He wasn't in his khaki uniform like the rest of us. He was wearing a suit, and his suitcases were on the floor next to him. When he lifted his head, he resembled a raccoon with his bruised eyes and swollen nose.

Another roommate asked him, "What the hell happened to you?"

He replied, "I have a broken nose and a concussion." He went on to say, "The doctor doesn't think I can continue boxing, and they are sending me home."

Guilt overwhelmed me because they could've chosen anyone else to do their bidding. I had mixed emotions and wanted to express my sorrow, but I let it go.

We said our goodbyes, and I wished him good luck. I will always remember how some instructors held personal vendettas against specific recruits and ruined their potential careers in law enforcement.

My next two fights were the most challenging. One opponent was a semi-pro boxer and the other a former high school football player. The boxer gave me the toughest match because neither one of us wanted to lose. He looked like a barroom brawler—not overly muscular but a rather big man. His punches were heavy but not bone-crushing. His strengths were that he threw lots of combinations to my head and body. The fight was strategic, and after ten minutes of maneuvering and slugging it out, we had garnered each other's respect.

The fight with the football player showed me that there are some genuinely tough men in this world. He was about forty pounds heavier than me and was just a big brute. He was somewhat slow but could damn sure take a punch. I hit him many times and as hard as I possibly could, and he didn't flinch. I would've hated to face off with him in a real fight.

After our fight was over, we walked out of the ring and headed to the water fountain. When we got to the back room, he said, "Thanks for taking it easy on me." I offered no emotion and sarcastically replied, "No problem." I was just glad it was over. I knew I could defend myself and was also pleased that I got my bell rung.

With the boxing segment completed, our training turned to ground fighting, which simulated a physical confrontation on the side of the roadway. The grappling was well suited for wrestlers, so I was at a distinct disadvantage.

We sat on the floor mats in our gym suits with leather gear, which consisted of a gun holster and a nine-millimeter plastic replica. The instructors didn't provide us with any specific directions but stressed the importance of not getting our weapon taken. When they told us to fight, we had to make our opponent surrender.

A few of my academy classmates struggled with their adversary and had their gun snatched from them. I couldn't see myself fighting that long with anyone while I had a weapon on my side.

When my time came, I rushed my opponent and struck him in his balls. I didn't want to hurt him severely, but this was a competition, and I didn't want to lose. Within seconds, he screamed, "Uncle!" He then crouched over and grimaced. I wasn't looking for any accolades, but I knew I didn't have time to play games. This exercise simulated a life-or-death scenario, and I walked away from it.

For the most part, they matched us evenly; however, the instructors didn't like a particular recruit and made him fight one of the biggest and most fit guys in the class. The bigger recruit's massive cranium and enormously chiseled body were freakishly impressive. Here I thought I had a big head. He appeared capable of physically destroying someone. When they were told to fight, he severely head-butted the smaller recruit. The bigger recruit had been given his marching orders, and he did what he needed to do. The match ended shortly after that.

They fought on another occasion; but this time, the big brute placed his fingers into the corners of the smaller recruit's mouth and tried to rip his jaws open. It was the most gruesome act of sanctioned violence I had seen. The instructors ended the match, and the smaller recruit sustained only minimal damage. He gained my utmost respect for not giving up. I would've screamed like hell.

As our journey continued, the academy instructors provided us with several opportunities to prove we could be trusted. Strict rules had to be adhered to if we intended to remain. Lights went out promptly at ten o'clock, and we had to go directly to bed.

One evening, I was up late and decided to take a shower—even though it was after curfew. I waited for the night-duty officer to go to bed and went to a vacant room. After getting out of the shower, I carelessly secured my towel and pranced back to my room. Unexpectedly, a female instructor yelled out, "What are you doing?"

I almost crapped on myself. I ran into another vacant room trying to get away, but she followed behind me. She emphatically asked, "What do you think you're doing?"

I quickly snapped to attention and nervously replied, "I'm sorry, ma'am. I just finished taking a shower." I then looked down and noticed that my loosely draped towel had fallen to the ground. I don't know if she realized it because she continued chastising me while I stood there butt-naked. It looked like I had just stepped out of a cold pool. I silently laughed it off, and maybe she did as well. After she had finished yelling at me, I grabbed my towel, covered up, and went to my room. Fortunately, no one else was awake.

During our training, if an instructor observed us messing around, we'd be punished. They caught us a few times, and we paid dearly by doing an hour and fifteen minutes of push-ups or jumping jacks.

On one occasion, we participated in progression drills, which were doing calisthenics, followed by running wind sprints, and then more calisthenics. It was an utterly exhausting exercise. As we stood waiting, the instructor told us that he had expected total participation. He then casually walked away and disappeared into a dorm room.

After completing the drills, the instructor returned and told us that he had been inside watching with a pair of binoculars. He then began calling out the names. Those recruits named were immediately dismissed from the class because they were caught cheating. Shocked by this revelation, I stood there thinking about what an instructor told us on the first day, "Look to your left, now look to your right. One of you will not be here in the end." Unfortunately, this was the wake-up call that some of us needed. If they cheated at something as trivial as an exercise, what else were they capable of doing?

Some days, they had us run in a drill formation for five miles. The pounding took its toll on my legs; but mentally, I removed any thoughts of failing. We had gone through so much, and recruits were still getting kicked out.

About two-thirds into the training, we had to qualify with our weapon. My prior Army Reserve training fully prepared me, but others weren't as fortunate.

The passing standard was 210 out of 300. I wondered where they came up with these numbers, but I guess it was paramount that everyone had to be proficient with the weapon that could ultimately save our lives. They gave us ample practice sessions to familiarize ourselves with the course. On qualification day, ten recruits stood next to each other as they barked out the firing sequence. Ear protection made it difficult trying to decipher their commands. One by one, we passed until a very popular recruit scored a 209. As with every test, they gave him a second chance; but again, he didn't score the mandatory 210, so he was sent home. Several recruits questioned why he couldn't be given an exception because he had done well up to that point. They exclaimed everyone had to meet the bare minimum; and since he failed, he had to go home.

Life didn't get any easier for some of us after that incident. Several recruits had problems controlling their weight, which I couldn't understand why. Given the amount of exercise we had completed, no one should've had a problem. In an attempt to embarrass them, the instructors placed them on a fictitious "fat man's list." Some of these guys were just big men; but according to the instructors, they were a bunch of wide-bodies, so their food consumption was limited.

The chow hall and eating customs were similar to those in military facilities. From the time we sat down, we had about two minutes to consume as much as we could and then quickly leave. There was no way that this practice was good for digestion, but I wasn't going to go on a crusade for an extra ten minutes of dining because the food sucked.

When we were in the mess hall, the instructors continually berated us. On a particular occasion, while standing in the chow line, an instructor approached me and asked, "Are you a Crisco oil duck fucker?" His snicker afterward suggested that he wanted a response.

I stood there looking at him with a "Boo-Boo the fool" expression on my face. I had no idea of what it was or why he thought I had been one. Maybe it was some perverted act he engaged in, but I wasn't going to ask; it would've only caused me problems. I believed it was a part of their twisted way of harassing us, and no one had been off limits. "No, sir!" I curtly responded.

The instructors continued with their folly; but by then, they had sent home the recruits incapable of staying.

As time progressed, the instructors gave us more liberties. We were able to shed our khakis to wear our blue uniforms, which displayed the state police patch on the right shoulder. Being in the uniform was a proud moment because it showed that we were close to graduation. Nevertheless, as a mind game, they periodically made us take them off so we'd realize that we weren't state troopers yet.

Another thing that most of us enjoyed was being able to call home. I rarely did. I knew my mom was busy working and taking care of the household, so I didn't want to bother her. I talked to her when I returned home on the weekends.

One evening, I happened to be walking in the hallway, and I overheard a conversation of a white recruit whose father was a high-ranking state trooper. The recruit said, "Mommy, I'm not like daddy, and I want to come home." In this case, the preferential treatment wasn't desired. I tried my best not to show any facial expressions as he looked up and noticed me walking past him. It appeared that his family forced him into something that he didn't want. In some ways, I guess there was more pressure on him to get through the academy than the rest of us; I was glad he stuck it out.

Most of the stress from the training subsided as we prepared for graduation. They always reminded us about who we represented, and we should be mindful of our behavior at all times. When I went home on the weekends, I only spent time with my closest friends because I knew they wouldn't be detrimental to my future career.

One weekend, I had a conversation with a friend regarding the academy. He commented that he thought I had changed and spoke differently. I knew my diction had improved due to my environment. I didn't hear slang, and my academy classmates made sure that every time I said the word "asking," they'd jokingly remind that it wasn't pronounced "axing." I had to remember to put the words "ask" and "king" together to pronounce it correctly. I also understood that as a state trooper, I'd be judged by a white male standard. I wouldn't realize the full impact of my academy experience until years later.

Graduation day was unbelievable. Adoring family members and friends filled every seat. The cheers were deafening as they announced the names of all the graduates. When they called my name, I proudly walked across the stage and received my badge. I thought about my father and wondered what he would've said to me.

Nevertheless, looking out into the audience and seeing the smiling faces of my mother and godmother made my day. Who would've ever thought that the kid from the pizzeria would become a New Jersey state trooper? I had just conquered my greatest opponent: me.

My state-police class had several recruits who had fathers, uncles, brothers, cousins, or friends that were enlisted members. This type of legacy hiring is what has plagued us for many years.

My class started out with about 250 recruits and graduated 131. The most glaring reality about it was that there were only twelve African-Americans, seven Hispanics, and five women.

Due to litigation, subsequent classes in the next three years saw a marked increase in the number of minorities allowed to enter the ranks. It didn't dawn on me that the previous low number of minorities might have been deliberate. Today, I compare their discrimination against black minorities to Article 1, Section 2, Paragraph 3 of the US Constitution, which gave three-fifth status to black people, who had to fight to be considered full human beings before fighting for rights that white people had at birth.

In my opinion, the outfit needs to do a better job of appreciating the tangible and intangible assets of minorities and women. We were the exploited huddled masses, and many of us came from inner cities and were just happy we had a job. It appeared that in prior years, they cared more about keeping the organization stocked with select family members and friends. Fortunately, the chance for an ordinary candidate regardless of race or gender increased because the process has been changed to a random selection to take away subjectivity. The reasons for my controversial opinion will become apparent in future chapters.

Chapter 11

The Culture

A sleeping conscience precipitates regression of progress.

The experience of traveling on an unknown road is challenging, especially if at times, this path had only been accessible to a particular group. In 1890, with the passing of the Police Enforcement Legislation, New Jersey incorporated its first state police agency.

From the outset, only white males 5'6" and taller were allowed to enter its ranks. The exclusions of others hadn't been by force of circumstance. The mechanism for the rarely discussed preferential treatment was cemented, which was eerily similar to a stance taken in an old Jim Crow sign I've seen from Dallas, Texas, that read: "NO Dogs—Negroes—Mexicans."

It wasn't until the early 1960s that the arc of history began to bend toward progressive change when a former military officer, P. Landon, became the first African-American to graduate from the academy. His inclusion was the beginning of the end of their racial superiority. Moreover, his achievement was such a monumental accomplishment that he received recognition in an issue of a prominent black publication.

The outfit's chronicled behavior preceded the Civil Rights Act of 1964, which forbade discrimination. In light of this, it may appear that I'm affording them credit for being forward thinkers; however, it is more a condemnation of its behavior toward others. They should tell this story to every incoming recruit class to exorcise all its discriminatory demons.

Undoubtedly, my viewpoints will offend some of my white colleagues whose favorable opinions make them believe that we are beyond reproach. However, we must keep in mind that history has consistently overlooked the black and brown perspective. I hope that they are mature enough to be open-minded to a different point of view. Nevertheless, at the time, I acknowledge that the outfit was similar to many other intolerant factions of society. While today we can see it as a great injustice and flawed tradition, back then, it was shamefully the norm.

In retrospect, Trooper Landon rode on the shoulders of civil rights and first unofficial Black Lives Matter activists Rosa Parks, Malcolm X, and Dr. Martin Luther King Jr. during a time when black people struggled to gain equality and justice.

Later in my career, I had the distinct pleasure of meeting Trooper Landon, who had been getting up there in age but still looked to be in excellent physical condition. I asked him if he'd ever considered writing a book about his experiences. He sadly claimed that he couldn't remember a lot of the details due to his age. However, he said that his employment was filled with both internal and external flagrant disrespect and discrimination.

Trooper Landon stated that while a high school degree was the only requirement for entrance, he had a college degree and later earned a doctorate. He maintained that they intentionally refused to promote him even though he had more qualifications than most of his contemporaries. He also claimed that white motorists attempted to physically assault him because they didn't appreciate a black state trooper telling them what to do. Given the history of African-Americans in law enforcement, I'm shocked that they gave him a gun and allowed him to arrest anyone other than black people. He subsequently filed a civil lawsuit after years of discrimination and later resigned.

During this time frame—which I refer to as the "raisins in the rice bowl era"—they had employed approximately seventeen hundred state troopers of whom thirteen were African-American, five Hispanic, and one female. That one woman also filed a civil lawsuit and later resigned.

As a staunch opponent of any discrimination, I won't sanitize or support any agency that intentionally disallowed minorities and females to join its ranks. Again, my stance may be an issue for some, but it needs to arouse the conscience of others about our past. At some point, the rejected groups will have to be made whole because it took too damn long for the NJSP to accept that its actions were undeniably wrong. Out of respect for Trooper Landon and those denied an opportunity for inclusion, I will only recognize our existence starting in the early 1960s.

My first duty assignment was Hacket Station located in West County, which is about sixty miles from my family's home. It took approximately an hour and fifteen minutes to get there. As a rule, your first station would be as far away from your home as possible. It was a tradition that we all had to endure.

On my first drive to the station, I took in the unfamiliar scenery. It was late in the evening, and I had been given the 11:00 p.m. to 7:00 a.m. shift and needed to be there by 10:00 p.m. The weather was cold with blustery winds, but the stars packed the night sky and were the guiding light for my travels. Swaying trees lined the sides of the roadway. My car's cassette player serenaded me with Patti Labelle's music in the background. A chill seeped in through an intentional crack in my window and allowed fresh air to subdue the contrasting hot air coming from the car vents. A few tractor trailers shared the right and center lanes because a law prohibited them from being in the left lane. The closer I got to the station, the more the area became quiet and desolate. I wondered if it was typical for this part of the state. If so, it would be a welcome change from the hustle and bustle of city life.

I had reached milepost 19 when unexpected flashing red lights appeared in my rearview mirror. Caught up in forecasting the coming events, when I looked down, my speedometer read "80 mph." *Damn it*! My butt cheeks clenched tightly because I knew I was in trouble. "Where the hell did he come from?" I asked myself. (I said "he" because I had never seen a woman state trooper in a patrol car.)

Frightened, I pulled over to the side of the road and waited for whomever I had disturbed. A slight glance in my side-view mirror reflected a uniform that I had just gotten acquainted with, and I knew shit was going to roll downhill and smother my ass. As this was my first day and I was in civilian attire, I had no clue about what to expect.

The state trooper walked up to my side window, blazed his flashlight into my eyes, and sternly said, "License, registration, and insurance card." I knew I should've had them ready, but I couldn't think straight.

With my hands shaking, I grabbed my wallet from my back pocket, pulled out the requested documents, and extended them out the window. I didn't want to give him a chance to go back to his car and write me a ticket, so I quickly interjected in a cracked voice, "Ex-excuse me, sir. I-I-I am on my way to the Hacket Station. Today is my first day." *Damn, I should've kept my mouth closed.*

He leaned over and said, "What is your name, Recruit?"

I wanted to say "Duh, you have my license. Can't you read?" However, I sheepishly responded, "Trooper Vincent Martin, sir."

He then became noticeably upset and hollered, "You aren't a state trooper yet!"

I knew that I had just graduated from the academy, so what the hell was his problem? I didn't know what to think, so I sat there while he verbally assaulted me.

After a while, he sounded like the obscured teacher in the Charlie Brown cartoons. All I heard for about a minute or so was the drowned-out, repetitive, and annoying noise of *womp, womp, womp, womp, womp, womp!*

He ended his tirade and said, "I am going to call ahead and tell your investigative officer you were speeding."

I incessantly apologized until he allowed me to leave. *Damn, he ruined my very first day. What an asshole!*

When I arrived at Hacket Station, I was still a little unnerved, but I soon met my squadmates and the person who'd teach me how to become a state trooper. Once a recruit graduates from the academy, he or she is assigned a senior state trooper (coach) to receive on-the-job training.

My coach was about 5'9" tall and weighed about 165 lbs. He looked physically fit in his uniform and had a well-defined blondish mustache. I couldn't wait to grow mine back. My initial sense was that he appeared to be a decent guy. Based on the friendly banter between my squadmates, they seemed to be tight-knit, which eased some of my concerns.

After going through the official formalities, my coach pulled me to the side to discuss my speeding incident. True to his word, that other trooper had made the telephone call. However, to my coach's credit, he told me that the guy was an idiot. He advised me to slow down and not to be too concerned. I was relieved because, on my first day, I didn't want to be labeled as being arrogant or—as they referred to it—salty. He then told me to get my cold weather gear (overcoat and gloves) because we had to respond to the scene of a possible motor vehicle accident.

I quickly unpacked all my uniforms and stored them in my assigned locker. My name, "Trooper V. Martin," was emblazoned on the front door. What a welcoming feeling.

I then went to the front of the building and asked the state trooper sitting in the radio room for our assigned car. From the back room, my coach yelled, "Grab the keys to car 205 off the board." I pulled the keys down, ran outside, and started it. I then moved over, sat in the passenger seat, and filled out the patrol chart with the odometer reading and radar unit serial numbers—as I had learned in the academy.

After ten minutes, my coach came out, got into the driver's seat, and said, "Starting tomorrow night, 'Martini,' you will drive."

Another nickname. Oh well. However, in time, I noticed most state troopers were given silly nicknames or name derivations as a part of the bonding process.

He then turned on the red flashing lights, and we sped out of the parking lot.

Driving to the scene, I mentally zoned out. I couldn't believe that I was going on my first official call. My thought process was interrupted when my coach said, "Pay attention to what you say and do tonight."

What did he think I was going to do? I immediately responded, "Yes, sir!"

When we arrived, I observed several volunteer emergency medical technicians (EMTs) standing around. I walked over, and one of them said, "Hey, Troop, there is a dead man in the pickup truck."

Even though they showed movies of autopsies in the academy, I was shocked to hear this my first night on the job. Is this what I signed up to do? I tentatively approached the dark-gray pickup truck and peered into the driver's icy glazed window and saw a white man, frozen stiff as a board, lying across the front seat. He was wearing a pair of jeans, a blue jacket, a gray shirt, and a red baseball cap. A thick, frozen, tannish mucous film lined his black mustache. I then noticed his shirt was untucked. I also eyed several rifles hanging from a gun rack across the rear window. I thought he had overdosed because I didn't see any blood; however, an EMT told me that the deceased had taken an M-80 firecracker and placed it against his stomach. The blast cracked one of his ribs, punctured his lung, and killed him. It must've been excruciating for him to die in that manner. I wondered what could've been going on in his life that made him go to such an extreme.

My coach told me the man left a suicide note on the front seat, which was for his wife and kids. I was moved to tears as I read the letter. I dried them quickly because they started to freeze as they rolled down my face.

He was thirty-three years old; and in his letter, he explained that he took his life because he was unable to provide for his family. Coincidentally, his name was Vincent, which screwed with my head. I was uncertain if I could handle seeing dead people, especially those who took their lives. Later, I discussed my apprehension with my coach. "Sir, is this normal?" I asked.

He looked at me and said, "I'm not going to say it's normal, but it does happen occasionally. Don't worry. You'll be okay. We all get used to it."

I suspected he knew I was going to see more of this in my career, and his words of encouragement temporarily helped me to reconcile my thoughts.

After my first set of midnights had ended, I worked the 7:00 a.m. to 3:00 p.m. shift. I arrived every morning around 6:00 a.m. because

I had the responsibility of taking out the trash and washing the dishes left in the sink from the midnight shift. My squadmates forewarned me that this was a tradition everyone had to do until a junior state trooper graduated from the academy. I didn't take it personally because I knew that it was a part of our tradition, and I didn't mind because I couldn't stand seeing dirty dishes in the sink. After completing my duties, I looked forward to getting on the road and learning more about my job.

My coach had a reputation for being a "crime dog," or someone with a keen ability for detecting illegal activity. He told me that the profile of individuals committing crimes in the Hacket Station area was a white male between the ages of eighteen and thirty. I didn't think it was a profile because it was a predominately white area, but this word would later become very controversial. He showed me what to look for regarding a person's physical appearance, types of cars, body language, and nervousness in speech patterns. When we stopped cars, it was fun watching the driver attempt to deceive us into thinking that everything was okay. I was astounded at how their eyes shifted and their lips quivered; and some sweated profusely even though it had been freezing outside.

After two months, I completed my training and was allowed to patrol on my own. My coach said, "Martini, you have been my best recruit. When you're out there on patrol, I want you to remember what I've taught you, and you'll do fine." I hoped he wasn't just trying to be nice because his words validated me, and my insecurities started to diminish.

The state troopers on my squad were very hawkish and wanted to make arrests. We understood it wasn't a game because gun violence was a real problem in West County. Makeshift memorials of deceased state troopers lined the sides of roadways throughout the state. I knew that if something had happened to them, then it could most certainly happen to me as well.

During my time at Hacket Station, I developed a reputation for making arrests, and I had garnered respect from my colleagues. My first arrest was for a driver's possession of a .25-caliber handgun. The driver's nervous body language tipped me off that something was wrong. I patted him down for my safety and uncovered the gun in his waistband. The arrest made me realize that I had a possible knack for detecting criminal behavior, but another incident caused me to question if I also had the potential to become a racial profiler.

While patrolling eastbound on Route 180, I saw a black Chevrolet Camaro traveling in the middle lane. I assumed the driver and passenger were black Jamaicans because of their long dreadlock hairstyles. I thought, *If I stop this car, it might have something illegal in it.* The occupants didn't fit the West County profile, but they looked suspicious traveling through a rural area.

I shamefully followed the car until it departed my patrol area. In retrospect, my inexperience showed me how easy it was for me—and probably other state troopers—to be influenced by appearances and stereotypes. It was unfair of me to treat them differently based on their appearance because I knew that I was different than most of my colleagues. There were not many black state troopers in the entire state, let alone at my station, but I recall the first time I understood that my "blackness" was viewed as being blue.

While in uniform, I had encountered numerous older white adults who were extremely friendly to me. Once, a little woman walked up to me and said, "Good morning. Let me see your name tag. Oh, good morning, Trooper Martin."

I replied, "Good morning, ma'am." Her pleasantness caught me by surprise because I wasn't used to it.

I later questioned my former coach as to the reason why people were so deferential. He said, "The clothes and gear you are wearing has a long-standing tradition in this area and commands respect."

That's when it dawned on me: I was a part of something truly unique. After that, I wasn't as concerned about working in West County anymore. I wore a distinctive uniform, and race didn't matter—or so I thought.

My work environment lacked diversity. I was one of two African-American males assigned to Hacket Station. The other guy was on a different squad. We never worked together due to our conflicting work schedules. However, the few times that we crossed paths, his only advice to me was "They will make off-colored remarks. Don't take it personally."

I suspected my colleagues had waited for me to complete my probationary period because, within days, I was the recipient of many racially motivated jokes. To an unsuspecting onlooker, a lot of the improper conduct could be construed as rookie hazing, but I didn't think it was funny at all.

Periodically, state troopers replaced their uniforms and equipment. A written request was required to make the exchange. I submitted the requisite documents for new clothing items. Nonetheless, a senior state trooper, unbeknownst to me, had revised all my paperwork and signed my name.

On my original clothing card, I requested a new blouse (jacket), a sand brown (leather cord), and several pairs of black socks. On his revised card, it read that I requested "a loincloth, sweatbands, and a six-foot spear." Also, in a doctored internal "special report" that was submitted as though written by me, he used derogatory, ignorant, and illiterate-sounding slang language to express my request to transfer to another station. Trying to convey my emotions wouldn't do justice to my state of mind. I have elected to include the exact text so readers can consider what impact his words would've had upon them if they were in my place.

> Title: Quest foe transfer: Dis righter be axen foe a transfers two eider da Turnpip ohr da Parkwiys for seberal reason. Da furse reason be dat dis honkey I be workin foe dasn't be understandin da needs an feelins ob a hot Negro stud witch I be. He be always tellin me to leebe dees green teeft, honkey wimins alone. He say I kin only be goin out wif da wons wif no teefs. Dat be find wif me, cept but moss ob dems be ole an ugly. Us hot Negro studs likes to be stikin hour massib members inta honkey wimins but dat be cruel an unfare punishment. Sekinly, I be feelin dat if I be back wif my own kine, witch be wear I belong anyways, I wood be

feelin moe cumforble, an not be always lookin ober my showders foe da Klan. Foe dees reason I be questin an medieight transfers to da earis down by my house. Spectfuly.

The documents were photocopied and posted on information boards at several road stations. It was difficult trying to dismiss the trooper's childish antics because I was embarrassed. I didn't outwardly make a big deal about it even though, inside, I was seething. I needed to have thick skin. I never shared my thoughts with anyone about how it affected me because I didn't want to start any trouble. They never punished the trooper even though many of our superiors knew about it. However, this incident showed me that I might have been a bit naive about being fully accepted. I knew that I probably couldn't change their opinions about African-American state troopers: it was their ignorance, so I didn't need to bother. His racist actions and my colleagues' acceptance would later become commonplace.

When I traveled to different stations, someone would invariably ask me, "Are you the same Martin in the report?" I wanted to tell them to kiss my ass because I got tired of defending myself. I needed to put it behind me because I had a five-year probationary period to complete, and I didn't want to give them any reason not reenlist me. I assumed that all minorities were screened to make sure we'd keep our mouths shut. I remembered my childhood days listening to my elders talk about the racist name-calling and second-class treatment that they had to put up with. I could now relate.

My initiation into the "state police family" was, at times, more challenging than I had expected. My upbringing in the City of Elkanda never prepared me for this rural lifestyle.

One afternoon, I investigated a deer and motor vehicle accident. The car was damaged, and the deer lay dead on the side of the road. I radioed my investigative officer and advised him of the circumstances. He instructed me to place the dead deer in the trunk of my troop car and bring it to the station. It didn't faze me because I thought it was an unwritten policy for removing dead animals from the roadway.

The deer weighed about 150 lbs., so I foolishly waited awhile because I believed that another state trooper had been dispatched to assist me. After twenty minutes or so, when no one showed up, I realized I had to lift it by myself. I was very cautious not to get my uniform dirty because, eventually, I'd have to go back on patrol.

I returned to the station and removed the carcass from the trunk and placed it in the garage. My investigative officer told me, "Hey, kid, take off that uniform and get into your khakis." I went to the locker room and did what he told me. When I returned, he handed me a four-inch knife and said, "Okay, gut the deer."

I quickly said, "You must be joking! You don't do this to Bambi, do you?"

He laughed at me and said, "You city boys."

A nauseous sensation crept in, and without looking, I had placed the knife at the midsection of the deer and cut it open. "I didn't sign up for this country stupidity," I mumbled under my breath.

Something warm oozed onto my hands, and when I turned to look, I observed brownish and pinkish deer guts everywhere, which almost caused me to puke. Some of my colleagues, who came to witness my initiation, laughed at my apprehension.

"What are you knuckleheads laughing at?" I screamed. It was disgusting, and I couldn't believe they did this for sport.

The remains of the deer didn't appear salvageable. I cut open the stomach and rectum and sliced the hindquarters. My investigative officer laughed as I stood there with the terrible stench of deer feces on my hands.

After removing all the innards, someone took the deer to the back of the garage and hung it from a suspended ceiling hook. The residual blood and whatever else was left inside dripped to the ground. I guessed I passed my initiation but swore I would never do it again. "Look at me! This is the last time! Do you hear me?"

It was evident that this practice would always be a part of their ritual. They laughed at my dispute, and someone jokingly commented, "Yeah, okay, Martini."

During the afternoon shift, my investigative officer made it mandatory that the squad ate dinner together. He was an excellent cook and had enjoyed preparing our meals. I helped set the table, and dinner was served.

We had baked beans, salad, bread, and something called venison. I wasn't familiar with this type of meat, but they told me that it was excellent. The mood was laid-back, as we were allowed to undo our ties and roll up our sleeves. I consumed my share of the dish, and to my amazement, the tender meat was probably the best I had ever tasted. Afterward, my investigative officer asked me if I had enjoyed it. I expressed my pleasure and then heard a muffled chuckle coming from my squadmates. I thought that I had said something funny until they told me—I had eaten Bambi. I quickly blocked that thought out of my mind and requested another serving.

The squad's camaraderie set the stage for what I expected to be the norm at all the road stations. I innocently thought that, as an organization, we'd take care of each other despite that senior state trooper's insensitive actions.

After fulfilling my initial probationary requirement, my time at Hacket Station came to a sad ending because it was mandatory that I transfer to another road station. I didn't want to leave because I became very fond of my colleagues and surroundings. I had developed a reputation for drug interdiction and looked forward to continuing my crime-fighting prowess at my new assignment, Freling Station. However, before I transferred, I received a congratulatory letter regarding a drug arrest I had made, which resulted in the confiscation of one ounce of cocaine valued at $2,000.

Although this wasn't a massive seizure, this letter of commendation only increased my enthusiasm to make more arrests. Our eagerness to eradicate drugs caused some of us to cut corners later on in our careers. Unknowingly, many of us subconsciously fell prey to the reward of the "dangling carrot."

Chapter 12

On-the-Job Realities

Face decisions or they may boomerang.

Freling Station was very similar to Hacket Station in that they both were general policing areas, but it didn't have an interstate highway to patrol. The criminal activity involved investigating burglaries, thefts, removing cows from the roadways, and other mundane calls for service. It wasn't an area conducive to significant drug arrests, which were usually made on highways traversing inner cities. Even though I knew the locals used drugs, I didn't think any of the major drug couriers lived in this part of the state.

The slow-paced working environment indicated that dull days were ahead. The county shut down at around eleven o'clock in the evening, and the only thing left open was a Dunkin Donuts. We made several coffee runs to keep ourselves awake. This is probably how the stereotype of cops drinking coffee and eating donuts started.

At Freling Station, I had the pleasure of working with coworkers from various parts of northern New Jersey. One person that taught me a lot in a short period was a former police officer. A true down-to-earth Latino, he shared a lot of his police experiences with me and opened my eyes to my new profession. The diversity in our formative years made for interesting conversation. However, there was one state trooper who shocked me regarding the harmful effects of allowing any child to attend a segregated school system.

While having breakfast at a local diner, he brought up the topic of race. He said that he had attended a predominately white regional high school and confided in me that he had only come into contact with a handful of black students. I didn't know where this conversation was going. He went on to say that the only thing he knew about black people was what he had viewed on the local news channels. He then said, "You are nothing like them." I didn't know whether I should've thanked him for what he thought was a compliment or dismiss his ignorant comment.

I then asked him to tell me what he thought about black people. He replied matter-of-factly, "I thought they were all terrible."

I looked at him not knowing what to think. I hoped my blank stare and facial expression made him feel a bit uneasy. In the back of my mind, I wanted to smack some sense into his ass to fulfill his prophecy. I couldn't believe that in the late 1980s, there were still people like him around. Going through high school, I never let the issue of race bother me until a white schoolmate called me a nigger, and I knocked his retainer out of his mouth. He later apologized, and we became friends again. Other than that, I didn't have a similar opinion of white people because I knew better.

Taking the high road, I assured him that it was just the media's tendency to stereotype people of color and that, unfortunately, like other misinformed people, he had been brainwashed to harbor these same perceptions. I hoped that he'd mature in the coming years and purge himself of his asinine misperceptions.

Most of my daily assignments at Freling Station were routine. There were times that I met some of the most exceptional people the county had to offer. Nevertheless, I also came across individuals who were clueless when it came to proper human behavior.

One day while on patrol, I responded to a call of a possible mentally troubled person. I was familiar with the address because the owner had frequently contacted the station in an ornery and drunken stupor. I expected to go there, quietly resolve her issue, and then leave. Usually, she heeded any warnings; but this day was different.

I pulled up to her residence and observed her standing on her lawn talking to herself. As I approached, she caught me off guard by taking a swing at my face. It was more humorous than threatening because she was very petite and looked awkward trying to fight with me. However, I couldn't allow her to get away with it, so I told her that I was going to place her under arrest.

I attempted to put handcuffs on her, but it was difficult trying to grab her flailing arms. "Stop fighting with me!" I yelled. In a slurred speech, she responded, "Hell no! Now get your damn hands off of me!" If that wasn't enough, I had to contend with her little white poodle trying to bite my pant leg.

By coincidence, an off-duty investigative officer drove by and observed me scuffling with her. He stepped out of his car, calmly walked up, and field goal kicked the dog across the lawn. Without saying a word, he then kindly assisted me in placing her in handcuffs. Feeling a bit tired from struggling, I seated her in the rear of my troop car and caught my breath. I then turned around to thank the investigative officer, but he was gone. I wondered if he was there or if I had been dreaming. I subsequently transported her back to the station.

Upon walking through the station's doors, I was bombarded with jokes from my colleagues. "Help, trooper needs assistance with an elderly lady," one guy said while hysterically laughing. Of course, the investigative officer told them a funnier version of what had happened. I shrugged it off and went on with my job. The jokes eventually died down, and I was glad that I was able to laugh at myself.

About a week later, the station received a complaint of a barroom brawl. They dispatched a few cars, but I was the first to arrive on the scene. As I pulled up, I heard a raucous noise coming from inside. I grabbed my PR-24 (baton) and headed for the door. The closest patrol was about ten minutes away, but I couldn't wait. From the loud commotion, it sounded like someone was getting the crap kicked out of him. I peeked inside the circular pane window and said to myself, "Yep, someone is getting the crap kicked out of him."

I snatched the door open, and a plume of thick cigarette smoke briefly blinded me and caused me to cough violently. I collected myself and then shouted, "Everybody put your hands where I can see them!" Country music was blaring on the jukebox, but a few of the patrons did as I asked; however, the fighters continued to go at it.

The two burly white men with thick beards appeared to have had too much to drink. They slowly wrestled each other around while bracing themselves against the bar. I removed my PR-24 from its holder and forcefully rapped it several times against the bar to get their attention. *Bam, bam, bam!* I then reiterated, "I said put your damn hands where I can see them, and I mean now!"

The fighters looked up and instantly stopped grappling.

The barroom patrons quieted down as I yelled at the owner, "Turn off the music!"

He quickly ran and snatched the jukebox electric cord from the wall socket. I looked around and observed everyone because I didn't want any unforeseen beer bottles thrown at me. The owner approached and told me what had happened. I then yelled to the combatants, "You two, outside. Right now!" They bowed their heads like whimpering puppies and staggered out the door.

Once outside, I arrested them for disorderly conduct. I was in the process of placing them in my car when my backup arrived, but he didn't look surprised. I jokingly asked, "What took you so long?"

He calmly said, "One barroom fight—only one trooper needed. Get used to it." While putting his car in gear and slowly driving away, he said, "You'll learn, boot. You'll learn."

As the weeks passed, I began to understand what it took to be a state trooper. Early one morning, another state trooper and I responded to a residence regarding a domestic violence call. Just as we walked up to ring the doorbell, we heard a man having a heated argument with a woman. Foregoing any constitutional issues, we rushed in and separated the two of them. After a brief discussion, it was apparent that the man's slurred speech and aggressive attitude was going to be problematic.

While I was attempting to calm him down, he told me, "Get the fuck out of my house."

Did he just give me the perfect excuse to kick his ass? I immediately flashed back to the violence in my family. Instantaneously, I pulled out my PR-24 and was about to thump him when a young boy, about ten years old, came from the back room and started yelling at the man. My partner and I stood there dumbfounded as this kid called his father an asshole and told him to get out of the house. The father then shamefacedly asked his son for some money to stay at a hotel. The kid ran to a back room and returned with a mason jar filled with cash. He handed his father about fifty dollars, and we escorted him from the house. Back then, it wasn't uncommon for the aggressor to be removed from the premises and told not to come back until they had cooled down. Luckily, times have changed. Everything in me told me to stomp the hell out of him to teach him a lesson, but the kid's method peacefully resolved the problem that night.

The job wasn't always filled with adrenaline and excitement. Occasionally, a report of an accident would be a welcome change of pace. On the midnight shift, two state troopers are assigned to patrol together. This particular evening, the state trooper assigned to the station received a telephone call from a panicked woman who claimed she had argued with her boyfriend, and he drove off drunk and angry. She described his car, his physical appearance, and the potential places he may have been headed. Typically, we would've just documented this information, but because he was possibly under the influence of alcohol, my colleague and I were dispatched to locate him.

Freling County is known for having dark and winding roads, making navigation difficult for anyone. After about an hour of searching, my partner and I gave up and resumed our routine patrol. I hoped the driver had made it to his destination and slept it off. We continued patrolling for about three hours until we were dispatched to a single car accident.

Just as we pulled up to the scene, I observed a few local first-aid volunteers with their blue flashing lights displayed on their dashboards. They were the bedrock of the community because they knew the area better than most. About a tenth of a mile down the road, I saw a car fully engulfed by fire. Bright orange flames and crackling noises were shooting from the engine and passenger compartment. I had expected an inevitable massive explosion, so I immediately radioed for a fire truck.

Oh no, please don't let someone be in there, I thought. Then my worst fears were acknowledged.

A man ran up to me and hysterically screamed, "Someone is in the car!" My partner and I attempted to get closer, but the flames were too intense. My heart was heavy knowing someone had burned to death. I just hoped that the person died quickly and didn't suffer as much.

Shortly after that, the fire truck arrived and extinguished the blaze. Sadly, the driver was burned beyond recognition. The only distinct body parts were bones and teeth. I contacted the station and requested the crime scene investigators and medical examiner. Upon closer inspection of the vehicle identification number, we learned that the car belonged to the man we had attempted to locate earlier.

As I stood there watching what everyone else was doing, it didn't appear that they were too affected. They casually chatted with one another while I silently struggled with what had happened. This was my first time seeing a burned body, but I understood how overexposure to terrible accident scenes could potentially desensitize me. I had hoped that I'd never lose my compassion, but I then recalled what my coach had told me a few months earlier: "We all get used to it."

The medical examiner eventually removed the body. Crime scene investigators gathered the remaining evidence, but I still had the unenviable task of informing the deceased man's family of his demise. No words could undo the damage; but this, too, was a part of the job.

I pulled up to the residence, and it seemed as though the family was expecting me. As I stepped out of my vehicle, a young woman started crying uncontrollably. I guess she was the one that made the call. An elderly gentleman pulled me to the side and told me that they already knew about the accident. I did what I could to comfort him and hoped that they'd eventually find solace believing that their loved one didn't suffer.

The routineness of police work made me look to my colleagues for outside excitement. We all wanted to be a part of the state police brotherhood, and late-night drinking (a.k.a. "choir practice") was a part of it. Unfortunately, the rendezvous spot was about sixty-five miles away from my home.

One Saturday, while off duty, I received a call from a colleague who invited me to a get-together. Though I dreaded traveling so far, I couldn't pass up the opportunity to bond with my squadmates. I brought along a friend to drive me home because I knew that I would be drinking a lot.

We arrived at the party, located in a fire station, around six o'clock in the evening. The atmosphere was friendly as head-bobbing rock music played in the background. It brought back memories of my military days.

A table with loads of food containers had been set up against a wall for self-service. I jokingly said, "Don't ask me to gut a deer." My coworkers laughed because they had heard about my prior experience. I then spotted a beer keg and got myself a drink.

I made my rounds and talked to the state troopers I knew and introduced myself to some I didn't. My friend also made himself at home and struck up conversations with many of the partygoers. I listened to my share of their state police "war stories" because I was relatively new and didn't have too many of my own to tell.

They bragged about fights, high-risk traffic stops, and rescues they had made during their respective careers. The senior state troopers appeared to have done everything, or so they led me to believe. The evening continued as people came and went, but a core of state troopers that lived in the area remained to finish off the beer.

I couldn't recall how much I drank because several hours had passed and I needed to go home, but I was drunk off my ass. I told one of my colleagues that I was going as I stumbled away to look for my friend, who was going to drive us home.

Locating him was difficult because, surprisingly, there were many people still hanging out and drinking at four o'clock in the morning. I then glanced over in the corner and found him asleep in a chair. I walked over to wake him up, and it was apparent that he was drunk from the smell of his hot breath. I kicked him a few times and slurred, "Hey, get up! You have to drive us home."

He opened his eyes, laughed, and then started to speak; but he garbled his words. He attempted to stand but failed as he staggered to catch his balance and fell back into the chair. My plans of being responsible went out the window. I was in no shape to drive, but I couldn't tell anyone; they would've accused me of being a lightweight.

"Hey, guys, I am outta here," I shouted.

Someone replied, "Okay, Martini. Drive safely, bro."

I had been drinking since midday and should've just slept it off in my car.

At this point, I blacked out, but I knew we got into my car and drove toward Route 180. The next thing I remembered was waking up on my living room floor. The door was wide open, and my car was correctly parked in the front of my house. I don't know how I got home but realized I had been fortunate that I didn't kill anyone. Regrettably, the pressure of being a new state trooper caused me to make a wrong decision that night. I had learned my lesson, but there were other matters that I needed to address.

My relationship with my brother had improved during the beginning part of my career. We weren't as close growing up because I was always working at the pizzeria. He became a corrections officer, which I believe bonded us. In retrospect, I would've never expected either one of us to be in law enforcement. For two young men from Elkanda with no college education, we were fortunate to have had secure and well-paying jobs. My mother couldn't have been prouder.

We had recently purchased new cars—he a Ford and I a Nissan. One evening, we hung out at a restaurant with some friends and left in our separate vehicles. While driving side by side, we began racing on the highway. Neither one of us was drunk, but the sibling competition spurred this stupidity.

My car's speedometer reached about ninety miles per hour when he started to pull away. Speeding wasn't new to me because I did it every day at work, but doing it in my vehicle made it exhilarating. I was in the center lane, and he was in the left lane. I damn sure wasn't going to let him beat me. I wanted to step on the gas pedal, but I was aware of a pending bend in the roadway. I slowed down, hoping that he would follow my lead.

When we hit the curve, out of the corner of my eye, I saw someone changing a tire in the left lane. I panicked and immediately moved over to the right lane. Instinctively, maybe like twin telepathy, he shifted lanes and narrowly missed hitting the driver in the roadway. In that instance, I recognized that what we had done was irresponsible and could've been tragic. We needed to make better decisions if we wanted to keep our jobs.

Within a year of graduating from the NJSP Academy, I had fulfilled my two required assignments. I then requested to be transferred somewhere closer to my home. Greenville Station was my next stop.

Chapter 13

Model of Diversity

Tolerance is a trait worthy of cherishing.

The Greenville Station covers forty-three miles of a toll road in the northern section of the state. Oversized signage guided you where to get off, and the numerous toll plazas directed where you would pay for usage of the clean commuter roadway. The location made commuting easy for me because, with minimal traffic, it was about fifteen minutes from my home.

My first day at the station, I was greeted by my new investigative officer and squadmates (some of whom were minorities) and my academy classmates. That wasn't even the best part. The station's personnel was diverse. You name it, we had it. There were people of different races and cultures working together in harmony. I looked forward to my new environment.

The roadway is a conduit to the shore, where many beachgoers trek every summer; but for me, it was an opportunity to meet many attractive women. I can't count the number of times women threw themselves at me. I suspected that my uniform—and not my average looks—enchanted them, but I didn't mind.

One summer morning, I stopped a blue convertible Ford Mustang for speeding and driving on the shoulder of the roadway. I walked up to the vehicle and observed a reasonably attractive young white woman sitting in the driver's seat. I kindly asked her, "License, registration, and insurance card, ma'am."

She replied, "I am so sorry, Officer." She had on a tight-fitting top that truly pronounced her cleavage. She then bent over and lifted her left leg to reach into her glove box. With her extremely skimpy blue-jean shorts on display, it appeared that she had smuggled a small, black, furry animal in her shorts. I got a prolonged bird's-eye view of her kitty cat because it was evident that she wasn't wearing any underwear. It looked rather painful having that stringy jean material pressing against her private part. Once she sat up straight, I took her documents and said, "Please remain here. I'll be with you in a moment."

I went back to my car and waited for the blood circulation to return to my brain. At no time did I ever consider giving her a break. To some degree, I tolerated speeding—but intentionally riding on the shoulder of the highway is just dangerous.

Upon my return, I handed her the tickets, and the look on her face said it all. The glowing smile had turned into a frown and constant eye rolling. I explained the court procedures and ended our interaction with "Have a nice day." I chuckled as she slammed her car into gear and drove off. This encounter was very memorable because she dared to believe that her beauty would get her off the hook.

Working on your own is fun because you're the boss, but teaming up with a partner on a midnight shift makes the night go faster. My partner was my classmate Trooper H. Avilla. He had also worked at Freling Station, but on a different squad. We had developed a close friendship on and off the job. He is of Puerto Rican descent and grew up in an inner city as well. He supplemented my knowledge of the Latino culture; and to this day, I consider myself an acculturated Afro-Latino. "Yo soy Afro-Boricua pa'que tu lo sepas!" (I am Afro-Puerto Rican, just so you know.)

As I learned more about him, it became evident our backgrounds and cultures were very similar. The commonalities, to name a few, were African-centric rhythmic music, foods rich in sodium and fat, and the all-too-familiar plastic seat covers on our family's living room furniture, which stuck to your skin during the summer.

Our relationship cemented my feelings regarding the benefits of having a diverse workforce because it isn't easy working with a partner. You must manage conflicting personalities, different work ethics, and quirks. Numerous circumstances proved we were compatible, but two distinct situations assured me that we'd be a great team.

One night, while patrolling, we came across a car that continually failed to maintain its lane. "Bro, what do you think?" I asked.

He responded, "Yeah, why not? Pull him over."

I drove because it was difficult staying awake while sitting in the passenger seat. He hit the button for the flashing lights and siren, and the other car immediately pulled to the side of the road.

I walked up to the driver's side of the car and asked the driver for his credentials. Trooper Avilla had taken up a position on the rear passenger side. As I spoke, the driver appeared to be high on something. I couldn't smell an odor of an alcoholic beverage, so I thought he might have smoked some marijuana. I then asked the driver to step out of the car so that I could administer some balance tests to confirm my suspicion of his impairment. I directed him to stand between his car and ours for safety concerns. I told him of my intuition, and he said, "Sir, I only had two beers." Some people who were caught drinking typically gave this response.

After providing him with specific instructions, he failed all the tests miserably. I glanced at Trooper Avilla and gave him a look that told him the man was going to be placed under arrest. When you partner with someone, you work these details out beforehand to catch the driver off guard.

I grabbed his arm and inadvertently dislocated my right thumb; unfortunately, it was my shooting hand. I had sustained this initial injury while in the academy. I didn't want to scream, but it hurt like hell. I snapped my thumb back into place and motioned to Trooper Avilla to watch him because I was going to go to the car to grab my PR-24. I sensed the driver was going to be disruptive and couldn't expose my injury.

I then ran back to the car, and when I turned around, the driver had become unruly. Trooper Avilla had jumped on him. I was genuinely shocked because he outwrestled the driver, who weighed approximately 270 lbs., and outweighed him by at least 110 lbs. and outweighed him by at least 110 lb. I dashed back and assisted with placing the man in handcuffs. I knew I had a great partner, but damn! I never imagined he was that tough.

The second situation we encountered could've turned deadly. We had stopped another motor vehicle just off Exit 157 in an abandoned lot. We went through our usual routine of approaching cars, me on the driver's side and he on the passenger's side. As the driver attempted to retrieve his wallet from his back pocket, Trooper Avilla noticed a handgun protruding from the side of the passenger's seat and immediately shouted, "Gun!"

We both instinctively drew our weapons, and he yelled, "Show me your hands!" The female passenger then casually grabbed the gun. At that precise moment, we could've shot her, but the all-too-familiar "I was in fear for my life" never set in for either one of us. Trooper Avilla snatched her door open and emphatically grabbed it from her hand. After careful inspection, it turned out to be a remarkable replication of a handgun.

He yelled, "What were you thinking?"

She jokingly retorted, "It's not a real gun."

I angrily responded, "How the hell are we supposed to know?"

After explaining that we could've possibly killed her, we let them leave with a stern warning. An almost tragic experience confirmed our mutual trust, but it was just another story that we could talk about at family functions.

The roadway had several rest stops located just off the main road. The restrooms served as conclaves for homosexuals to meet and have sex in the stalls. It became so controversial that we had plainclothes undercover state troopers work overtime details to catch them soliciting sex from unsuspecting men. It was funny watching my colleagues act effeminate to lure in potential clients. I served on the arrest team because I couldn't keep myself from laughing.

One of the most disturbing aspects of the detail was when I caught off-duty police officers giving blow jobs to men in the rest area parking lots. Often, I had kicked them out with a threat of reporting them to their respective police departments. What they did in their personal lives was none of my concern, but they should've been smarter than to do it in public and risk exposure.

The Greenville Station had a reputation for having competitive state troopers who enjoyed playing football, softball, and basketball. I played all three sports, and it gave me the opportunity to develop long-lasting relationships with some exceptional individuals.

Some of us competed in more challenging nonconventional sports. My colleagues conned me into running half-marathons and competing in biathlons (run and bike), which assisted me in maintaining physical conditioning.

Our work environment should've served as the model for all stations. Nevertheless, due to the diversity, I later found out that some white state troopers from other areas referred to the Greenville Station as "Coonfield." A few displayed Adolf Hitler memorabilia in their lockers and talked openly about their fondness for the man. Since their views may have bothered others, I appreciated their openness. They never tried to disguise their true feelings, and I knew how to deal with them. The NJSP provided a sanctuary for some of these bigots who weren't used to the different cultures, ways of communicating, styles of fashion, and mannerisms. I knew we were different, but they couldn't appreciate how we made our mere existence a central component of the working environment. It wasn't like we sang James Brown's song "Say It Loud—I'm Black and I'm Proud." We assimilated into the NJSP culture but brought our flair to it; however, I knew that I couldn't be the old me.

One day, I came to the station having forgotten to remove an earring that I had sported for many years. After walking through the front door, the station squadron officer noticed the gold stud and adamantly yelled, "Troopers don't wear earrings. Now get out!" I immediately ran back to my car and took it out. I didn't want to garner any future negative attention.

While adjusting to my new surroundings, it became apparent, based on numerous monthly arrests, that drug interdiction was necessary. This ardent perception was in response to the president's Anti–Drug

Abuse Act of 1986 and the commander solicitor's 1987 Reform Drug Act, which amounted to a zero tolerance for drug possession. A video was produced in response to the commander solicitor's drug policy, which was viewed by every state trooper. We knew what they expected from us regarding arresting drug couriers.

This new mandate was synonymous with unleashing the hounds. Many state troopers appreciated taking criminals off the roadway, but this proclamation elevated arresting people to a higher level. Every person of color and poor white people were vulnerable.

In the academy, they trained us on how to detect drug couriers. To bolster this directive, a select cadre of seasoned state troopers was assigned to a newly formed "Illicit Interdiction Unit" and fanned out to road stations to identify state troopers who were good at drug interdiction. They selected me because of my arrest numbers.

The coveted Drug Interceptor of the Year Award—commonly bestowed upon the state trooper with the most criminal arrests—became most state troopers' motivation. It consisted of a rectangular ribbon that was proudly displayed on the recipient's uniform, and it probably cost about five dollars. Most state troopers aspired to at least be in the running. It not only represented exemplary drug interdiction for that particular year but it also placed you in the company of state troopers thought to be the best of the best.

On several occasions, I overheard conversations between my colleagues concerning places to look for probable illegal drug activity. One guy said, "We can catch them coming down Route 180 to the Green Salamander because they are trying to avoid the Black Dragon." Our patrol area had always been considered just a commuter road. The prospects of capturing individuals with large amounts of drugs were slim, but circumstances changed when drug dealers altered their travel routes.

We often parked our patrol cars at toll plazas and waited for those fitting the Greenville Station profile, which was a black or Hispanic male regardless of age. I was able to recognize those who probably sold drugs because they looked similar to the drug dealers in my neighborhood.

There were no distinguishable marked entrance lanes to the toll plazas, and most violated a motor vehicle statute for failure to maintain their lane. I never challenged the legitimacy of this violation because I wanted to arrest criminals. On several occasions, I caught suspects with a small amount of marijuana, and I made them dump it on the side of the highway. I should've arrested them to pad my stats, but it was for their personal use, and the effect wasn't any different than having a drink of alcohol. I wanted to grab the mega load of more potent drugs. To justify my actions, I made them either sing a song or do push-ups. It was the funniest thing ever watching their incredulity about not going to jail, but I couldn't see ruining their lives for a trivial offense. I didn't fully comprehend my complicity in the practice of racial profiling because a lot of our problems festered in the dark. I honestly believed drug interdiction worked, but I didn't realize the ramifications of race relations.

One afternoon, a white stretch limousine pulled up to the toll plaza, and I spotted a large imitation foxtail hanging from its rearview mirror. This was a view obstruction, and it provided me with probable cause to stop the car. I learned to use this trivial, but legal, motor vehicle violation to defend my actions. As the car drove toward me, I motioned for the driver to pull over. I intended to give him a warning to account for my time and let him depart.

As the car pulled ahead of me, I noticed suspicious movement in the back passenger compartment. The windows were tinted, so I didn't have a clear view. It seemed rather odd for all that commotion to be occurring. When the driver pulled over to the shoulder of the roadway, I immediately opened the rear door for my safety. I then observed two young black males kneeling on the back seat; they were attempting to shove a large clear plastic bag, which was filled with a white powdery substance, between the seats. I instantly drew my weapon and ordered them out of the car. I realized what they were attempting to do but was unsure if they had any guns.

As they exited, I secured the first passenger in handcuffs while simultaneously telling the other guy, "I'll shoot you if you move!" Afterward, I retrieved my second pair of handcuffs and secured the other passenger. I then yelled at the driver and his front-seat passenger to get out of the car and sit on the curb. The scene was hectic. I was fortunate that there were only two criminals.

With the suspects cuffed, I asked the driver where he had picked up his passengers and where he was in the process of taking them. In broken English, he said, "I pick 'em up, take them city, and bring 'em back." His response corroborated the intelligence information about what the drug dealers were doing.

Backup arrived shortly after that and transported the subjects to the station for processing. I then retrieved their drugs and a brown paper bag containing about two hundred plastic vials, which I suspected were going to be used to package the drugs for distribution. They must've assumed that they wouldn't be pulled over in a limousine. I gave the driver a written warning for the view obstruction and released him and his passenger because I didn't believe they were complicit. My act of kindness would later be scrutinized.

When I returned to the station, I formally charged both subjects with possession of a controlled dangerous substance and with the intent to distribute. After formal processing, I lodged them in the county jail pending a court hearing.

In the coming months, I received a letter commending me on an arrest that I had made. It was letters like this that made most of us want to become the prototype of the "Super Trooper." Several months after the praise, I was subpoenaed to testify in Begent County Superior Court. As this was a suppression hearing, the defendant had an opportunity to have evidence thrown out on a technicality. I was thoroughly prepped by the assistant prosecutor assigned to the case.

The public defender who represented one of the defendants rested his defense on the fact that I didn't have a legitimate reason for opening the car's back door.

This guy can't be for real, I thought. I tried to explain that once I observed the suspicious movement in the rear passenger compartment, I became fearful for my safety and needed to see what they were doing.

The judge interrupted and asked, "Trooper Martin, did you give the driver a ticket for the view obstruction?"

I said, "No, Your Honor. I gave him a warning because I didn't think he was involved."

He quickly responded, "Well, you had no right to open that door because you didn't have probable cause."

I reiterated my position, but I got nowhere with him. He suppressed the evidence because he said it was an illegal search.

I believed that I had done everything by the book and didn't expect to lose. I thought, *How could he just throw it out and let this scumbag go free?* Coincidentally, the defendant was brought to the courtroom in an orange prison jumpsuit because he had been locked up in Camus County on similar charges. When he heard the judge had suppressed the evidence, the little bastard looked at me and smiled.

The judge's decision ripped away my passion for drug interdiction. Although it was my fault for not following the rules, it wasn't worth risking my life removing drug dealers from the streets only to have judges release them. As my zest to eradicate the highways of drug runners had subsided, the practice of drug interdiction continued until the NJSP was publicly taken to task.

In 1989, Germany experienced a historical phenomenon when they demolished the Berlin Wall, which permitted East and West Germany to become reunited. This globally publicized event allowed everyone to see some of their hidden secrets regarding their previous separation. Similarly, that same year, the NJSP experienced a contentious unveiling when a reporter from Channel 9 News televised an exposé regarding allegations of racial profiling. The blatant overcriminalization of minorities finally came to a head.

A camera crew covertly followed several state troopers on the Black Dragon toll road. They recorded the races of individuals stopped for purported motor vehicle violations. According to published data, the reporter surmised that state troopers had stopped an inordinate number of African-American and Hispanic male motorists. Interviews conducted with several of the drivers found an overwhelming impression that they believed they were pulled over solely because of their race. What did he expect? Our superiors gave us a zero tolerance mandate that cleared the path for violating certain individuals' Fourth Amendment rights. At the time, we didn't have advanced technology (i.e., dashboard car cameras or body microphones) to document our behavior. Unfiltered consent was our method of indoctrination into the quasi-criminal practice of the Blue Wall of Silence.

During this time frame, I didn't blame many of my colleagues because we were taught to profile, but I should've been more informed. Nevertheless, I knew that more than a handful of state troopers suffered from what I've coined as the "punkification of policing." They are the ones that were probably bullied as children and sought out the police profession to exact revenge. They took it upon themselves and violated minorities' rights by beating and falsely arresting them. Some were mean individuals, but I speculated that the sporadic allegations of steroid use had enhanced their brutality, and their rage was just a by-product. Who knows? However, these hooligans knew that they could get away with it because, at the time, their despicable actions weren't captured on a video camera. More importantly, they understood that the criminal injustice system would sympathize with the all-too-familiar cry: "I feared for my safety." While in many cases, this concern is believable, some used it to take advantage of others. It is this type of individual that never should've been allowed to wear our uniform (or any uniform), but they slipped through the cracks because of nepotism and cronyism.

It wasn't too long afterward that drug arrests declined. While I wanted to be considered a crime dog, I knew that it would put my career at risk. With the enhanced spotlight on racial profiling, I didn't want to get singled out for added scrutiny. Therefore, I took the advice of a colleague who had warned me about arresting suspects based on race, and I immediately discontinued our standard of drug interdiction.

Instinctively, I knew that we would try to rebrand our actions to make it more acceptable to our critics. Expectedly, our arrogance resurfaced about a decade later and cost taxpayers millions of dollars in civil lawsuit settlements. I soon realized that our superiors acted on this premise: "Go ahead and sue me. It's not my money."

While crime and drugs were destroying many communities, minorities were the only ones targeted. In retrospect, I believe many African-American and Hispanic state troopers (including me) were emasculated cowards for not confronting our superiors about racial profiling. Most of us rode into the outfit on the same concealing Trojan horse because we wanted to be accepted. Our complicity perpetuated the overcrowding of prisons, which intentionally removed minority male figures from inner-city households. Mindlessly, back then, I thought that my deeds were honorable.

After going through my brief "lock 'em up" phase, I got back to patrolling and investigating accidents. Most of the accidents weren't severe and were cleared up within moments. However, one evening, two young men stopped at the station to report that they may have hit an animal.

I jumped into a troop car along with a senior state trooper and drove them back to where they believed the accident had occurred. After driving southbound approximately four miles, we came upon a dark object near the center median. I turned on the car's spotlight, and I observed the remains of a human body, and my heart sank. The passengers saw it too and screamed uncontrollably. I called for a backup unit to secure the scene. We then dropped the passengers off at the station and returned.

It was my first fatal pedestrian accident investigation. The victim's body was lying across the shoulder and the left lane of the highway. The body had been decapitated, and its lower left leg and right arm were severed. Pools of blood had seeped into cracks in the roadway and splattered onto the grass. I nervously looked for the head because I didn't know how I was going to react when I found it. I methodically used my flashlight and searched the scene. As I paused for a moment, I shone my light on the opposite side of the roadway, which was more than one hundred feet away, and something caught my eye. I ran across the northbound lanes and found the male victim's head sitting upright in a natural position on the grass berm. How the hell did it get all the way over here? The driver of the car had to have been excessively speeding when he struck and catapulted the victim's head. My stomach knotted up as I stared at his face. I had hoped that the head wouldn't wink at me or start talking.

The crime scene investigators responded to make sense of what happened while I stood by and watched them work. They were cavalier about picking up the victim's remains because the body parts represented just an investigation to them. One investigator grabbed the hair of the victim's head, which had its tongue dangling from the mouth, and walked it across the roadway. I fought back the urge to puke. It made me recall, again, the words of my former coach: "We all get used to it."

They cleared the scene and reopened the roadway. I returned to the station and interviewed the driver, who was still plainly shaken. I assured him that he wouldn't be charged because it was a horrible accident and that pedestrians are not allowed on the roadway. I telephoned his father to pick them up from the station. My job had just begun because I needed to find out the identity of the victim.

After going through his belongings, I learned that he lived locally and contacted his family. The victim's sister told me that he left his girlfriend's house after arguing. He then went to a bar, got drunk, and was kicked out. I surmised, based on the bar's proximity to the girlfriend's home, that he attempted to return to her house by crossing the highway and was struck. It was unfortunate that his life ended so tragically.

In the coming weeks, for unknown reasons, I had a recurring nightmare that involved my being in a gunfight with a faceless male who was about to shoot me. Every attempt at shooting him first was a failure. I could never muster up enough hand strength to pull the trigger and kill him. My inevitable demise always came without any definite closure. I'd then wake up terribly frightened and sometimes in a cold sweat. Afterward, I'd be apprehensive about going to work because it might be the day that I'd encounter the villain.

It wasn't until several years later that I finally killed him and was able to move on without concern. Sadly, traumatic incidents that I couldn't discard had been stored in my subconscious, and these caused many sleepless nights.

Chapter 14

Outside the Lines

Smarten up because stupidity is a choice as well.

After two years of working at the Greenville Station, they assigned me to a summons-driven unit: Ticket Patrol. I, along with three other state troopers, had been selected because of our willingness to write a lot of tickets and arrest drunk drivers. I missed working with my former squadmates, but this was a great opportunity that I couldn't turn down.

My new colleagues and I got along well. We had similar engaging personalities and took pride in making sure our uniforms and leather gear always looked outstanding. As a perk, they gave me an unmarked light-blue Chevrolet patrol car. On workdays, we met at a designated place to discuss patrol assignments. Our job was to *crush* the motoring public by writing a lot of summonses, which should've decreased the number of accidents and excessive speeding. In theory, it was an excellent idea; but I was smart enough to know that the more tickets we wrote, the more revenue was generated for the State of New Jersey, and it probably offset some of our salaries. *What a brilliant con game.*

One afternoon, as I prepared to go to work, I heard a man's scream coming from outside. I peered out my window and saw my elderly next-door neighbor running down the street and yelling for someone to stop. Instinctively, I grabbed my gun and handcuffs and then darted out the door. I caught up with him and asked, "What happened?"

Breathing heavily, he said, "Someone broke into my house!" He gave me the physical description of a young black male wearing blue jeans and a light-blue T-shirt. I then jumped into my troop car and scoured the neighborhood.

While driving around, I saw a black male that bore a striking resemblance to my neighbor's description of the burglar. As I approached the guy, I noticed it was a friend. I yelled out, "James, hold up. I need to talk to you!" I jumped out of my car and asked, "Where did you just come from?" He panted heavily but didn't say a word. I asked him again, "Where did you just come from?"

He blurted out, "Please, Vincent! Just kick my ass. Don't lock me up."

I responded in disgust, "I can't believe you broke into their house!" *I should've kicked his ass as he requested.*

I went to grab hold of his wrist, and he attempted to break away. I locked on to his arm and in a stern voice told him, "I will kick your ass if you try to resist!" I then placed him in handcuffs, opened the front passenger side door, and pushed him inside. My emotions were running high, and I wanted him to be quiet.

We then drove back to my neighbor's house while he piteously begged me to let him go. It was difficult trying to separate my Elkanda upbringing because the inner-city part of me said to kick the shit out of him and let him go.

When I drove up, my neighbor spotted us and yelled, "That's him! That's him!" He then attempted to punch him, and I immediately yanked James out of the way. In any other circumstance, I would've let him beat the shit out of James, but I couldn't turn a blind eye. I told him, "Don't worry. He will get his very soon."

Two Elkanda police officers pulled up, and I told them the details. I knew that James was going to catch a beating because that is the way they did things. Whether they took him to jail or not wasn't my concern. At that moment, I realized that even my police authority couldn't stop crime from occurring on my street. Moreover, I understood that if I locked up the wrong person, it could mean severe repercussions for my family. It was sobering knowing that someone could retaliate, but I was confused about what to do and hoped that nothing else would occur. However, it wouldn't be long before a life-or-death situation confronted me.

After finishing an afternoon shift, I pulled up to my house and noticed a dark-colored car cruising up the street. I was about to get out of my unmarked troop car when the other vehicle made a U-turn and almost hit me. I yelled out, "You asshole!" I was in my state police uniform and knew the driver saw me. When he bolted, I got back into my car and chased him down the street. The next set of events was like something out of a movie; you had to be there to believe it.

I drove down the road with my siren blasting and lights flashing. The car then crossed the center aisle and drove in the opposite direction of traffic. I quickly got my wits about me and was about to let that driver go when I noticed a second car backing up the street in a reckless manner. I didn't know what these guys were doing. It seemed as though they were out joyriding in stolen cars.

Sensing something terrible was going to happen, I pulled over, and the car barely missed me. I then drove down the street and turned around to chase that car. As soon as I began driving, another vehicle, with its engine revving loudly, stopped in front of me about one hundred feet away. I slammed on my brakes and put my car in park. I then removed my shotgun from its floor-mounted rack and jumped out.

My heart pounded in my chest like a sledgehammer kept hitting me. I positioned myself in front of my car, raised the shotgun, and pointed it at the driver's head. I knew if he was going to try to run me down that I wasn't going to make it easy for him. As the third car came toward me, I saw two heads pop up from the rear seat.

"Please don't force me to shoot you, you assholes," I mouthed. I braced myself because I didn't know what they were going to do or, more importantly, what I was going to do to them.

The car's tires screeched, and smoke billowed. I didn't want to shoot them, but I'd be damned if they made me back down. Something inside of me said, "Get out of the way and live to see another day."

As the car came racing toward me, I quickly jumped to the side, and he narrowly missed crashing into my car. I gathered myself while standing on the sidewalk. I couldn't believe what had just happened. I ultimately let them go, but the craziness didn't stop.

On another occasion, I was on patrol when I received an urgent message over the police radio. My brother called the station to inform me that someone had broken into our house. I sped home and met with him to get the details. He said one of the neighborhood kids broke in and had stolen a VCR and ransacked the place. He told me who the kid was, and I immediately drove to his apartment building. It didn't dawn on me that I was in my state police uniform. I just wanted to kick the kid's ass and get our stuff back.

I ran up the stairs to his apartment, banged on the door, and yelled, "Police, open up!" A middle-aged woman opened the door with a startled look on her face. "Where is your son?" I angrily asked.

"He's not home," she nervously responded.

Of course, I didn't believe her. I then sidestepped her and walked to a rear bedroom, where I located him cowering behind a dresser. "Get your punk ass up!" I shouted. I approached him and was about to punch him in his face, but something told me to stop. At that moment, I realized that I was about to commit an assault and had already violated his civil liberties by entering his home without a warrant.

Setting aside my irrational behavior, I gathered my thoughts and turned around without uttering another word. I then walked toward the front door and spoke with the kid's mother. I apologetically told her, "Ma'am, I am truly sorry for my behavior."

We had a brief conversation about her *problem child*—as she referred to him. She said that she couldn't control him and was afraid that he would eventually get himself hurt or killed. I suggested that she find him a job or have him enlist in the military. I shared with her some of the options that helped keep me out of trouble at his age. I then departed from her home thinking that I could've been that kid several years earlier.

As I walked out of the building, I noticed a crowd of my friends had gathered. A few of them asked me why I didn't hurt him, but I silently walked back to my car and returned to work.

The actions of some of the neighborhood menaces were getting out of control and caused me grave concern. One day, while sitting on my front steps enjoying a day off, I heard a loud commotion. Before long, a young man ran up the street and suddenly collapsed. I yelled, "Are you all right?"

I sat there waiting for him to get to his feet, but when he didn't move, I ran over and reached down to check on him. He faintly moaned, and then I saw a kitchen steak knife protruding from his stomach. He had unwisely attempted to pull it out and had started bleeding profusely. His body then went limp, and his eyes started flickering. I asked him what happened, but he didn't say anything.

I yelled to my mother, "Call 911 and tell them I'm on my way to City Hospital with an injured kid."

I ran to my car and opened the door. I then went back, picked the teenager up, and placed him in the passenger seat. The hospital was only a few minutes away. I had hoped that I could get him there in time. I looked over at him and said, "Hold on, you'll be all right."

Once I got to the emergency room, two hospital attendants met me at the front door. They removed the kid from my car, placed him on a gurney, and rushed him into a back room. I told the nurse that I didn't know what had happened and provided her with my information. I then returned home to get more details.

As I pulled up to my house, I saw several Elkanda police officers milling around. I approached one of them and told him what had transpired. I pointed to where the kid tossed the knife and then asked, "Do you know what happened?"

He said that two guys fought over a girl, and one had stabbed the other. He then made a radio call to the hospital and informed me that the kid had died. I couldn't believe it; he couldn't have been more than sixteen years old.

Due to the number of incidents that had happened, I began rethinking my living arrangements. I enjoyed living at home, but I knew it was just a matter of time before something more serious would happen. One series of incidents sealed my decision to leave.

For about a month, every Saturday, I called the Elkanda Police Department and let them know that the neighborhood hoodlums had parked a stolen car in front of my house. Unfortunately, I gave in to their subtle message of intimidation and couldn't place my family in danger any longer. There was no doubt that if I caught one of those bastards, they were going to get hurt, and I didn't need the drama.

I told my family of my decision and subsequently moved to the Town of Fords in Central New Jersey. After twenty-six years, I cut the umbilical cord and moved out of my mom's house and into a spacious one-bedroom apartment located off Route 1. It was minutes away from my patrol area and made getting to work easier.

Chapter 15

Rules Need Not Apply

Being different sometimes has setbacks.

My position on the Ticket Patrol gave me the flexibility of roaming the highway undetected. The traffic always flowed at an above-average speed, so I only caught those that distinguished themselves from the norm.

One evening, I left my apartment to start a midnight shift. I drove in the right lane to watch the other drivers. At milepost 131 northbound, a gray-colored car with two white male occupants sped by me. I lay back and started to pace them. When the driver increased the distance between our cars, I settled in behind him. After following him for about a mile, I turned on my flashing lights and siren. Like a frightened animal, the driver took off, and his speed increased to over one hundred miles per hour. I contacted the Greenville Station and advised them that I was going to be in a pursuit.

After a brief chase, the car exited off 131A and drove toward Edial Township. I continually communicated my precise whereabouts because I didn't know who was in the car or why they attempted to elude me.

The car made numerous erratic left and right turns. The adrenaline boost exhilarated me because of the unknown. The driver then drove down a cul-de-sac, and I knew their journey had ended. He slowed down and then came to a screeching stop.

I turned on the loudspeaker in my car and yelled, "Driver and passenger, get out with your hands up where I can see them!"

The passenger door opened abruptly, and a young white male took off running. He wasn't my most significant concern because he wasn't driving. The driver then jumped out and ran in the opposite direction. I chased after him as he ran toward a backyard. Fortunately, the house had numerous motion sensor lights installed, and it lit up like a Christmas tree. I found the driver crouched down behind a thick green bush.

With my weapon drawn and hands trembling, I yelled several times, "Show me your hands! Show me your hands!"

He immediately jumped to his feet, but I couldn't see his hands. He was a little more than six feet tall and very slender. Nevertheless, for whatever reason, I knew I couldn't shoot him. The circumstances didn't warrant that reaction. He then looked at me and started crying.

I asked him, "What the hell are you doing?"

He sobbed. "I didn't mean to do it. I'm sorry. I'm sorry." By his response, I knew he was just a kid.

I screamed, "I could've shot you! What were you thinking?"

He started shaking uncontrollably and tearfully told me that he had taken his dad's car without permission. From his reaction, I could only imagine how much trouble would be in his future. I jotted down his information and had the dispatcher contact his parents. I toyed with the idea of locking him up but decided against it because I remembered taking my mom's car years earlier and couldn't be a hypocrite. He needed to be home to receive the punishment he deserved.

I placed him in my car and then drove around the neighborhood until I spotted the passenger. When he saw his friend seated in the front, he bowed his head and slowly walked toward us. I quickly patted him down and sat him in the back seat.

Our brief time together provided me with the perfect opportunity to teach them a lesson. I shared horrific stories of other kids who had stolen cars and were killed trying to evade the police. I didn't know if I had gotten through to them, but I gave it my best effort.

Pulling up to his home, I noticed his parents standing outside awaiting my arrival. I shared my philosophy that everyone needed at least one break. I gave them the address where their car was parked and then shook hands with the father. I returned to my car hoping that he would kick his son's ass just on general principle alone.

To say that every interaction I had with the motoring public went off without a hitch would be disingenuous. A chance meeting with an elderly motorist made me cynical about the integrity of our judicial system.

One evening while patrolling, a red Mercedes-Benz entered the roadway from an on-ramp at a high rate of speed. I moved over three lanes, positioned myself in the left lane, and paced the car for approximately two miles before stopping it in Palermo Township.

I walked up to the driver's side of the car and politely said, "Good evening, sir. I'm Trooper Martin. Do you know why I stopped you?"

He replied, "No, Officer. Did I do something wrong?"

I told him, "I pulled you over for speeding and carelessly cutting across three lanes of traffic."

After obtaining his driving credentials, I advised him that he'd receive two summonses. His incredulous disposition changed instantaneously, followed by an angry facial expression typical of an unhappy motorist.

Shortly after that, I handed the tickets to him and explained the necessary information for his probable contestation. He gave me a stern look as he took the tickets and drove away.

About a month later, as expected, I received a subpoena to appear in court. As with every infraction, I had made notations on the back copy of my summons to refresh my memory. I recorded that the driver was the only person in the car and had made no incriminating remarks.

On the day of court, I presented my car's certification regarding the accuracy of the speedometer, which I used to pace his vehicle. I testified to the facts and that it was a textbook stop. I then waited to hear the rebuttal story.

The defendant told a very different version of the events, which made me wonder if his age had affected his memory. He also presented an elderly female witness to corroborate his fabricated story. I couldn't imagine two senior citizens committing perjury. *Damn was I naive.* However, as with most court cases, the police officer is often given the benefit of the doubt, unless there were extenuating circumstances. I sat next to the prosecutor arrogantly awaiting the guilty verdict.

Palermo Township was an excellent place to write tickets because of the relationship that many state troopers had with the prosecutor and judge. We usually didn't have our judgment questioned because of our professional reputation. When the result was about to be read, the judge commended me on my testimony but announced, "I am going to find the defendant not guilty."

Did I hear him correctly? Stunned, I leaned over and told the prosecutor that I needed to speak with him. I then walked to his office and waited. I kept my composure because I didn't know if I had done anything wrong.

When he walked in, he had an uneasy look on his face. I asked, "What just happened in there?" He said that he wanted to apologize for not filling me in before the court proceeding. He then presented me with a letter that the defendant sent to the court.

In his letter, he made a point to state that a black state trooper gave him two tickets and claimed I called him "red face." He also suggested that I may have been either "drunk, high, or hyperactive." He said I was driving in a marked unit and wasn't wearing my hat. Lastly, he asserted that his passenger would attest to his allegations.

After reading it, however, I stood momentarily trying to comprehend his words. Other than acknowledging that a black state trooper had given him two tickets, everything else in the letter was a total fabrication. The wording was very suspect because the defendant emphasized that I wasn't wearing a hat, which was untrue. Someone told him that our badges are fastened to our hats, and we must wear them or get in trouble. He also lied about having a passenger in his car.

Moreover, he claimed I was in a marked troop car. I guess his vision was going bad because I was in my light-blue unmarked vehicle. I could've accepted his lies, but what had bothered me the most was his racist accusation. At that moment, I understood what some of my white colleagues experienced when a minority motorist falsely accused them of being a racist.

The defendant's actions stung me to my core. Nevertheless, he accomplished what he set out to do. I suspected he and the judge might have been friends because he was a township resident. The prosecutor could've asked me to allow the defendant to pay a fine, like so many other cases. However, he embarrassed me and called my integrity into question.

I walked out of the courthouse dispirited but knew that I had done my job correctly. I located a trash can and ripped up the letter and tossed it in the garbage. In personal protest against perceived corruption, I never wrote another ticket in that town again.

While writing motor vehicle violations was the crux of my job, I wouldn't be a party to what my warrant agent demanded that the Ticket Patrol members do just to remain on the squad.

We typically wrote about eighty tickets per month with most of them being moving violations, which assessed points to the driver. I understood the financial cost related to my actions and couldn't in good conscience screw the motoring public. I issued more of the nonmoving violations (i.e., no seat belt and overdue inspection sticker summonses), but our warrant agent had other plans. He told my supervisor that we had to increase our output to 150 tickets per month. Ordinarily, we'd have given him what he wanted, but screw him. I didn't want to make him look good to his superiors. Within three months, his constant demanding of "more, more, more" fell on deaf ears, and he strategically removed all of us.

Chapter 16

Contrasting Treatment

Don't let another's view of you alter your identity.

My Ticket Patrol assignment ended after three years, and I returned to a squad at the Greenville Station. I opted to move to the Town of Greenville because it was closer to work.

After driving around town, I spotted several For Rent signs displayed on front lawns. A prospective apartment near the local high school caught my attention. The building had four stories with magnificently detailed architecture. The grounds were immaculate, so I thought they kept the interior just as neat. The potential of living in a relatively crime-free neighborhood seemed imminent.

I subsequently met with the building's superintendent, a middle-aged white male, who showed me two spacious vacant apartments. I came in my uniform to increase my chances. As I walked around, I envisioned my new furniture and the big television and mega sound system that I'd eventually buy to fill the space.

We made small talk, and then he asked about the status of my credit. I wasn't aware that things like this mattered, but I told him it was excellent because I always paid my bills on time. I didn't want to be that person standing in line at a store, about to pay with a credit card, only to have the clerk decline it—how embarrassing. He said the apartments were available and that he'd call me in about a week with all the particulars. I thanked him and patiently waited for his telephone call.

A week and a half had passed and no call, so I returned to find out what delayed his decision. We met in front of the building, and again I asked about the apartments. With furrowed brows and a stern vocal tone, he replied, "I rented them already!"

I didn't know what to say at that moment. I could only imagine what others may have faced if they, too, attempted to rent an apartment in this building. His agitated attitude was unprofessional because I was a potential renter. I deserved to live in a safe neighborhood like everyone else. Still and all, I thanked him for his time and dejectedly walked away.

I eventually rented a spacious one-bedroom apartment near the town center. It upsets me to think that in my official position, I didn't stand up for myself. This experience was one of many whereby discrimination reared its ugly head while I had been in and out of my uniform.

While off duty, I made it a point to be as inconspicuous as possible. I dressed casually in jeans and collared shirts and tried not to perpetuate existing stereotypes about young black males (i.e., playing my car stereo loudly, speaking slang, and hanging out on street corners with friends). However, sometimes, just my mere presence bothered others.

On numerous occasions, I had observed white females either lock their car doors or cross the street as I approached. As disturbing as these situations could be for some, I got used to it because I considered it their issue and not mine. Still, an isolated incident at a novelty store in a suburban town made me question whether it was something more.

While standing in line waiting to pay for some items, a little white elderly woman directly in front of me turned around, noticed me, and immediately clutched her pocketbook. I knew that many black males probably experienced this situation, but damn, I was a state trooper. The scared look on her face disoriented me. I couldn't answer for her possible past experiences, but I wanted to alleviate her concerns. Nevertheless, I wouldn't, under any circumstances, have expected what happened to me after being pulled over by a fellow police officer.

One night I had driven to my (then) girlfriend's house, one of the few black families that lived in the quaint little borough. At about 9:00 p.m., I crossed over Route 252 and drove through a yellow light. As I continued, I heard a police siren and observed flashing red lights in my rearview mirror. *Surprisingly, I got that funny feeling in my stomach that most get when they are nervous about something; however, I was in law enforcement, so it seemed a bit strange.*

I pulled over immediately and reached into my back pocket to retrieve my wallet, which contained my badge and driving credentials. I turned on my car's interior light, set my badge on the dashboard, and placed my hands on the steering wheel. Looking in my driver's side view mirror, I watched a white police officer exit his vehicle and immediately put his hand on his weapon as he approached my car. He cautiously walked up and said, "License, registration, and insurance card."

I didn't want to make him nervous or give him a reason to say that he was in fear for his life, so I let him know that everything was in my wallet. He was a young officer like me, so I expected him to look at my credentials, and then we'd have a brief conversation about our respective departments. However, with a stern facial expression, he then grabbed my wallet and went through it as if he was specifically searching for something other than my driving credentials. I sat speechlessly and watched him in disbelief. *I guess the "brothers in blue" blanket of protection didn't apply to me.*

After rummaging, he flippantly threw my wallet into my lap and casually walked away. *No, he didn't!* It took every ounce of discipline not to jump out and drop-kick him in the back of his neck. I wondered if it was a "local police versus state police" matter, but I wasn't naive. Regardless, I made sure that I never went through another yellow light in his town.

Chapter 17

Serendipity

You only have one chance to do it right the first time.

The law enforcement profession is exhilarating and unmatched by most occupations. I've been involved in many felony car chases and made numerous arrests; however, my most rewarding experience happened early on in my career.

While patrolling southbound, traffic began to get congested. I thought an accident had occurred a few miles in front of me, so I kept up with the flow. I then spotted Trooper D. Daisy and Trooper M. Mume standing in the middle of the roadway. Trooper Mume was directing traffic, and Trooper Daisy appeared to be speaking with someone.

I pulled my car to the shoulder of the road, exited, and walked toward Trooper Daisy, who had been talking to a short and frail-looking young black male standing on top of a cement ledge overpass. As he walked back and forth very deliberately, his exaggerated hand gestures implied that something was wrong. His face was sullen, and he appeared agitated. Unbeknownst to me at the time, there was a crowd of onlookers at the bottom of the overpass holding a rather large blanket to catch him, just in case he jumped or fell. I continued moving around trying not to get his attention. However, the rubberneckers yelled for him to jump and kept diverting the guy's attention. I stared at the guy and hoped that he'd eventually come to his senses and get down.

Trooper Daisy was frantically trying to tell him whatever it took to save his life. I gathered from their conversation that he had recently broken up with his girlfriend and was having a difficult time finding a job. I realized he was probably experiencing what most young people went through, but he had a tough time coping.

The discussion went on for approximately ten minutes, and as I inched closer, he watched my every move. Trooper Daisy continued speaking and kept him occupied. I was about three feet away from him when I turned, looked up, and asked, "Hey, what's going on?" He then focused his attention on me. At that point, I became the lead negotiator.

He watched me very intently and periodically peeked over the side of the overpass. I snapped my fingers to regain his attention and said, "I have friends who are looking for people to hire. Do you want me to get you a job?" He smiled momentarily as if my words had registered. I then said, "Relationships always have their ups and downs. I know she still cares for you, and she wouldn't want you to hurt yourself."

He mumbled something, but I couldn't understand. I went on to say, "I can help you get her back." I desperately said anything that kept him engaged. I positioned myself about a foot away from him and watched as he again looked down at the crowd. I was unsure as to what to do, but I took one more step, quickly grabbed him off the overpass, and immediately put his face down on the hood of the marked troop car. His body went limp as I placed him in handcuffs, but he appeared to be relieved that the ordeal was over. I then assured him that everything would be okay as I placed him in the back seat of Trooper Daisy's car.

I stepped to the side to collect my thoughts and didn't realize the joyous applause emanating from the crowd beneath and the passing rubberneckers. It was indeed an enjoyable experience knowing I had just saved his life. I didn't know him, but I knew he needed help, and fortunately, we were there.

An ambulance arrived and took him to a mental hospital for a psychological evaluation. As I stood around speaking with my colleagues, I realized that many police officers go through an entire career without saving someone. Working that day was a godsend. Surprisingly, someone videotaped the incident from underneath the overpass and sent it to the station at a later date.

We cleared the scene, and I went back to the station to log in my patrol stats. My supervisor was there, and we discussed what had happened earlier. He told me he would put me in for a "beige badge," which they gave to state troopers who had performed an extraordinary act of bravery or who did something exceptional. The ultimate decision lay in the hands of an awards board comprised of upper-echelon commissioned officers. He secured a copy of the video and submitted it with a detailed report. The real reward for me was that I saved someone's life.

About a month later, the station warrant agent told me that I had to meet with the troop squadron officer to receive a letter of commendation. I was unaware if there was a difference between a letter of commendation and a beige badge.

The following week, Trooper Daisy and I met with the troop squadron officer. He thanked us for a job well done and presented me with a letter of commendation. In the letter, his focus seemed to be on the fact that the young man was black, which baffled me because that played no role in my deeds. A photographer ultimately took our picture as we shook hands, but I was still waiting for the beige badge. After twenty minutes of going through the obligatory handshakes and "attaboy" festivities, I departed wondering if there was a misunderstanding.

I returned to the Greenville Station and asked a colleague about the process. He told me that I had to be recommended for it, which I had been. However, it appeared that my actions weren't worthy enough in their eyes. What I found unbelievable was that my former investigative officer performed a Heimlich maneuver on a choking kid at a restaurant, and they bestowed the ribbon upon him, which I deemed more than appropriate. This snubbing underscored the arbitrary and differential treatment I had observed over the years.

Chapter 18

Getting Out of My Way

Setting a bar for success is self-defeating.

While working at the Greenville Station, I realized many of my coworkers either had a college degree or were in pursuit of one. Early on, a lot of state troopers negatively referred to them as "college boys." It appeared that they were fearful that having a degree would place them in a better position to get promoted. As for me, I was in my early twenties and very content with just having a high school diploma.

Sadly, I have no distinct recollection of my high school days and can only recall two of my teachers. I just made the fiftieth percentile of my graduating class of 321 and barely had a C average. I was the product of a social promotion having nothing to do with my classroom effort. Even so, I took full responsibility for my failures because I could've done better.

My official academy grade average was a C+. Many recruits also had a similar standing, but my 76 numerical score placed me next to last. This information cast a dark cloud on my confidence, or lack thereof.

Intellectual prowess had never been my strongest asset. On the other hand, my oldest sister, Faith, an honor student, was ranked 14 out of 200 in her high school graduating class. She was also a member of Operation PUSH and was a Market University School of Nursing graduate. She always told me that education was the key to success. I admired her intelligence and ability to overcome adversity.

Faith had an autoimmune disease that primarily affects women, which surfaced when she was twenty-one years old. I later learned that people who have this disease are born with it. It attacks the person's immune system and is sometimes fatal. While she agonized over this horrible condition, she never let it define her. Even more remarkable was the fact that when it caused her to become physically challenged, she returned to school, attained a paralegal degree, and subsequently provided free services to indigent clients.

I didn't immediately recognize the signs of her debilitating disease. She appeared healthy when I visited her and my brother-in-law at their home. After a few years, however, I noticed puffiness in her cheeks and an unusual amount of hair growth. She told me that her doctors prescribed steroidal medication that had many side effects; and due to the disease, she experienced kidney failure and underwent weekly dialysis treatments. Regardless of what she had gone through, she maintained a positive outlook on life.

I had spoken to her often about what it was like to be a college student. While her preaching should've encouraged me, I was more focused on making money. It was always Faith's mission to see my brother and me graduate from college. I vividly remember her dragging us to get registered at Market University.

"Why do we have to do this?" I asked.

"Because I'll be damned if I am going to be the only one in this family to get a college education," she emphatically replied.

I didn't like going to class in high school and wasn't delusional enough to think I could maintain a college workload. However, I knew not to cross her once she had made up her mind.

We stood in line at the registrar's office, and when our turn came, a counselor asked, "What did they score on the Scholastic Aptitude Test?"

My sister replied, "They've never taken the SAT."

I didn't know what the hell they were discussing.

The woman then said, "Well, I am sorry, but they will not be able to register."

Amen, maybe she'll get off of this education thing; but she was undeterred. She kindly thanked the woman and yanked us out of the building. I thought we would be heading back home, but she said that a county college was down the street, so we headed there next. Again, we stood in a line waiting to speak with a counselor—this time with greater success.

South Community College was a place that gave high school underachievers like me a second chance, and it sparked my love for higher education. My brother and I had been out of school for approximately four years and needed assistance. The counselor explained that it was okay that we didn't take the SAT because we'd take a few remedial classes and could matriculate at a later date.

Marticu-what? I still didn't know what these big words meant.

My sister flashed a relieved grin and excitedly told the woman, "Please register them!"

I didn't know what to expect, but seeing her smile was worth it.

I wasn't a good student, but her confidence motivated me to see it through. After taking a few courses in the first semester, we became Criminal Justice majors.

The second semester, I read a lot of books that were devoid of nonwhite people and wondered why. Growing up, I never thought about race—with the one exception when a seventh-grade classmate called me a nigger, and I knocked his retainer out of his mouth. Ultimately, I learned about the contributions that we made to the world but were never adequately given recognition for.

As a law enforcement officer, my consciousness changed after someone gave me *The Autobiography of Malcolm X*. Reading this book made me loathe February's Black History Month because it reminded me of what my ancestors had gone through via Jim Crow policies. Pictures depicting white cops beating unarmed black men and women haunted me. Similarly, gruesome videos of dogs chewing on the extremities of black folks gnawed at my psyche. However, over time, I channeled my anger and came to grips with our intentional exclusion from American history books.

In my Western Civilization English course, I read books about the poet and playwright William Shakespeare. Initially, his eloquent vocabulary made it difficult for me to follow. Fortunately, my professor—a slightly bald middle-aged man with a witty personality—made the stories easy for the class to understand. As a result, I also learned about Jiddu Krishnamurti, a British Indian philosopher, whose book *Think on These Things* provided me with a unique perspective on education. In essence, Krishnamurti claimed that regardless of how many earned initials you have at the end of your name, if you don't cause a change in someone's life, then it is all for naught. His philosophy later became the driving force for my altruism and entrance into the teaching profession.

As a part of the required curriculum, I enrolled in an Art Appreciation course. The professor, an African-American female, proudly wore dreadlock braids and was well versed in her discipline. She opened my eyes to several artists from different periods in history. Before long, I became familiar with Van Gogh's *Starry Night*, Frida Kahlo's *Las Dos Fridas*, Georgia O'Keefe's *Canyon with Crows*, and a multitude of art genres. She also introduced me to African-American artists such as Romare Bearden and Jacob Lawrence. I was proud to know that someone who looked like me could produce such fabulous works of art. I just hoped that one day, a handsome price would be paid for their work, as it is for a Picasso or a Rembrandt.

It was because of her that I imagined a vast world outside the United States. She shared stories about art galleries in Germany, France, Italy, and other European countries. I listened intently and daydreamed about visiting similar places. She gave me a spirited desire to not only learn about different cultures but to experience them firsthand.

Years later, I traveled to Hagan, Germany, and observed Turkish and African people, who appeared out of place. I ignorantly expected everyone to have blonde hair and blue eyes, but I admired the diversity. My trip to Prague, Czech Republic, exposed me to the famous Charles Bridge and Prague Castle. A border crossing to Bratislava in the Slovak Republic exposed me to a country not unlike that of the Czech Republic, which had recently overcome many decades of communist rule. The ubiquitous graffiti, Dunkin Donuts, and McDonald's showed me how globalization had influenced them and would ultimately destroy their uniqueness.

An excursion from the Slovak Republic to Vienna, Austria, showed me that the Austrian police were curious about black males. While crossing the border with an African-British friend, they detained us for more than two hours. We had traveled with two Slovakian female companions, and this also may have been an issue for the Österreichische Polizei (Austrian Police). Interestingly enough, our friends expressed extreme sorrow for what they witnessed and had voiced a few choice words with the officers.

A cross-country trek from Germany to Belgium and France allowed me to visit the Koln Cathedral, the Eiffel Tower, and the Arc de Triomphe. My annual trips to Cranfield, England, ultimately made it my second home, and I returned to spend the holidays with friends. A relaxing escape to Aalborg, Denmark, showed me that women sunbathing topless wasn't a big deal for them, but it excited the hell out of me. Lastly, in later years, my school trips to Italy, Greece, Spain, Portugal, Ireland, Hungary, Wales, and Amsterdam increased my knowledge of lands that had been previously foreign to me. Each destination left me with fond memories and had exposed me to many new things. However, my ultimate goal is to set foot on the continent of Africa before I depart this life.

After seven years of attending South Community College on a part-time basis, I had attained two degrees: an Associate of Science in Physical Education and an Associate of Science in Social Science. I should've been happy, but before graduating, my sister was hospitalized.

Over the coming months, my mother and I traveled to Maryland every weekend to spend time with her and my brother-in-law, who had provided unwavering support while she battled her illness.

Faith's agonizing facial expressions showed us that she was in tremendous pain as she struggled to stay alive. Unable to speak, she wrote things down on a piece of paper and used her eyes and brief smiles to express her thoughts. I will never forget her bravery and strength. I am moved to tears as I remember her commitment to looking after me, even on her deathbed. She was unselfish and didn't want to see us depressed about her inevitable passing.

Regrettably, in her final days, Faith's condition significantly deteriorated. My last words to her were "I know you are holding on for us. Please do what you think is best. We will be okay." She looked at me and blinked her eyes, which told me she understood that she didn't have to fight anymore. I departed from the hospital grievously knowing that I'd never see my sister alive again.

The following week, I traveled to Boston, Massachusetts, to attend a street gang conference. I called home to get an update on her condition. The phone rang a few times before my mom answered. "Hey, just checking in to see how Faith is doing." There was a momentary silence, and I immediately knew something was wrong. "Ma, what's going on?"

She said, "She's gone."

I stood there with the phone in my hand. "When?" I asked.

She replied, "Early this morning. We knew it was going to happen, but she's not suffering anymore." My mother's tone sounded composed, but her sadness had been apparent. She maintained her strength for the rest of the family.

Faith's wake was held in Maryland about a week later. As I walked up to the casket, I bent down and kissed her. I then whispered, "Thank you for everything you've done for me. I love you and will forever miss you." She will always be the wind beneath my wings in every sense. Just before her thirty-fourth birthday, we buried her where many of my mother's immediate family were laid to rest.

More than anything, I wished she could've seen me walk across the stage and receive my college degrees. Due to her passing, I chose not to participate in my commencement ceremony.

After graduating from South Community College in 1994, I transferred to Valley University to pursue a bachelor of arts degree in sociology.

While I enjoyed going to classes, I had a hard time dealing with a few arrogant and short-tempered professors. I'd never come across so many people who were undeniably impressed with their titles.

One professor told me to sit down and shut up as I walked into the classroom and said hello to a classmate. Quite naturally, I sat down and closed my mouth because I wanted to get a good grade. *I guess she forgot that I paid her salary.* There were plenty of times I wanted to share with her the concept of having a bit more thoughtfulness because of the way she disrespected other students. However, I took her arrogance in stride and pressed on with my studies.

On certain days, I went to school completely exhausted from working a midnight shift. My situation was no different from other students, who worked full-time and went to school part-time.

At the beginning of 1997, I completed my studies and received my bachelor's degree. I couldn't wait to get out, but my journey wasn't over. I had aspirations of attaining the rank of vice marshal, and due to our educational standards policy, I decided that I had to continue.

The policy established an official attempt at codifying the first objective criterion for promotion. It required that every candidate have at least 120 credits to be considered for promotion to warrant agent, a bachelor's degree for promotion to squadron officer, and a master's degree for the rank of vice marshal. The rank of assistant chief leader was a position afforded to someone at the chief leader's discretion. The governor has the pleasure of choosing their candidate for chief leader.

The policy didn't become official until 2006, so it provided ample time for everyone to comply. It also paved the way for us to become a more professional organization—like our federal agency counterparts. However, over the years, the policy was intentionally manipulated, and it became the impetus for several state troopers filing civil lawsuits.

In the spring of 1997, I applied to McDermott University for graduate school, an arena that no one from my immediate family had ever attempted. I needed to prove to myself that I was capable of completing it. I passed the required admissions test and began attending classes at several off-site facilities, which McDermott University provided at reduced tuition.

As a part-time student, I wanted to complete my graduate degree as soon as possible because I was burning out from the grueling schedule. I doubled my course load, and in the spring of 1998, I attained a master's degree in education. I partook in the graduation ceremony because I knew Faith was looking down on me and was just as proud of my accomplishments. I didn't think anyone else in my immediate family was interested in participating, so I didn't want to bother them.

They held the graduation ceremony at a massive stadium. When I saw the McDermott University draped banners, gratification and relief gripped my soul.

The graduate and undergraduate students wore black robes, and the doctoral recipients wore blue gowns. Family members and friends cheered as they introduced us to the crowd. While we marched down the aisle to take our seats, flashbulbs went off, and screams of joy echoed in the arena. After about an hour of formalities, I beamed with pride when they called out my name, and I walked across the stage to accept my degree. A feat that I believed had been unattainable was now my reality. I had finally arrived.

With my master's degree in hand, I had also satisfied the educational requirement for teaching at a community college. During my time at South Community College, I befriended the Criminal Justice chairperson and reached out to her to see if there were any available teaching positions. I had an official interview and expressed my intense desire for giving back to the college because of the education I had received. She was very receptive and ultimately assigned me an Introduction to Criminal Justice course.

The first day of class, I had arrived fifteen minutes before the students and sat at my desk to get a feel for my new position. I couldn't remove the big smile on my face. There were about thirty desks in the classroom, and it appeared that nothing had changed since I last attended.

As students filed in, I looked at their faces and wondered if I had that same lost look on my first day as a student. I immediately set them at ease with a little joke and assured them it was going to be okay.

While teaching far exceeded my academic expectations, I continued to hear a little voice in my head asking me, "If Faith were alive, what would she advise you to do?"

I knew the answer.

Chapter 19

No Boundaries

Strive to be better than you were the day before.

In the fall of 1998, McDermott University accepted me into their doctoral program, but as a fail-safe, I also looked into their postgraduate degree, which required thirty-six additional credits. My concern was that if I didn't get the doctorate, a post–master's degree would've sufficed.

Working forty hours per week, teaching an undergraduate course at South Community College and taking graduate courses seemed daunting. However, surprisingly, in the fall of 2000, I completed my fifth degree. I had surpassed all my educational expectations, but I couldn't leave the task of attaining a doctoral degree incomplete.

Nevertheless, within three years, I had completed the coursework and began preparing for the comprehensive exam—a requirement for starting to write my dissertation. Many doctoral students quit the process for an array of reasons. I still had reservations, so I took a break before taking the exam.

However, my hiatus caused me to think about my future goals for teaching. I knew that my lack of having a criminal justice graduate degree might factor into whether or not I got a full-time position teaching criminal justice at a four-year institution. As a result, in the spring of 2003, Abernathy State University accepted me into their graduate program.

Sometime in 2006, while still in the midst of taking criminal justice coursework, I met another police officer in the McDermott University doctoral program. I was curious about whether he was taking the comprehensive exam. He told me about another option, which required writing a forty-page detailed assessment report that needed to outline a resolution to a particular issue within the educational field. This solution was better suited for me, and I excitedly rekindled my doctoral studies.

Over the course of thirty days, I conducted my research. I stayed up every night making revisions, and I challenged myself to solidify whether I needed to drop my dreams of being referred to as "Dr. Martin."

When I finalized the report, I walked to the post office to mail it to the three specified readers, who were McDermott University professors from different departments. They'd judge my research paper on three levels: Passed—no revisions, Passed—minor revisions, or Failed. It just had to be perfect.

I anxiously stood in front of the mailbox, wondering if I had done a thorough job. My hands shook as I got up the nerve and opened the lid to shove the manila envelopes inside. I let out a sigh of relief once the documents left my hands; it was no longer up to me.

After approximately three weeks, I received an official letter from a professor in the doctoral program. With trembling hands, I ripped it open and read as fast as I could. When I got to the end, it proclaimed, "Passed—no revisions." I grabbed my face and yelled, "I passed!" I danced around my condo like a damn fool. It erased all those years of being told that I probably took the place of a more qualified white state police recruit. I had stepped out of my self-imposed "I'm not good enough" line.

I overcame the first hurdle, but I still had to decide on a research topic for my dissertation. Previously, I had analyzed our education promotion policy, which they used for selecting potential leaders. I suspected the system had been subjective, and I utilized the additional research as the premise for my dissertation.

I assembled a required four-member dissertation committee. A participant's selection was crucial because of the potential for personality conflicts, which made the process stressful for the doctoral student. I chose two former professors and two former doctoral graduates as my committee; they were all friends.

With the stress of forming my committee behind me, I moved on to my research. I, being naive once more, believed that my inquiry regarding the educational promotion policy would be welcomed because it was publicly available via the State's Open Public Records Act.

In early 2007, I submitted a formal request to receive their permission to utilize my colleagues as my study group. I didn't anticipate any difficulty because other doctoral students had received unfettered access and approval.

For the next few months, I tirelessly worked on writing and submitting drafts to my respective committee members. I openly accepted their corrective criticism and made the necessary revisions; but after three months, I still hadn't received permission to distribute my questionnaire. Confused and concerned, I submitted two more requests but received neither a confirmation nor denial. At that point, I figured they didn't want my research discussed.

After relaying my suspicions to my lead committee member, we decided it wasn't worth fighting and agreed that the study would only address retired personnel because I didn't need permission to speak with them. My research was unbiased because I used data from retired African-American state troopers, retired white state troopers, and open-sourced documents, thus increasing its reliability and validity.

Later in 2007, I completed my final dissertation revision. My committee members told me they were satisfied with my corrections and that I had a month to prepare.

About a month later, my oral dissertation defense day had arrived. I could've invited family members, but I opted to go alone. I had been used to my hermit status, and again, I didn't want to inconvenience anyone.

I arrived about half an hour early to make sure they set the conference room up correctly. As I walked through the opaque glass doors, I noticed that an extensive collection of black dissertation books lined the bookshelves. The names of former students—who had probably given their defense in this same room—were stenciled in gold on the binders, which made the books appear very professional.

My committee members and doctoral colleagues arrived soon afterward, and we exchanged a few brief pleasantries. All the while, I tried my best to exhibit a confident facade; but deep down inside, I was nervous as hell. I then took up my position at the head of the table to begin.

With seven people in the room (including me), I had thirty minutes to defend my dissertation. I started to tell the guests my name when I suddenly heard a loud repetition of sounds at the door. *Knock, knock, knock!* Unbeknownst to me, the lead committee member had invited some of his students to hear my defense. My anxiety increased tenfold as seventeen additional students situated themselves in the remaining chairs.

Looking around at their strange faces, I told myself, "You can do this. You've come too far to fail."

The lead committee member then said, "When you are ready, you can begin."

I took a moment and bowed my head. I sat there for a few seconds and calmed down. I then looked up, introduced myself, and gave a brief history of my sister's influence on my educational endeavors and why I chose my subject matter. I glanced around the room, and the warm, reassuring facial expressions confirmed that I was going to be okay. Then I presented my research.

My findings criticized the promotional system as being subjective and untimely. All my respondents believed that implementing a promotional examination was unfair. Most felt that the education promotion policy should've been grandfathered in for those already employed.

Some of the respondents said they couldn't attain a college degree because they worked ten-hour rotating shifts. They claimed that trying to maintain a regular sleeping pattern, as well as handling common issues related to family life, was difficult. Also, they asserted that they paid for their children's education, so it would've been cost-prohibitive. However, they had no standing regarding this challenge because they had been reimbursed. I also shared that the respondents who were compliant said their professional and educational credentials weren't recognized until after they had retired, which contrasted the policy's intent.

Following the allotted thirty minutes, I fielded questions from the committee, which lasted an additional thirty minutes. At the end of my defense, the lead committee member said, "If there are no more questions, I want to be the first to say congratulations, Dr. Martin."

Those two words echoed in my ears: "Dr. Martin." All my hard work had paid off. I wanted to cry, but I knew it was neither the time nor the place.

After the festivities were over and all had departed from the room, I was left to think about what had transpired. I put my head in my hands and thanked Faith.

In the summer of 2007, I had the distinct pleasure of attending McDermott University's graduation ceremony at the Intercontinental Arena. I fulfilled my ultimate goal of attaining my doctorate. By far, it was the most extraordinary event in my life. Again, no one from my family attended the ceremony, but being with my classmates removed any solitary feelings.

I couldn't fathom why the NJSP didn't permit me to pursue my original research. Upon reflection, nevertheless, I understood that they had always been secretive about internal matters. Once the reality of being promoted factored into the equation, survival of the fittest took precedence, and the worst in some state troopers became apparent. A better option would've been openness and a fair promotional policy, thereby significantly reducing the rampant nepotism and cronyism.

Ironically, several months after my defense, I received a memo granting me permission for my research. The memo placed the blame for the delay on the Office of Professional Lawyers. *What rubbish.* There was no doubt that someone wanted to save face.

In the intervening years, I completed my coursework at Abernathy State University. Writing my thesis was very cathartic because my adviser encouraged me to document what had happened to me regarding my whistle-blowing experience. In the latter part of spring 2009, I graduated and received a Master of Science in Criminal Justice.

Over the course of twenty-two years of formal education, my social life and personal life suffered. School became my mistress. While I toiled at attending classes, writing research papers, and teaching, I unintentionally neglected sporadic girlfriends, who struggled with my internal drive—but I tried my best.

The significant financial cost of accumulating several degrees almost made me an indentured servant to fancy pieces of paper. After receiving minimal tuition reimbursement, I took advantage of my pension system's low interest rate and borrowed large sums of money on numerous occasions to cover the cost. My friends often asked why I made such a commitment. I could only say that I needed to show that my entrance exam score of 61 wasn't a predictor of what I could achieve. I consciously decided not to live down to their expectations of minorities. However, the thought of failure became my vaccination for overcoming adversity, and it freed me from some of the insecurity restraints that had mentally arrested me for several years.

My only regret is that during my bouts of isolation and selfishness, I deprived my mother the opportunity to see me graduate and for her to tell me that she was proud of me.

Chapter 20

Divergence

Perpetuating stereotypes retards progress.

Over the years, the outfit has matured from its days of patrolling on horses and motorcycles. Today, it is a highly diversified organization that provides more than 120 different career paths. Some state troopers pursue opportunities to transition from a patrol to being an inquirer. I didn't have any expectation of relinquishing my uniform because (1) I liked interacting with people on the highway, and (2) the honor of wearing it was immeasurable. However, I reconsidered my position after a surprising telephone conversation.

In mid-1993, while at the Greenville Station, I had received a telephone call from a supervisor in the Middle Protection Unit regarding an inquirer's position. It has always been one of the premier units because of its high-profile duties. He mentioned that he had heard about me from other inquirers and wanted to know if I would be interested in a transfer. I thought it was a prank, but after listening to his tone and articulation, I knew he was telling the truth.

He said that their responsibilities included covert surveillance of subversive groups, monitoring civil unrest in inner cities, and conducting executive protection details. On the surface, it sounded interesting. *How could I not accept?* Within a week, they officially transferred me;

however, I couldn't imagine the friction that I would endure in light of my new position.

Upon my arrival, I noticed that the company head was African-American. *What a welcome surprise.* The Middle Protection Unit shared office space with another unit, which conducted background investigations into organized crime figures in the solid hazardous waste industry. I had anticipated a smooth welcoming into both units because they, too, had an African-American assigned to their office. I had hoped that they had paved the way for other minorities, but that wasn't the case.

There were times when I came to the office and tried to be friendly with my officemates, only to be ignored by some of the white inquirers. After several incidents, I knew it wasn't my imagination. It was some time later that I learned that the cold shoulder had been intentional because a few of the inquirers had applied for my position. I didn't take it personally because I remained under the fraternal illusion that I was a part of the "blue-and-gold" family. *Only time would tell.*

After familiarizing myself with the new assignment, I was curious to know why they had selected me. I asked a former colleague, whom I had worked with at the Greenville Station. He said that he had attended a unit meeting with other inquirers, and they were asked to submit the name of a "qualified" minority candidate. He went on to say that he and Inquirer R. Chivalric submitted my name. I knew Inquirer Chivalric from his days working on the Black Dragon toll road. He stated that one of the prerequisites was that the candidate had to be articulate. I had heard this phrase used many times, but I later learned that speaking "articulately" was a code word for a perceived qualified minority. I asked him why it was critical that they sought out a minority. He said that a group of African-American state troopers had filed a complaint with the Federal Work Intervention Commission, which accused the NJSP of widespread racial discrimination and racial profiling. They also testified before a subcommittee of politicians that discrimination existed for them in the areas of specialized jobs, educational opportunities, and promotions.

I had worked with some of the members of the group, and they asked me to join their group, but I declined. I didn't feel as strongly because I had been given a few unrequested opportunities based on my race. Nevertheless, I knew that a few of them were being targeted and harassed by internal complaints that sullied their reputation.

Some of their assigned station lockers were filled with salt and had racist caricatures of black men displayed on them. I had expected a backlash to suppress their opposition to maintain compliance from any future *hell-raisers*. Even so, I had only been a state trooper for approximately seven years, and I didn't want to take a chance and have that same spotlight put on me.

They conveyed to all of us, "If the discrimination isn't presently happening to you, it will eventually." These words were prophetic and ultimately became my reality. As they stood fighting the injustice, I remained seated. I could only imagine the disdain they may have had for those of us that chose to do nothing. Early on, I suffered from self-inflicted cowardice and deserved their disapproval.

After a few months in the unit, I realized that our investigative functions were unique. We monitored inner cities for potential civil unrest and investigated threats against the governor, superior court judges, state troopers, and politicians. We also tracked alleged subversive groups, which sometimes placed me in precarious and conflicting situations.

For example, we monitored a controversial Muslim minister whose inflammatory words frightened white people. When my supervisors learned that he was going to speak at a local college, they had dispatched another African-American (who had recently transferred to the unit) and me to attempt to infiltrate the gathering. The minister espoused anti–police brutality rhetoric, which didn't bother me because I knew that some cops enjoyed beating black people. But it was his anti–law enforcement position that disturbed me because those fixated on hurting police officers couldn't care less about race.

During his opening remarks at a local gathering, the minister noticed us sitting in the audience. He said, "I would like for everyone to know that we have two *Uncle Toms* seated in the third row."

At that moment, I wanted to bow my head in shame. I glanced around and noticed the eyes of disgust piercing straight through me. The words "race traitor" rang out in my ears. I knew that I wasn't the first state trooper they subjected to this role, but I wondered if my predecessors, too, had felt the disgust. Our "secret police" actions could be viewed as comparable to our federal counterpart's COINTELPRO surveillance of domestic political organizations from the late 1950s through the 1970s. Through the use of the 1967 Freedom of Information Act, we now know how deceitful our counterparts were back then.

We also extended our scrutiny to a legendary black activist and a controversial alleged confidential police informant. They were unrelenting in expressing their concerns regarding racial profiling, but I didn't know if they were frauds because they were beloved in the black community. Of the two, the activist appeared more genuine. I later came to revere him for politically advocating on behalf of people of color. I am fortunate to have monitored him because shortly after that, he passed away due to prostate cancer. He cemented his legacy in civil rights because he co-coined the term "institutional racism," which is still relevant but often misunderstood.

As for the alleged confidential police informant, he and his entourage shut down a major roadway due to widespread allegations of racial profiling, but his actions are still very suspect to me.

An assignment like this had its advantages and disadvantages. I was at the forefront of all investigations whenever black people were involved, but what troubled me was why they feared black people more so than others. I grappled with my identity as a young African-American man and slowly lost my individuality to appease my superiors. I needed to learn the art of compromise if I wanted to remain in the unit.

Unsurprisingly, one of our greatest provocateurs came from an unpredictable fathers' rights group. They waged a battle with the courts concerning their parental authority. A few of its members sent threatening letters to judges who were involved in their respective child custody hearings. I found many of these men to be responsible individuals who weren't given equal standing by the courts. Some of them claimed they were only a paycheck in their children's lives.

While monitoring a court session, one father told me, "I am forced to pay hundreds of dollars a month for my children, but I can't visit them when I want. I need to see my kids for more than just a few hours every week."

I asked him, "Isn't there a better way to resolve this matter rather than threatening a judge?"

He quickly responded, "They couldn't care less about us! Confronting them is the only way to get their damn attention!"

I ended the conversation by telling him, "Just know that if you continue going about it this way, I will be back."

He quipped, "See you soon."

I chuckled and walked away.

A secondary function of our unit was to assist other agencies with executive dignitary details in New Jersey. One of the benefits was getting my picture taken to show to family and friends. My job was secretive, so the pictures supported my stories.

In 1994, the United States hosted the FIFA World Cup, which is soccer's equivalent of the NFL Super Bowl. They assigned me to one of the teams as an intelligence officer. My duty had been to forward any information about the team to my superiors. Fortunately, they were the fan favorites and were treated like royalty, which made my job easy. They made it to the finals in California but were defeated by a superior team. This experience was unforgettable because I grew as an inquirer.

In the course of my assignment, I didn't fully comprehend the level of integrity they expected of me. Early on, I needed to alienate myself from some of my neighborhood associates because of the risk that some of their behavior might come back and gnaw at me. Midway through my assignment, unbeknownst to me, that is what happened.

During an undercover criminal investigation, a confidential informant alleged that a state trooper named "Martin" had purportedly assisted some local criminals. The allegations were serious and, if substantiated, could've landed me in prison.

The confidential informant supposedly told my close *friend*, an undercover narcotics inquirer, that I had given a State Trooper Fraternal Association sticker to a drug courier. It is a blue-and-gold triangular sticker that can be affixed to the front or back windshield of a car. It is similar to a Policemen's Benevolent Association sticker, which is given out excessively to many friends of law enforcement officers with an expectation of "professional courtesy." Most people are unfamiliar with ours unless they are personal friends with a state trooper. The possession of it by a criminal isn't a crime, but it calls the association into question.

For several months, without my knowledge, members of my unit conducted a secret internal criminal investigation.

As the investigation progressed, they didn't find any evidence that suggested I did anything wrong or had any involvement. The department manager, Squadron Officer E. Moreh, reviewed the findings of the investigation and questioned why no effort was made to clear my name.

But how did my name surface?

Squadron Officer Moreh interviewed everyone involved in the investigation, including my friend and his female supervisor. The confidential informant had been incarcerated on two separate occasions in one of the State's correctional facilities. At the time, my brother worked as a corrections officer, and the confidential informant was housed on his tier. My brother said that he might've told him I was a state trooper. *I understood because a lot of our neighborhood associates were incarcerated in that prison.*

I relayed this information to Squadron Officer Moreh, who later determined that my friend's failure to accurately assess the situation caused the allegation against me. I didn't know the confidential informant, and a simple Q&A could've quickly squashed the investigation. This experience left me shattered because what I couldn't fathom was how my friend could've ever assumed that I might be remotely involved in something so criminal. We had gone through so much together, both in the academy and after we had graduated, and I believed he knew enough about my character that should've shut this down before it even started. The stigma of an Internal Affairs investigation could've left a cloud of suspicion hanging over my career. Once accused, always a suspect. To this day, neither one of us has brought up the subject, nor does he know that I have a copy of the report detailing his actions.

Ultimately, Squadron Officer Moreh determined that the sticker belonged to another state trooper named Vincent, who was a relative of the targeted suspect.

Chapter 21

Life's Realisms

Don't give self-pity the time of day.

While working in the Middle Protection Unit, I had an impromptu conversation with another inquirer about a nonprofit organization called Camp Cheery, where he had volunteered. He said it was a one-week camp that catered to approximately two hundred kids who have, or had, cancer. He went on to say, "There aren't many counselors who can relate to some of the black and Hispanic kids. Would you be interested in volunteering?"

I wondered what he saw in me that made him believe I'd be a good candidate. But it didn't matter—within days, I signed up.

It was about a three-hour drive from my home to the camp. The scenic trip resembled much of the territory in the northern part of New Jersey. My only apprehension was whether I'd be able to handle seeing children with health-related issues.

Upon arrival, the picturesque camp validated my expectations. A large calm lake was the centerpiece of the sprawling land. Although the camp served as a training facility for high school football teams and a getaway for a contingent of wealthy kids during the year, it was our private oasis while we were there.

The camp's director assigned me and two other counselors to a group of thirteen-year-old boys. I remembered that age and recalled how much trouble I had caused, and I couldn't put anything past the kids in our bunk. I could've easily seen myself giving the kids a wedgie or placing shaving cream on their faces while they slept, so I had to keep my eyes open.

Chartered buses transported the kids to camp from several area hospitals throughout the state. They arrived around noontime and scrambled to their assigned cabins to be with their friends. We had a greeting session to ease some of the fears of any first-year camper.

For the rest of the day, we mixed and mingled with other kids and counselors. Their happiness was evident in their contagious smiles and laughter. I made sure I knew all my boys' names and a little bit about things they liked to do. Later in the day, we escorted them to a few planned activities and then to the dining hall for dinner.

While sitting at our tables and waiting for further instructions, I noticed a young woman standing on top of a table. She had her hand raised, and automatically everyone became silent. She then began rhythmically singing a song, and everyone then went into a call-and-response version. The kids yelled at the top of their lungs. Their excitement gave me chills. The only thing that could've topped that was a full-fledged food fight.

Eventually, we lined up by our assigned tables and served the meal. Things quieted down while we ate. Looking around and seeing the smiles on the kids' faces as they interacted with their friends brought me inner joy. Afterward, we hung out in front of our bunk and talked until it was time to go to bed. The upcoming days seemed promising.

Every morning, we were awakened around seven o'clock to get ready for breakfast. Without fail, barring any rain, the sound of chirping birds and the chill of morning dew stimulated my senses.

After breakfast, we went to our scheduled activities, which included football, golf, basketball, archery, swimming, soccer, volleyball, and woodshop. I had hoped my campers would get worn out afterward, but they always caught a second wind. They stayed up all night talking about girls, school, and sports. I, on the other hand, was drained; but I couldn't miss out on this bonding moment. I think the real reason they stayed up was my annoyingly loud snoring. Everything was going well until they gave us some bad news.

A little girl—whom I had seen being pushed around in a wheelchair—became seriously ill. We had spoken on a few occasions, and she appeared to be in good spirits. She told me that she begged her parents to allow her to attend camp because she wanted to be with her friends. The smile on her face illuminated when she was around her bunkmates. Observing her watch them from her stationary position touched my heart. Rallying around her was a fantastic display of unconditional love and friendship. Unfortunately, during camp, her condition flared up, and she later died at an area hospital.

They instructed us on how to relieve the despair of the remaining grieving children, but remarkably, they were better prepared to confront it than some of us. They understood that it was more of their immediate reality than ours.

The last day of camp was mentally challenging. As we said goodbye to one another, I got caught up in the emotions and broke down and cried uncontrollably. I equated the sorrow to departing from a funeral knowing that you'd never see that person again. Another male counselor pulled me to the side and gave me a comforting hug. At that moment, I needed the consoling because I couldn't comprehend my behavior. He convinced me that it was a reasonable response and that he, too, had experienced it when he first volunteered.

As the kids boarded the buses, I cherished looking at their faces and bright smiles as they waved goodbye. If I could turn back the hands of time, this would've been the perfect occasion because I didn't want them to leave. However, I sadly accepted the fact that some of them would never return.

My relationship with Camp Cheery lasted for fourteen years. I couldn't stay away because the kids had become an integral part of my life. Every year brought more excitement as I drove through the gates expecting to see all the returning campers. However, as the years passed and more kids succumbed to their illnesses, the thought of them dying began to wear on my soul. Mentally, I couldn't take the heartache anymore, and I ended my volunteerism in 2009; but I still keep in touch with the campers that I had seen grow up before my eyes.

Chapter 22

Peter Principle

One's actions - not status - equates to leadership.

In every large-scale organization, you'll find a generous share of individuals who lack interpersonal skills and yet get promoted to their level of incompetence. Unfortunately, my supervisor turned out to be that person.

Investigative Officer P. Hinge had been assigned to the unit several years before I got there. He dressed like a monogrammed banker and carried himself with a high level of cocksureness. He was, by far, the most arrogant person that I had ever worked with in my career.

While presenting a bias crime lecture at in-service training, he made a favorable remark about a former fascist dictator. His failed attempt at humor shocked everyone. *I guess he thought he had like-minded individuals in the audience, but he was sadly mistaken because a few white state troopers complained about his comments.* He later received a verbal reprimand for his insensitive remark.

Conversely, his investigative competence brought credibility to our unit because he was a capable inquirer, but his lack of people skills always seemed to get him in trouble. As time passed, I observed his rude and snobbish actions toward colleagues and civilians. He talked down to them when he felt the need to do so, but his despicable behavior didn't stop there. The confrontations between us were numerous, but two particular incidents stood out and solidified my perception of him as an incompetent supervisor.

One afternoon, Investigative Officer Hinge called a colleague and me into his office for a meeting. His desk had copies of our reports littered all over it, so I expected the meeting to be about our cases. However, I soon realized that he had a different agenda. While sitting across from him, he emphatically claimed that he disagreed with our squadron officer's decision to remove another inquirer from his squad. He went on to say, "It's like I have to treat you and him special because you are black." His comments shocked me because all I required was to be treated with respect regardless of my rank or race, but I let him vent.

Afterward, I redirected the meeting to our reports. All the while, my jaw and fists tensed up, and I couldn't wait to get away. When the meeting concluded, I immediately reported him to our supervisors. There was no way that I would allow him to talk to me in that manner, let alone in front of someone else. I didn't expect he'd receive any disciplinary action, but someone needed to school him on behaving properly.

Unfortunately, they attempted to defuse the situation by saying that no one else felt that way. As the leaders, they had the authority to shut him down and make him adhere to common decency practices. Nevertheless, at that moment, I recognized that they didn't like being questioned, primarily by someone who could *articulate* their shortcomings.

Around this time, I began documenting everything he did in a ledger. His actions were getting progressively hostile toward me, and just in case I ever needed to recall facts about what he said and how his supervisors failed to do anything about his behavior, I'd have my recollection of the events.

In the following weeks, we monitored an annual judicial conference held at a luxurious hotel. For three days, we provided security for the annual in-service training conference of superior court judges. Our job had been to investigate suspicious telephone calls, direct bomb sweeps of the hotel, conduct background checks on hotel employees, and supervise uniformed state troopers.

The first day went well until Investigative Officer Hinge arrived. Still reeling from our previous encounter, he entered the hotel and immediately approached me and questioned whether I had heard him calling me on the state police radio. I didn't have a portable radio with me because it wasn't customary. He appeared somewhat agitated from the grimace on his face. He then walked to the front table, snatched a radio, and briskly returned and shoved it in my hand. I knew there wasn't anything I could do, aside from throwing it at him, and I just had to deal with the repercussions. *I still had three long days ahead of me.*

On the second day, I worked with Inquirer Chivalric, and things appeared to be getting better. The judges attended all-day judicial seminars, so downtime was plentiful. Midway through the morning, I told him that I needed a bathroom break and went to our assigned hotel room. This time, I had a portable radio just in case. There were other uniformed state troopers in the room, so I hung out with them.

When I returned, I noticed Investigative Officer Hinge standing in the middle of the hallway and giving me a dirty look. *Not again.* He then motioned with his finger for me to come to him. *There is no way he is gesturing for me. I'm not a damn kid!* I looked left and right, hoping to find someone next to me. Possibly sensing that I wasn't going to comply, he assertively walked over to me and said, "You'd better stop leaving your post!" He then got in my face and menacingly said, "Stop acting like a baby."

He had no clue as to my deep-seated hatred for being talked down to, especially from someone who thought that they were better than others. I sternly told him, "You need to speak to me professionally." I'd seen other state troopers buckle to this bullying behavior, but I wasn't the one. We were about the same size, so it would've been a fair fight if we came to blows.

He then "ordered" me to report to the office the following day, to sign a "negative" performance notice for leaving my post. A performance notice is equivalent to a slap on the wrist, so I wasn't too concerned.

The rest of the day, my colleagues observed me erratically pacing the front hallway and highly suggested that I just let it go. I went home that night overwhelmed with the notion of kicking his ass, but I knew that I'd get fired if I put my hands on him.

The next day, we participated in what they deemed a "conflict resolution" meeting with our squadron officer and other squad supervisors. In the encounter, Investigative Officer Hinge was adamant about reprimanding me and exclaimed, "I can discipline him how I see fit. I am his superior." His emphasis on being my "superior" irked the hell out of me.

I had expressed my concern about him getting in my face and his previous comment about having to treat me special because I was *black*. When the squadron officer asked him about his comment, he claimed that I had taken his words out of context. The squadron officer then said, "Vincent, I think you are overly sensitive."

What did he just say? His attitude was appalling and unsurprising at the same time. I knew he wouldn't understand, so I remained quiet.

The squadron officer deemed the gathering an impasse and suggested that I report Investigative Officer Hinge to the Work Intervention Unit.

Later that afternoon, I anxiously met with two members of the Work Intervention Unit, who recommended that I participate in their conflict resolution process. I was tired of talking; I wanted something done about him.

The stress of dealing with him, I am sure, is what later led to my high blood pressure diagnosis. Our relationship didn't get any better, and after several months, they subsequently transferred me to a federal Anti Radical Team. However, nothing happened to him, and they later promoted him to warrant agent.

I looked forward to the new challenges ahead of me. While my investigative efforts changed to terrorism, I soon came to realize that our law enforcement focus would target a different community.

Chapter 23

Heightened Alert

Listen to the voice of reason when personal sanity fails.

In the fall of 1999, the governor hired a high-ranking federal official (who was also a former State employee) as the new chief leader of the NJSP. Ordinarily, I would've referred to him as an African-American, but he always made it a point to remind us that he was half-European, so I didn't want to be insensitive. Why he was chosen to lead the NJSP was anybody's guess. However, he received a unanimous vote from the New Jersey Senate—the governor got her man.

My inclusion on the Anti Radical Team was, by far, one of the most exciting assignments of my career. Foremost was the fact that it brought me back to the City of Elkanda. Also, I was a part of a team of investigators from federal, state, county, and local agencies, which afforded me the opportunity to observe the best investigative practices.

I went through an exhaustive six-month federal background check. They explored every aspect of my life—from finances to overseas travel. They needed to know everything about me. Afterward, I received *top secret* and *CIA* security clearances. I was also sworn in as a US marshal because I needed federal authority to arrest suspects who lived in other states and countries.

The feds had always intrigued me. From their documented history, many in the African-American community didn't view them in a favorable light. I don't think any law enforcement agency could withstand scrutiny. However, I learned that while most special agents just wanted to do their job, their higher-ups would always have the last say.

While conducting an investigation, evidence is sometimes gathered by following up on information provided by concerned citizens. It isn't often that an alleged terrorist would self-report, but that is what happened in April 2000.

A dispatcher on the Anti Radical Team received a telephone call from a local police department regarding an individual claiming to have information about the alleged monstrous terrorist Osama bin Laden. No one believed it, but they immediately sent two agents to relay him back to the office.

Umar Shah was a Pakistani-British national who told an elaborate story. When I first saw him, I thought, *No way can this little guy be a terrorist.* He had on blue jeans, a gray shirt, and a white "kufi" cap. His modest stature of about 5'5" tall and his weighing about 140 lbs., threw me off, but who said that pure evil had to come in a giant package?

We drove him to a restaurant in Edison to have dinner and relax. We didn't want to overwhelm him the first day with probing questions. Even though Shah spoke English, his strong accent and soft voice made him difficult to understand. Luckily, my colleague from the Prosecutor's Office spoke his native language and translated when necessary. Later, we put him up in a hotel and assigned two Anti Radical Team members to guard him 24-7.

The following day, we transported him back to our office and debriefed him. Shah claimed that while in London, an unknown man approached him and asked if he knew about Osama bin Laden. His acknowledgment then set the ball in motion. He said that they flew him to Lahore, Pakistan, where he was trained by al-Qaida operatives to commit an act of terrorism that would test our security measures. Once the plans were in place, Shah said that he traveled from London's Heathrow Airport to JFK Airport, where he was supposed to meet his handlers for further instructions. It was while on the plane that he observed a young woman with a small child, and then he had second thoughts. He then tearfully whispered, "My wife recently gave birth to our first baby, and I couldn't go through with it."

Confused and scared, he said, "Once I got to New York, I took a bus to Atlantic City and gambled away the money they gave me." He went on to say that he was afraid that something would happen to his family because he had failed in his mission. His story was very descriptive, which meant he was either telling the truth or was an excellent liar. Shah subsequently passed two polygraph tests, and from his passport, we verified his travel.

We allowed him to keep his scheduled meeting with his alleged handlers at JFK Airport. We set up surveillance at the terminal and waited patiently for the meeting, but no one showed. Doubt set in, and some of the Anti Radical Team members believed it was just a hoax. I still thought he was telling the truth because his story was too compelling, and his body language seemed sincere.

After several weeks, federal administrators decided we could no longer detain him. We were instructed to send him back to England for further investigation by the British officials. We could've done much more to explore his allegations, but who was I to question their authority?

Chapter 24

Revelations

Arrogance can obscure the conspicuous.

On September 10, 2001, while teaching a class at South Community College, a student brought up the topic of terrorism. Although I couldn't speak about any ongoing investigations on the Anti Radical Team, I told my class that based on some of the information that we had received, I believed that something catastrophic was going to happen. I had no idea that my words would become prophetic.

The following day, my colleagues and I were in a meeting at the local police and fire academy. Suddenly, several pagers randomly emitted resonating sounds. It was eerily similar to a scene in Denzel Washington's movie *The Siege*. They told us that a small airplane accidentally crashed into the World Trade Center. I pictured a small Cessna aircraft dangling from a window on the fiftieth floor. However, several minutes later, we were ordered back to the Elkanda office because of a possible terrorist attack. My stomach knotted up as we dashed out the doors.

I traveled eastbound on Route 79 en route to the office and pulled over to the side of the road, along with hundreds of other concerned drivers, to frantically gaze at the Twin Towers. Words can't express the sorrow knowing that as the planes hit both buildings, scores of innocent people instantaneously died. Many of us stood there motionless until that final moment when we watched the second building crumble to the ground and plumes of white smoke ascended to the heavens.

At that moment, I thought about an ex-girlfriend, whom I believed had worked in one of the towers. Thank goodness, the next day, she called and told me she was safe. Sorrowfully, though, two of my former university professors—who were police officers—were among the dead.

When I returned to the office, an entire floor had been converted into a command post. Desks were removed and replaced with long conference tables, which accommodated numerous *secured* telephone lines. Support personnel and special agents weren't allowed to talk on regular phones due to the sensitive nature of the operation. Large flip charts were put in place to document a timeline of the events. In my many years in law enforcement, I had never seen an operation work with such precision.

Within a couple of hours, the telephones rang constantly, and leads were coming in by the hundreds. Even though the outside world was in chaos, we were determined to identify the perpetrators.

Several Anti Radical Team members teamed up and were dispatched to investigate every lead. It was an around-the-clock operation because our efforts to solve this investigation were undeniable. As a result, another community of color would experience the shamefulness of racial profiling.

One of the first leads that I investigated came from an anonymous caller who complained about a "Middle Eastern-looking" male standing on the corner near our office. Downtown Elkanda had plenty of immigrants milling around, so I didn't think much about it when my counterpart and I were dispatched to go "check him out."

We walked up to the unknown man, and I identified myself. He was approximately 6'1" tall and weighed a solid 250 lbs. He had very muscular shoulders and biceps, so I hoped he wouldn't be a hothead. We had a brief conversation, and he claimed that he was waiting for a friend to give him a ride. I didn't sense anything suspicious up to that point because his story sounded reasonable. I then asked him for his identification, and the bells and whistles began to go off.

Dr. Vincent Lucas Martin

He gave me what appeared to be an expired Egyptian military ID card and said that he was a former police officer as well. His calm demeanor then changed. His poker face was exposed as we fired more interrogating questions at him and he stumbled continuously trying to answer them.

I pulled my partner to the side and suggested that we take him upstairs for follow-up questioning. It was a stretch, but he didn't have a valid ID, and I thought we were justified in making the inquiry. After a brief discussion and pat down for any potential weapons, we quietly walked him into the office building.

After a more thorough background investigation, we learned that he was a military intelligence officer. He didn't provide us with a valid reason for coming to the United States and overstaying, so we eventually lodged him in a county jail for being in the country on an expired visa. He'd languish there for more than a year before being deported. While I believed my actions were justified in this matter, my moral compass began to go awry.

As more leads came in, a noticeable pattern developed. Men of Middle Eastern descent became our primary focus, even though no formal group, at that time, had taken responsibility. Muslim spiritual leaders knew we targeted them, but we tried to convince them otherwise.

We used electronic surveillance to help with our investigative mission. A team of federal attorneys was assigned to facilitate legal matters. Nevertheless, some of the methods we utilized for detaining alleged terrorists troubled me. Several suspects were jailed for months without a formal court hearing. They were served meals containing pork, which went against their religious beliefs. In protest, many detainees went on hunger strikes. I completely understood their reaction to our insensitivity because we should've treated them better. They were presumed innocent until proven guilty—or so the Constitution said.

In early 2002, I was promoted to investigative officer and took on supervisory responsibilities regarding the other state police personnel assigned to the Anti Radical Team. My workload doubled due to investigative and administrative duties, but I enjoyed it.

My Anti Radical Team supervisor detached me to assist with the investigation in the death of a reporter from an acclaimed news organization. The reporter had been working in India and had been captured and executed. My task was to monitor his credit card usage after his death in an attempt to track down his captors. Having watched the World Trade Center crumble to the ground, I didn't think anything else could mentally bother me. Regrettably, there was no action on his account after the abduction.

About a month later, everyone on the Anti Radical Team was summoned to a meeting to view an internet video posted by his captors. I watched as a masked man grabbed the reporter by his hair, plunged a large knife into his throat, and then vigorously cut back and forth. With each stroke, blood squirted out everywhere. Surprisingly, he remained stoic until they severed his head. Unfortunately, I didn't know if they'd use this video as a tool to extort money from future American hostages. I am incredibly proud of him for not giving those bastards any satisfaction in seeing him beg for his life.

Numerous leads took our efforts down different paths and unraveled other suspected terrorist organizations. Ultimately, it had been determined that nineteen individuals were allegedly responsible for the 9/11 tragedies. But conspiracies abound; we will never know what happened. Sadly, any effort on our part won't stop those hell-bent on harming us. If we don't seriously reevaluate our foreign policy and rethink our military actions in other countries, it will be just a matter of time before they attack us again.

My role on the Anti Radical Team kept me speculating as to what was to come next, but another telephone call altered those plans.

Chapter 25

Recycled Newcomer

Screwups move up.

While conducting a follow-up investigation at a local jail, I received a telephone call from Warrant Agent T. Deal, whom I had known for more than ten years.

"Hey, Vincent, are you busy?" he asked.

I responded, "No, sir. How can I help you?"

He said, "Well, the incoming governor is appointing a new chief leader, and I wanted to know if you would be interested in heading up his security detail."

I asked, "Why me?"

The new assignment would add two hours a day to my commute, and I'd lose the annual fifteen thousand dollars additional salary allotted for working on the Anti Radical Team.

After thinking about it briefly, I told him, "Sir, I appreciate you considering me. Of course, I would be interested!" I accepted his offer because I saw it as a challenge.

The head of the NJSP is a politically influential person who only answers to the governor and commander solicitor. Over the years, the titleholder acted more like a dictator than a real leader and abused their power when it came to dispensing punishment to enlisted personnel.

As per state statute Title 3A, the only person afforded the designation of chief leader is someone from within the NJSP. Anyone appointed from outside the ranks would be called Chief. In fairness to all state troopers, they need to defang the disciplinary portion of Title 3A and bestow its authority upon the Office of Administrative Law, which is unbiased and could render an impartial decision in significant disciplinary cases. Moreover, if the governor wants to bring in someone from outside to lead the outfit, that person should be beyond reproach and not another favor promised.

Chief J. Delfrio went through an obligatory New Jersey Senate confirmation hearing before his close vote appointment. The publicity given to his nomination was unprecedented because he had many personal issues that became political fodder for the media. The noncommissioned officer and state trooper unions came out against him due to his alleged affiliation with organized crime figures and conviction for assaulting another cop. Conversely, as politics would have it, the commissioned officers' union backed him. *I wondered why. Hmm?*

In March 2002, I finally met Chief Delfrio, a former city police director. My first impression was that he was either a banker or a *GQ* model. *How could he afford to dress like that on a cop's salary?* His suit was impeccable, and the sparkle coming from his cufflinks almost blinded me. I had conducted executive protection details for many dignitaries, but this guy carried a gun. So why would he need protection?

Typically, I'd pick him up at his palatial residence; his home was one of five on the block. I immediately sensed something was wrong as I walked into his brand-new abode and saw a damn near life-sized self-portrait of him hanging from his vestibule wall. *You gotta be kidding me—talk about being vain.*

Most mornings, I drove him to his gym. Wall-to-wall mirrors furnished ample opportunities for him to look at himself. I have to admit, for a man in his late fifties, he had an impressively chiseled body. I appreciated cops wanting to stay in shape, but this guy was just infatuated with himself. After his daily one-hour workout session, accompanying hair primping, and manipulating his tie's placement, we made the trek to his office.

During our time together, he displayed several personalities. For instance, when we were in transit, he was the Latino born and raised in the *hood*, who had fought for everything he had received. He spoke with bravado and continuously called state troopers *yahoos* and claimed, "You guys eat your own!" He had referenced the infighting between North and South state trooper factions. When he spoke with junior members, he was the caring newcomer willing to listen to their concerns. He attempted to demonstrate that as an outsider, he would make the necessary changes to ensure our future success.

At times, he made it apparent that he couldn't control his temper. On numerous occasions, he exclaimed, "I am going to launch some motherfuckers out of here!" Once, he summoned a few high-ranking individuals to his office and had them sit in an outer lobby for hours— only to later cancel the meeting. He was childish, but some of them got what they deserved because they had advocated for him.

Driving him around and listening to his cell phone conversations was another fiasco that made me question his motives. I recall an instance while driving him home, he received a phone call from a prominent Patch County executive. It was common for him to speak to other law enforcement officials, but this conversation sounded suspicious.

They spoke about bringing the NJSP Transportation Unit into the Patch County area. Chief Delfrio then said, "We could make a lot of money."

In the context of that comment, I was unsure as to what he meant. Just the same, I had never heard any state trooper speak about making money for something we did as an ordinary course of business. It seemed to me that a quid pro quo (*favor for something*) was taking place. Even though at the time, we were under a federal consent decree, the government never accused us of being a corrupt agency. His possible actions offended me because it seemed that he was attempting to bring corruption to our organization. I believed my disgusted facial expression was evident as I stared at him, rolled my eyes, and continued to drive. Little was said after he completed his telephone call. I eventually dropped him off at his ornate palace and couldn't wait for him to get the hell out of the car.

The following morning, his personnel director called me to the office and reassigned me. My new assignment was as administrative officer for Warrant Agent A. Deal, who, within three months, had been promoted to assistant chief leader. I asked if I had done anything wrong, and she responded, "No, we are just making a few changes."

I damn near ran out of the office because the inevitable shit was going to hit the fan, and I wanted no part of it.

Once I transferred to Assistant Chief Leader Deal's office, I assisted him with two inner-city crime initiatives that were designed to decrease crime rates with the supplementation of state police personnel. For example, when the state police patrolled rural areas, we implemented a prototypical community-policing model. We responded with *school safety officers* and *bicycle patrols* to quell any problems. On the contrary, in the inner cities, we sent an occupying force of tactical units with Kevlar helmets and riot gear because it was about *kicking some ass.*

Assistant Chief Leader Deal and I worked well together. I did most of his administrative tasks while he managed the initiatives. Nevertheless, I continued to interact with my former colleagues.

One day, I walked into their office and observed an overtime pay report on a desk. I was shocked to read that a particular individual— whom they had recently punished for inflating his hours—had been paid for an inordinate amount of overtime. *I guess he didn't learn.* I knew that he hadn't worked that many hours, so how could he justify getting paid? He couldn't because this was theft.

During this time, I had befriended the newly appointed African-American Commander Solicitor, P. Hamper, and requested an audience with him to discuss my concerns.

In our meeting, I told him, "Sir, I have my suspicions about certain members in the Chief's Office who may be padding their time sheets."

He asked, "What evidence do you have?"

I relayed what I viewed on the pay report, and he cavalierly replied, "Okay, don't worry. They will do themselves in."

It seemed like he already knew something was not right, but I had expected more from the highest-ranking law enforcement officer. He could've easily have asked me to get a copy of the report or have someone discreetly conduct an audit, but he gave no viable solutions. If this was going to be his response to corruption, we were in for a long ride. His inaction surprised me because he touted himself as someone who was going to do things differently.

As things moved along, due to political infighting, the relationship between Chief Delfrio and Assistant Chief Leader Deal had soured. He relegated Assistant Chief Leader Deal to a dingy office in the southern part of the state and transferred me to the Work Intervention Unit.

My assignment in the Chief's Office lasted approximately three months. In that time, numerous state troopers had met with the personnel director and subsequently secured either a specialist assignment or a promotion. Our deceptive promotional system has continuously placed inept and unprofessional individuals into leadership positions. I know this happens in mainstream society, but I foolishly believed that we had a selection process to address this matter.

While in office, Chief Delfrio had to contend with the thirteen African-American state troopers who had previously filed a lawsuit. With the help of a famed celebrity attorney, they settled their litigation, and it cost taxpayers millions of dollars. In later years, the attorney also settled another sizeable lawsuit filed by four minority males in an alleged racial profiling incident.

Chief Delfrio resigned after seven months due to pressure from the state police unions and *unfriendly* politicians. While his superintendence was not superb, he disrupted the good ole boy network. It would've been interesting to see what he could've accomplished. However, in his short stint as the boss, he promoted a few of the self-centered company personnel, which maintained some of the constant problems.

Chapter 26

Adulterated Process

Honesty and integrity shouldn't have an expiration date.

The Work Intervention Unit is responsible for investigating allegations of sexual harassment, hostile work environment, and racial discrimination. It is similar to the Internal Matters Bureau (later renamed the Office of Official Police Ethics), which investigates internal corruption. Most state troopers shied away from these particular assignments because they entailed investigating their workmates. I wasn't holier-than-thou, but I wanted to do my part to get rid of the discrimination and target those who believed this hideous behavior was acceptable.

Over the years, my colleagues had referred to me as "shad," "mud duck," "moon cricket," "colored," and "Crisco oil duck fucker." Some of these terms were new to me, and I wondered if their parents taught them this nonsense while they were growing up in their households.

To add to the ignorance, a former squad investigative officer, when referring to my Hispanic classmate, told me, "I remember when I allowed you and that Spic to ride together." All their casual racist comments were unsettling because they appeared extremely comfortable saying them. I had no choice but to deal with it.

Before my chance transfer, I had, on several occasions, verbally expressed an interest in the Work Intervention Unit and the Office of Official Police Ethics. Superiors repeatedly told me, "There are no openings right now." However, many state troopers got drafted, even though they wanted no part of the assignment. No one ever gave a legitimate reason why they never considered me.

I submitted numerous official transfer requests, but they were all ignored. In one such petition, the names were redacted on all résumés of potential candidates. According to a warrant agent who sat on the selection board, once they revealed the names, I was their number one candidate. However, when they submitted my name to the chief leader's office for consideration, they gave the position to someone else.

A few years later, in the fall of 2001, while I was still assigned to the Anti Radical Team, the Work Intervention Unit requested new candidates. Fifteen highly qualified inquirers and I officially applied. I had doubts about the prospect of being selected because I had filed a complaint against Investigative Officer Hinge, which was in the process of being investigated.

While preparing for my interview, I received an unexpected telephone call from Warrant Agent M. Drimmer of the Work Intervention Unit, to inquire whether I still wanted to proceed with my complaint. I reluctantly told him that I wasn't going to pursue it because so much time had passed. Did he think that I was stupid?

The day of my interview, Squadron Officer R. Rivers (Hispanic) chaired the panel along with Investigative First Officer T. Kriecher (African-American), Supervisory Assistant Commander Solicitor (SACS) L. Hodan (Caucasian), and Warrant Agent Drimmer (African-American). The diversity of the interviewers initially seemed refreshing.

I entered the room, greeted them, and took my seat at the elongated brown conference table. Sparing no time, Squadron Officer Rivers then asked me about the State's policy regarding discrimination, harassment, and hostile work environment. I had read it several times and could almost recite it verbatim. I replied, "There is a zero tolerance for any violation of the policy." I kept the answer short because if I started making exceptions, then I might appear too lenient.

They also wanted to know if I'd have any reservations investigating colleagues. I had separated my job from my friends much earlier in my career, and this wouldn't have been a problem either. We then spoke about some of the pitfalls of time management, and I assured them that I would be capable of handling the caseload. Throughout my career, I had always been aware that I was going to be judged differently than most of my colleagues, so I made it a point to get my work in on time.

The rest of the interview went without incident, but I had a strange feeling in my gut about Investigative First Officer Kriecher. When he asked me questions, he never looked directly at me; instead, it appeared that he had dismissed me as someone he didn't consider to be worthy. Once the interview ended, I stood up and thanked everyone for the opportunity.

As I departed, Warrant Agent Drimmer met me in the hallway and told me that SACS Hodan was very impressed with my answers. After some small talk, I shook his hand and thanked him, but I intuitively knew that I wasn't going to be selected.

Over the years, I saw how some minority commissioned officers changed personalities once they cracked the glass ceiling. Often, they made lofty promises and never delivered on any of them. I didn't appreciate this type of behavior because your word should be your bond. It is probably unfair of me to hold them to a higher standard, but it is just something about them that I immediately recognized.

About a month later, they made their selection; and as expected, they didn't choose me. I surmised that I wasn't the best candidate. Nonetheless, a couple of weeks had passed, and by luck, I ran into Squadron Officer Rivers and asked, "What did I do wrong?"

After looking around to see who was nearby, he whispered, "I will deny ever saying this, but we treat our own worse than we treat others." He didn't elaborate and quickly walked away toward a group of state troopers. His brief response didn't immediately faze me, but eventually, I knew something wasn't right.

Shortly after that, I had lunch with a colleague and expressed my thoughts about the Work Intervention Unit interview process. I vented but didn't expect anything to come of our conversation. Nevertheless, he told Warrant Agent Drimmer about my concerns, and within days, I was summoned to Division Headquarters.

I walked into his office, and we spoke briefly about trivial matters from our former days at Greenville Station. His demeanor then changed, and he said, "I heard that you didn't think I treated you fairly. Why do you feel that way?"

I repeated what Squadron Officer Rivers told me and replied, "I figured he was referring to you."

At that moment, he retrieved a box from behind his desk, removed some documents, and said, "Look at these."

The box contained the scoring sheets for all the interviewees. I observed that a perfect score was an 80, and then I looked at the scores that they gave me. I received an 80 from Squadron Officer Rivers and SACS Hodan. He gave me a 78, and Investigative First Officer Kriecher gave me a 72. While his 78 wasn't so bad, I wasn't pleased with Investigative First Officer Kriecher's low score and questioned why he did it.

Warrant Agent Drimmer responded, "Squadron Officer Rivers and I got into a heated discussion with him because we didn't think he scored you fairly. I just want you to know it wasn't me who did this to you."

Again, another coward's way of placing blame on someone else. He and Squadron Officer Rivers outranked Investigative First Officer Kriecher and could've easily made him change his score.

They gave the position to (then) Inquirer K. Nieps, a white male that looked liked a middle linebacker for a professional football team. He was the most senior candidate but one of the least educated in the process. At the time, it didn't dawn on me that he and Warrant Agent Drimmer were best friends. I wanted the position, but I couldn't argue with their choice because he was a nice guy and an excellent investigator. My quest to get into the unit had been unsuccessful—or so I thought.

Chapter 27

Presumption of Compliance

Stem the tide of ethical uncertainty.

In June 2002, I officially transferred to the Work Intervention Unit, which was staffed with politically appointed investigators from the Office of Police Fairness and handpicked NJSP inquirers. Both entities reported directly to the Office of Professional Lawyers. I had speculated that since the unit came under the purview of the Chief's Office, I didn't have to go through a selection process. In essence, I was being dumped there as punishment for daring to give the boss an unfriendly stare. Looking back, I think the transfer had been destined.

My initial days in the unit, I thought, were pretty much going to be routine, but it turned out to be so much more. My state police colleagues—(now) Investigative Officer K. Nieps, Warrant Agent A. Wenyal, and Investigative First Officer B. Midos—were all very close, so I had to get to know them. I already knew Warrant Agent Drimmer, but prior to the 2001 interview process, I hadn't seen him in years.

About two weeks into being assigned to the office, I observed all of them standing in the doorway of an assistant commander solicitor's office. I walked over, and Warrant Agent Drimmer said, "This is one of the assistant commander solicitors you'll be working with." He then pointed to a Gay Pride poster hanging on the wall, and they quietly snickered. I realized that as men, we sometimes ridiculed each other;

but given it was the Work Intervention Unit, I couldn't believe they made fun of him.

Over the course of the approximately fifteen years that I'd known Warrant Agent Drimmer, he always made me feel uncomfortable being alone in his presence. There were several instances where he made sexual overtures toward me (e.g., asking me out on dates or scratching the middle of my palm when we shook hands). I wanted to believe he was joking, but the intensity and frequency made me question his sexuality. I didn't know any openly gay state troopers, so if he were in the closet, it would've explained a lot of his behavior. Back then, I repeatedly told him to stop playing, but he continued the more I objected.

After several months, Warrant Agent Drimmer scheduled a unit meeting. As I walked into the office, he pulled me to the side and said, "You are doing an excellent job, and the assistant commander solicitors are pleased with your work product." He went on to say, "Based on your credentials, you are going to get the next promotion to investigative first officer."

I thought, *Where is this coming from?* They had promoted me about six months earlier, but I wasn't going to object because others had received "double bumps" (*back-to-back promotions*).

As I became more acclimated to our reporting system, it wasn't long before I realized that conducting an investigation was time-consuming and stressful for everyone involved.

The person who complains (complainant) is frustrated and has made the ultimate decision to file a complaint. The principal (*target of investigation*) is angry because their conduct had possibly violated the State's Work Intervention Unit policy. The witness is also upset because they became an integral part of an investigation, which they didn't initiate. Lastly, the investigator must be aware of completing the investigation within the required time frame.

We had to summarize and transcribe the facts of the investigation into a very detailed and lengthy report. I wasn't a stenographer, and I knew I couldn't write down everything they said verbatim. It would've been much easier if we were allowed to utilize a recording device. It later became apparent that they didn't record interviews by design because this had been their way of controlling these investigations. The Office of Professional Lawyers supervised every investigation but steered the most egregious ones to their chosen investigator—to protect the State should a lawsuit ensue at a later date.

As part of my internal training, I attended several classes regarding Work Intervention Unit policy. For some odd reason, it appeared that most in attendance were women and minorities. Nonetheless, it was enlightening to hear our instructors talk about what would happen to those violating the policy. I thought they meant what they said about fundamental honesty in our investigations, but it ended up being all a bunch of lies. In reality, the training focused on employer liability rather than prevention.

Work Intervention Unit guidelines mandated that an investigation be completed in approximately six to nine months. However, I noticed that some investigations took an unreasonable amount of time to be completed—some as many as three years. As the new inquirer in the unit, I didn't question it until the politically motivated actions of (then) "acting" chief leader F. Merdin—whom the governor had considered for the chief leader's position after Chief Delfrio resigned—exposed the level of corruption within the Work Intervention Unit. (Note: An "acting" designation is given until the official promotion is posted.)

Our office had received a complaint of hazing from a rookie Hispanic state trooper who was a former police officer. My initial impression was for him to get over it. Institutionally, we've used hazing as a character builder. We emptied garbage cans, washed troop cars, gutted dead deer, and did other trivial things that made senior state troopers laugh. However, when a white female state trooper at the same station alleged she was sexually harassed, A/Chief Leader Merdin gave our office strict instructions to resolve these complaints as soon as possible. We were ordered to suspend our cases and assist with the investigation.

Several assistant commander solicitors were assigned to the case, which was unprecedented. They instructed us as to what questions needed to be answered. We weren't given any leeway to conduct an impartial investigation. It became evident that whoever was responsible wouldn't have a chance of receiving justice. I was disturbed by our actions because the process had become politicized.

We completed the investigation in less than a month, and they suspended the two accused principals without pay. Again, this, too, was unprecedented. These were two low-ranking state troopers, and they made an example of them.

The aftermath summed up what could be expected of the cases we investigated. The two complainants were no longer employed with the NJSP. The Hispanic state trooper resigned after filing a civil lawsuit and returned to his former department. He claimed that he could no longer deal with the discrimination. *(Years later, his lawsuit was thrown out of court by a trial court judge because he failed to prove that they discriminated against him because of his race.)* The white female state trooper—who also filed a civil lawsuit—settled her case out of court for $325,000 and retired with an ordinary disability pension.

By the time our office returned to some normalcy, Warrant Agent Drimmer had been promoted to squadron officer and moved to Division Headquarters. I thought my problems with him were over. To my annoyance, they were only beginning.

One afternoon, I went to his office to discuss an ongoing investigation. I knocked, and as I slowly opened the door, I saw him sitting behind his desk. He looked up, noticed me, and flashed a sinister smile. I was about to sit down when he patted his leg and said, "Come over here and sit on my lap." My immediate reaction was to get up and leave. Instead, I told him to stop it; but again, it appeared my words had no effect. He laughed it off, and we eventually discussed the investigation.

I was in a bind because I had no one to tell about his behavior. He was in charge. Similar to how they dismissed female state troopers when they complained about sexual harassment, I didn't think anyone would've taken my complaint seriously. Also, never in my wildest imagination did it dawn on me that his previous promise of promotion was his way of possibly trying to groom me.

The inquirers in the unit were very close and occasionally went out for lunch. One afternoon, while dining at an Italian restaurant,

Squadron Officer Drimmer spoke in a noticeably high-pitched tone and made feminine gestures with his hands. I was agitated because he did it in the presence of our colleagues, and they said nothing. It was the first time he had acted like this besides our one-on-one interactions. At that point, I realized my colleagues had condoned his womanish mimicry. There were other occasions his behavior irritated me, but the incident that most offended me was when we traveled in his car to meet our office colleagues. I reluctantly accepted his offer to drive because my car was in the mechanic's garage.

As I entered the passenger side and was about to sit down, he extended his arm and attempted to touch my leg, but I moved instinctively. Again, I told him to stop, but I guess the reflection in my voice wasn't stern enough, so he laughed and continued to drive. I blamed myself for not kicking his ass, but it wasn't worth losing my job for a brief moment of stress relief.

The last reported incident of his inappropriate conduct occurred at our annual holiday party. I was hesitant to make an appearance, but due to members from other units participating, I believed that he would be on his best behavior. Initially, the event was very festive, and everyone appeared to be having a splendid time. We sat at opposite ends of the same table, but it didn't take long for his foolishness to start again.

Squadron Officer Drimmer looked at Investigative Officer Nieps, blew him a kiss, and lip-synched in a flamboyant manner, "I love you." While their behavior didn't directly affect me, it bothered me because our office had recently suspended a state trooper for a similar unbecoming act.

As his behavior became more blatantly obnoxious, I decided not to accept any more invitations to office functions. My firm stance affected my colleagues' perception of me, but I couldn't be a hypocrite by ignoring their behavior while punishing those found guilty of violating the State's Work Intervention Unit policy. No one should be made to work in such a hostile environment, which is why this situation was so demeaning. We were supposed to prohibit this from happening, and I couldn't do anything to thwart his nonsense.

While I struggled with going to the office and getting my work done, I continued investigating my cases and found it necessary to take them home to complete within the allotted time frame. However, after listening to numerous depressing stories from complainants, I realized that I suffered from "vicarious traumatization," which is characterized as secondary stress.

I heard stories from state troopers about being denied promotions due to an array of reasons. Some female state troopers shared their traumatic tales concerning inappropriate comments about female body parts and aggressive behavior regarding supervisors wanting sexual relationships. Investigating complaints against my colleagues, coupled with Squadron Officer Drimmer's sexual harassment, drained me mentally.

During this time, I had experienced stomach pains and noticed spots of blood in my stool. I thought I had a severe case of hemorrhoids and tried to deal with it. However, after a while, I knew something was seriously wrong. I soon had uncontrollable urges to go to the bathroom. Seeing all that blood in the toilet frightened me. I consulted with a gastroenterologist, who diagnosed me with an inflammatory bowel disease—*ulcerative colitis*. I didn't know if the disease was disabling or potentially fatal. It hampered my quality of life because I always needed to be near a toilet.

My doctor placed me on a high dosage of Prednisone, a steroidal medication that had horrific side effects. I developed black blotches on my shins and an unsightly dark scar on my right jawbone. I thought it was skin cancer, but a subsequent biopsy was negative. On certain days, it was difficult getting out of bed because my knees, right hip, and shoulder joints became arthritic and hurt like hell. Nevertheless, in spite of everything that happened, I maintained my professionalism at work but found myself being a bit standoffish in the office.

Chapter 28

The Unveiling

Introduce hypocrisy to integrity.

As my supervisor assigned me more cases, I noticed that some of the principals in my investigations knew more than they should've regarding the complaints lodged against them. It all came to a head when I had interviewed the assistant chief leader that had been rumored to be the next chief leader, and he told me that Warrant Agent Wenyal had called him and briefed him on the investigation, which I had not even started. He had no right to take away the element of surprise and undermine me. Warrant Agent Wenyal's actions were patently unfair to the complainant. These were confidential investigations and should have remained that way. I immediately relayed my revelations to a supervisor in the Office of Professional Lawyers. She had a duty to correct this subversion of the investigative process, but her response was to have a unit meeting and suggest to everyone that no more "heads up" calls were to be made to anyone.

After that event, it became apparent that something was gravely awry in how cases were investigated. I started to observe a pattern in the practice of racially disparate punishments meted out against policy violators. In particular, I noted two separate investigations that had similar circumstances but very different results.

A female radio dispatcher reported that her white male NJSP supervisor viewed sexually explicit pictures on his computer in plain view of her and other female dispatchers. She also alleged that he openly discussed his sexual prowess over the course of three years, which she felt was offensive and unprofessional.

My subsequent investigation confirmed that the supervisor's behavior created a hostile work environment. I could only imagine their frustration with the workplace he created.

The Office of Official Police Ethics received the case to assign the appropriate disciplinary action. Typically, I never followed up on what punishment was received, but the assistant commander solicitor assigned to the case had inquired. I expected the supervisor to get at least a thirty-day suspension and an immediate transfer away from the dispatchers.

I contacted their office and spoke with the company head. He said the supervisor received a "written reprimand," which is equivalent to a slap on the wrist and no transfer. This punishment was uncharacteristic for such an egregious transgression. I was dumbfounded because I knew of an African-American state trooper who had received a two-week suspension and a three-year promotion restriction for a single policy violation. As a consequence, I drafted a report detailing my frustrations and concerns with our internal process.

When discussing race or the inconvenient truth of slavery, you can almost guarantee that you will run into a buzz saw and watch your stock amongst some of your white colleagues plummet. I had no idea what turmoil my revelations were going to cause. However, before submitting the report, I wanted someone to read it to make sure I had thoroughly expressed my misgivings. I had developed a good working relationship with one of the office assistant commander solicitors, and I asked her to review it. Afterward, she suggested that I allow her supervisor, SACS D. Esel, an opportunity to examine it as well. I didn't expect her to have a problem with it because she was an African-American.

About an hour later, I met with SACS Esel and two of her assistants in a closed-door meeting. It was like going to the principal's office to get punished. My righteousness was seemingly about to get me in trouble, but I didn't care.

I sat in front of SACS Esel and waited for her to share her perspective. She didn't look happy and endeavored to mask her feelings with a fake smile. She tried to appease me by stating that my report was well written and she respected my viewpoint. She went on to say, "I would appreciate it if you don't submit the report because it would be discoverable."

In laymen's terms, once I sent the document, anyone who filed a legitimate request concerning the issues I addressed would have access to my report. I did a double take in my head and remained stoic because I didn't want her to view my facial incredulity.

As a supervisory assistant commander solicitor and an officer of the court, she took an oath to uphold the law, but did she just ask me to disregard evidence of a policy violation? I then glanced at the other assistant commander solicitors to see if they had a similar look of shock, but they quickly cut their eyes away from me.

I needed a valid explanation as to why she thought it was okay not to report it, but all I received was legal mumbo-jumbo that made absolutely no sense. Her response caught me off guard, and I told her I needed a day to think about it. After the meeting was over, I departed, thinking, *Vincent, what have you done now?*

The next day, after conferring with a few respected colleagues about the potential repercussions, I returned to her office and told her that I had decided against submitting it. I wasn't going to win this fight. My "agenda"—as a colleague later referred to it—was exposed.

As time passed and things seemed to quiet down, they assigned me a straightforward case involving two feuding squadron officers. I know my supervisors didn't expect it to go anywhere because it was a "he said, she said" situation.

A female squadron officer alleged that another state trooper told her that a male squadron officer called her a *cunt*. Understanding that policing is male dominant, I don't know any woman who'd accept being called this disgusting word.

I reluctantly interviewed the male squadron officer because I knew what he'd say. Before I even got the words out of my mouth, he emphatically denied it. I then interviewed the witness, who confirmed the comment. I asked him why he felt so strongly about coming forward.

He said, "I have two daughters, and I wouldn't want anyone talking to them in that manner."

I couldn't believe what he said and damn near had to pinch myself to make sure I was awake. I respected his integrity because it was unusual for a witness to implicate another state police member lest they'd risk future promotional opportunities. My supervisors didn't expect him to be forthcoming either.

After completing the investigation, I briefed SACS Esel on my findings. She told me, "I want you to meet with the squadron officer and strongly advise him to retire before we finalize the report." The preferential treatment didn't shock me. Historically, commissioned officers retired to greener pastures unscathed. Within a few hours, I met with the squadron officer and firmly suggested that he put in his papers.

About a month later, he officially retired and began collecting his full pension. The charges were substantiated, and they placed a letter of censure in his personnel file, which should've barred him from getting another State job. However, he later became the personal driver for a well-connected politician.

Shortly after that, they assigned me an age-discrimination case, which had been filed in 2001 and later became a lawsuit. The complainant never received a fair opportunity to transfer to an inquirer's unit because the units wanted someone younger. Once I received the file, I opened it prepared to find a lot of documents. To my dismay, there was only one piece of paper inside. I looked at the name of the previous investigator and noted it was Warrant Agent Wenyal, whom I later met with to discuss this matter.

Innocently, I had expected him to provide me with documents from a private file. After a brief discussion, I asked him. "Sir, I think I may have picked up the wrong file. Do you have any backup reports?"

He replied, "I didn't do much work on the case."

That was an understatement! I was troubled by the amount of time that had elapsed before this matter became a civil lawsuit.

I met with the complainant to discuss his thoughts regarding redress. He became visibly upset when I told him what they did. I'd be pissed off as well. He then provided me with several *forty-five-day extension letters* that were sent to him by the Office of Professional Lawyers, requesting additional time to complete his investigation. The letters extended the time frame for the case to be completed and placed the investigation past the statute of limitations, thus making it difficult to pursue if he ever filed a lawsuit.

At that point, I needed to make him whole again. I asked, "What would it take to make you feel better about the way they treated you?"

He paused for a moment and then responded, "I'd be satisfied with a transfer to the Office of Official Police Ethics and an immediate promotion to investigative first officer."

I advised SACS Esel and (now) Warrant Agent Kriecher (from the Office of the Chief Leader) about the complainant's request, and they assured me that it was feasible. However, within a short period, he was transferred, but his promotion wasn't attached. I was in the process of starting the investigation when SACS Esel told me they reassigned the case to Investigative Officer Nieps. Their reasoning was asinine, but in the grander scheme of things, it made sense.

Previously, the complainant had interviewed for the Middle Protection Unit (when I was still assigned to the unit). I sat on the interview board and recommended that he get the position, but it was given to another inquirer. According to SACS Esel, because I had been on the interview panel, they claimed it was a conflict of interest even though he didn't get the job.

Another reason given for removing me from the investigation was that I'd be away for approximately three months attending the Federal Training Academy. The complainant said he would wait until I returned, but they disregarded his petition. The Office of Professional Lawyers sabotaged cases because they wanted to maintain control by assigning them to handpicked inquirers.

This case was easy to solve. The most relevant evidence to secure was the ages of those that got the positions instead of the complainant. It was no surprise that Investigative Officer Nieps never asked that specific question of any of the recipients, and the case was unsubstantiated.

The complainant didn't receive the results of this investigation until the latter part of 2005, which was approximately four years after he filed it.

Chapter 29

Federal Training Academy

Display mettle in the face of your resolve.

For more than forty years, on a yearly basis, the NJSP have been sending about four state troopers to the Federal Training Academy. Historically, those that graduated were customarily promoted one or two times within the commissioned officer rank. As this was my first application, I knew it was going to be a difficult task. In all the years that they sent candidates, only one black state trooper had ever attended.

The selection process was competitive because so many had applied. Every applicant had to go through an extensive federal background investigation. I didn't have any issues because I already had a *top secret* security clearance while assigned to the Anti Radical Team. Also, we had to submit a résumé and a 250-word essay regarding our management philosophy. A review board comprised of graduates ranked the applicants and sent the final list to the chief leader for approval. Most waited at least four years before being chosen. I was overjoyed when they told me that they selected me from a list of approximately thirty candidates.

Applicants had to meet specific physical standards before attending. My medical condition kept flaring up, and its remission seemed bleak. The prescribed Prednisone medication caused me to balloon up to 250 lbs., and my knees had become arthritic. As a six-feet-tall, thirty-nine-year-old male, I couldn't weigh more than 204 lbs., if I wanted to attend. Every time I glanced in the mirror, Shamu the whale appeared; but I was determined to get in shape.

My diet changed dramatically. I stayed away from my comfort foods: pancakes, pasta, rice, cereal, and bagels. Initially, it was difficult; but after a while, I didn't miss them. My days got longer because I got up at five o'clock every morning and worked out. I was on a mission, and nothing was going to stop me. Surprisingly, within six months, I dropped the weight.

In the summer of 2003, I drove south on Highway I-95 en route to the Federal Training Academy. I had mixed emotions because I was about to embark upon a remarkable journey, but my self-doubt crept in again. I was going to be among some of the best that the law enforcement profession had to offer, and I wondered if I could compete.

Along the way, I stopped at a gas station to refuel. I pulled up to the pump, rolled down my window, and watched as the attendant loosened my gas cap. He then casually walked up to my window and asked, "How much, sir?" As I was telling him to fill it up, a sharp sting on my top lip distracted me. I brushed away whatever had bitten me and immediately grabbed my mouth. For a brief moment, the pain was excruciating, but I gathered myself and paid the attendant and was on my way.

As I pulled back onto the highway, I glanced in the rearview mirror and noticed that my lip had swelled up like a balloon. "Damn it!" I screamed out. I was only two hours away from the academy, and I knew that the swelling wouldn't go down for days. I wanted to make a good first impression, but this wasn't in my plans.

I eventually drove onto the academy grounds, which looked more like a university campus. My mental tension eased somewhat because I was in a familiar setting, but my lip still looked laughably huge.

Some of my classmates were removing their gear from the trunks of their cars and walking to the front entrance. I knew that I couldn't disguise my appearance, so I sucked it up, grabbed my stuff and headed for the front door as well. I expected all eyes were going to be on me once I got inside—and not because I was remarkably handsome. Also, these were fellow cops, and I knew that once we got comfortable with each other, they were going to bust my chops. I wanted a paper bag to put over my head.

We queued up at the reception desk to register. I stood behind a cop from Florida who noticed my lip and said, "Wow, what in the world happened to you?"

I smiled and responded, "Nothing. Why?"

He laughed, and so did I. We then formally introduced ourselves and headed for the dining hall.

The Federal Training Academy had prepared an elaborate reception, and by then, my lip had already been seen by most. They gave everyone an ID holder with our names and departments displayed on the front. Mine should've been "Investigative Officer Fat Lip Martin—New Jersey State Police."

A Federal Training Academy representative explained the upcoming events and stated that we'd take our official individual and section pictures the following day. There was no way that my lip was going to go down by then. *Damn!*

I looked around and observed about 250 police officers that represented thirty-eight countries. I was overwhelmed and couldn't believe that I was a part of the group. *What an honor!* My goal was to have as much fun as I possibly could and to learn about law enforcement's best practices from my more experienced colleagues.

During our first week, everyone went through a pretest of running, push-ups, sit-ups, and stretching. After completing the required exercises, I set out jogging on the rubberized racetrack. About a quarter of a mile into the run, my breathing was labored and my vision blurred. I became lightheaded but fought through the discomfort. I completed the run in eighteen minutes, which I usually ran in under eleven minutes. As I made my way back to the locker room, I was uncharacteristically exhausted.

I staggered through the doors, flopped down on a wooden bench, and tried to catch my breath. A man sitting next to me said, "You don't look well. Your skin is gray." He called for an instructor to check on me, who also noted my discoloration.

I thought, *How can a black man turn gray?*

A staff doctor was summoned to check my vitals, and they subsequently took me to the emergency room for further examination.

A preliminary test revealed that my blood pressure had dropped, and the doctor questioned me about my medical history. I told him about the medications I had been taking and my extended weight loss. He subsequently contacted my primary care physician, who authorized readjusting my medication. Afterward, I was released and told not to exert myself too much.

In due time, I slowly recovered and kept up with the fitness requirements despite my ulcerative colitis, which miraculously went into remission. It had been a welcome relief, and I was able to focus on my studies.

As a part of the academics, an instructor suggested that we share professional experiences with our classmates. In one of my courses, they asked me to lead a discussion group related to organizational behavior. The venue was perfect to discuss the problems that I had endured in my unit, and to ascertain if other agencies were experiencing similar issues. I needed to get some advice from some of the commanders concerning what they'd do in my position.

In telling my story, I left out issues concerning being sexually harassed because I didn't think it was the appropriate forum. Nonetheless, I discussed the intentional stalling of investigations, the disparate punishments, and the financial impact of the civil litigation on taxpayers. After providing them with the facts, my classmates unanimously decided I should bring my concerns to the chief leader.

During my time at the academy, a special agent class had also been training. Most of the prospective agents were in their early to mid-thirties and had left promising careers in the private sector. Their training was in stark contrast to most police academies. Many of them walked around talking socially to one another while going to their respective classes. I didn't see any stress of being thrown out. I didn't know what to think because it appeared that they had already been accepted and were going through the motions. It made me appreciate the NJSP's selection process more because only those that could "cut it" were able to graduate.

Most of my experiences at the academy were enlightening. I shared stories with police officers from all over the world. A lot of our networking took place in a section called the "Boardroom." We spent many nights getting blasted and doing juvenile crap. On one such occasion, several of us ran to the parking lot and placed empty beer cans on police car antennas. Our lousy behavior solidified the stereotypes about police officers and alcohol, but it served as a tool for bonding.

At the beginning of the tenth week, we prepared ourselves to complete the "Mud Chase Dare." It was comprised of a 3.1-mile run and 3 miles of maneuvering through a military-style obstacle course. Although it wasn't mandatory, everyone in my class competed.

The day we ran, the course was muddy and slippery. Our start times were staggered based on our level of fitness. My time placed me in the middle of the pack. I warmed up, and after about ten minutes, my group headed out. I had only one goal in mind, and that was to complete the course.

We ran over mounds of dirt and climbed hills of varying sizes while eagerly awaiting to get to the finish line. As I approached the hand-over-hand rope-climbing event, I stopped momentarily to catch my breath. Now I knew why others claimed it was difficult. It took all my reserve strength to complete this task, only to stomach-crawl through a deep puddle of muddy water. I could've opted to walk around it, but I didn't want to cheat myself out of saying that I completed the entire course. I ran with a classmate from Chicago, and we cheered each other on along the way. The dangling overhead ropes, above a full puddle of smelly water, didn't provide much room for us to escape the stench. By this time, my energy eluded me and nausea set in, but we still had a long run ahead.

We talked to each other while running to keep our minds off wanting to stop. It was rewarding that we finished, but we also had an ulterior motive. Anyone that completed the course received a painted brick with his or her session number on it. *I got mine!*

After ten weeks, one of the proudest moments of my law enforcement career came when I walked across the stage and received my graduation certificate. Hearing the applause from an audience that didn't even know me gave me goose bumps. I had given up hope of having support from friends and family; it wasn't that they didn't want to come, but I had just gotten so used to doing things alone that it didn't bother me anymore.

My private conversations with a few seasoned police chiefs regarding my troubles assured me of what I needed to do upon my return.

I didn't know what the NJSP would do to me after I put them on notice of my concerns, but I wasn't going to be sidetracked by fear. Come what may, I knew that I was going to do the right thing. This decision was my proverbial crossroads.

Chapter 30

Now What?

Exposing the obvious overrides implicit collusion.

When I had returned to my office, there were no indications that the investigations and practice of not punishing superiors for violations of the Work Intervention Unit policy were ever going to change. Lamentably, four weeks after getting reacclimated, my ulcerative colitis flared up again. There was a direct correlation between working in the office and my declining health. I want to think my intestinal problems were unique, but other state troopers who had also battled the NJSP told me that they, too, suffered from similar intestinal ailments.

In October 2003, I went out on administrative leave (sick leave) because the bleeding had become excessive, and at times, the pain was unbearable. Moreover, I couldn't stop forecasting harrowing worst-case scenarios, and my reflections kept me awake at night.

I had spoken with a few colleagues who were also having problems with their NJSP supervisors, and they suggested I reach out to a counselor from the Member Help Group, which supposedly provided counseling services for State employees. I decided to go down this unfamiliar terrain because I had nowhere else to turn. I didn't think it could do any harm, so I scheduled a meeting with a counselor: Ms. J. Polly.

Our initial meeting took place at a hospital in Elkanda. I rode the elevator to the fourth floor, and as I exited the doors, I began to question my actions. Who was this person that I was going to talk to, and what would she do with the information? I had no answers, so I just went with it.

I expected her office to be a serene environment with a long plush brown couch and tan fluffy throw pillows, but it was to the contrary. The hard, uncomfortable chair I sat in was similar to those in my grammar school. The walls were a somber grayish tone, and there were no cheerful staged paintings. It seemed like a room for conducting an interrogation, but I was in a vulnerable mental state and couldn't read the indicators. Nevertheless, for some unknown reason, I couldn't wait to bare my soul.

The first question she asked me was "Where have you been?"

I replied, "What do you mean?"

She said, "The average state trooper comes to my office after approximately twelve years."

Foolishly, my eighteen-year absence was indicative of my misguided trust of the NJSP. It wasn't until my exposure to the Work Intervention Unit that reality set in, and I realized that there were serious issues that needed addressing. I never expected to be in a position where I'd be exposing our internal corruption.

I told her about how the investigations were stalled to allow superiors to retire without being punished, and how black state troopers were being punished disproportionately compared to white state troopers. Her passive facial expression led me to believe that she wasn't shocked. I thought, due to her meeting with other state troopers, she had probably heard just about every possible complaint. She suggested that I speak with Chief Leader J. Ralesny, who had replaced A/Chief Leader Merdin. She claimed that she had developed a good relationship with him because they met on a monthly basis to discuss Member Help Group issues.

She then asked, "What resolution are you seeking?" I didn't know what she meant. She then clarified, "What do you want because this has happened to you?"

I thought about it for a moment and then responded, "Even though I am only an investigative officer, a promotion to the rank of warrant agent would suffice." She looked a bit perplexed, so I explained, "Once this information gets out, there are going to be some upset people. I firmly believe that a promotion to the rank of warrant agent would possibly protect me from some of the inevitable retaliation."

I didn't call for any institutional changes because I knew they wanted to maintain the status quo. I knew they'd view my promotional request as blackmail, but I assumed that once I divulged the internal problems, a target would be placed on my back, and it would grow exponentially.

Ms. Polly then replied, "Okay, I will relay your message."

Afterward, we signed a confidentiality waiver, which stated that I could only discuss my concerns with Chief Leader Ralesny. I wanted to put the Work Intervention Unit on blast, but I realized that it was best to allow the system to police itself.

I scheduled a meeting with Chief Leader Ralesny in fall 2003. Upon arriving at Division Headquarters, I met with his personnel director, Squadron Officer T. Ribbon. With a cocky smirk, he said, "The chief leader is in a meeting and can't meet with you today."

Squadron Officer Ribbon symbolized the classic case of someone who overcompensated for his lack of genetic height. While I'm not qualified to diagnose mental issues, his small stature and arrogant demeanor presented well for someone hell-bent on asserting their authority. He strutted toward me with an air of dominance and told me to write my concerns on a piece of paper, and he'd give it to the chief leader. I looked at him incredulously because he could've made the same request by telephone and saved me a damn trip.

I believed Chief Leader Ralesny had to shield himself from any appearance of impropriety, and maybe that's why he sent him to intercept me, but I was determined. I then nonchalantly provided him with a copy of the confidentiality waiver form and said, "Sir, if the chief leader can't meet with me, I will gladly come back another day." He appeared upset and again asked me to put my concerns in writing, but I respectfully reiterated my position.

There was a silent disagreeable pause as he looked up and waited for me to follow through with his request. Because he didn't give me a direct order, he couldn't charge me with insubordination, which could've gotten me suspended. I stared at him to let him know that I was serious. After a brief moment, he allowed me to leave; but I believed my insistence upset him, and I knew that I was going to pay for it eventually.

Days later, I received a telephone call from the chief leader's office advising that they rescheduled the meeting and that someone from the command staff would also be present. I told the person on the phone that I would only be comfortable speaking in the presence of two specific individuals that I trusted. One of them had retired, but the other had been available.

At the end of 2003, I met with Chief Leader Ralesny and Squadron Officer G. Nandora. I had known Chief Leader Ralesny since 1998 when he was an investigative officer. We had chatted many times about graduate school because he had attained a doctoral degree. I thought we had a good relationship because we also had worked on the Anti Radical Team together and that we'd be able to resolve this matter so I could get back to doing my job.

We sat down at his conference table and discussed a few pleasantries with Squadron Officer Nandora, whom I had known when she headed up the Work Intervention Unit in the late 1990s. I respected her integrity and needed her presence because I believed it was the protocol for him to have a witness in private meetings.

From the outset, I asked him to disregard anything that the Member Help Group counselor shared regarding our prior meeting. I knew she had apprised him of my promotion request, and I didn't want my earlier comments to cloud why I had come to him. I then exclaimed, "What has happened within the Work Intervention Unit should be a primary concern for the division and not just me. I want all state troopers, regardless of race or rank, treated fairly."

He said that he appreciated me bringing my concerns to his attention. I had no reason to believe that he wasn't sincere. I went on to tell him about the disparate treatment of minority state troopers and that Warrant Agent Kriecher, who is also African-American, had racially discriminated against me. I also advised him of the involvement of the Office of Professional Lawyers in issuing forty-five-day extension letters to complainants to intentionally stall Work Intervention Unit investigations. Lastly, I told him about the sexual harassment by Squadron Officer Drimmer. I wasn't going to be shamed and stigmatized by someone else's actions. Hopefully, my vocalization would shed light on this matter because there may have been other victims.

Chief Leader Ralesny's blank look troubled me. Squadron Officer Nandora's unresponsiveness was just as unsettling. I thought, *"Was this a poker game?"* I wanted my concerns internally handled because I was still a team player, and I desperately wanted to move on in my career. While I knew I'd be alone in this fight, I wasn't going to be stingy with the truth; they couldn't filter my voice.

Afterward, we shook hands, and he said, "I'll get back to you regarding what I'm going to do." My convenient ignorance gave me a false sense of relief that I had gotten all of that out in the open. Even though, at that moment, while I didn't realize that I had become an official whistle-blower, I kept the faith in his leadership. I believed that he wasn't going to wait for things to fix themselves; instead, he was going to do it. Little did I know how profound the real meaning of his words would come back to haunt me.

Chapter 31

Endless Nonsense

Fairness need not be for a select few.

As I convalesced at home, I had a lot of time to think about my future. I focused on starting a networking organization for African-American and Hispanic state troopers. The organized unions appeared to represent more of the majority and curried favor with the administration. Many of us were members of the Nationwide Minority Troopers Coalition, which had been formed to establish communication among minority state troopers from different states. With the help of two colleagues, we cofounded its newest chapter. We believed that if we formed an organization separate from our bargaining union, we'd have a say in how they treated minorities.

We convened a meeting at a large church, which was provided by one of the attendees, and a significant number of minority state troopers attended. I spoke to the group about the need to start a separate organization that wouldn't interfere with our dues-paying bargaining unit. After a thorough discussion about the mission of the chapter, we held elections.

A few individuals felt as strongly about the chapter as I did and ran for the respective executive board positions. I wanted us to be very boisterous and shed light on some of our internal problems. As a cofounder and whistle-blower, it probably would've been seen as self-serving if I had run for president. Ultimately, I was elected to the executive board.

Once we were up and running, the vision for the organization didn't come to fruition. My stupidity made me think that others would put their careers on the line to challenge the system. In hindsight, considering the outfit's record of targeting rabble-rousers, I couldn't blame them.

We presented a few ceremonial proclamation plaques to a select group of former state troopers. However, we lacked political influence, which I thought had been the intended goal. I wanted the organization to be our voice, but not once did we come to the assistance of a member who had been in dire need. Instead, we isolated them from the group as if they suffered from a "black" plague. We needed to rally around them similar to our effort of giving coats to the needy in our communities.

Over time, the group became bifurcated. The anointed minorities flaunted their rank while the non-promoted minorities tried to ingratiate themselves into the "inner circle." My stomach churned as I watched some of them try to portray themselves as the group's saviors. They should've known that it was a similar strategy used during times of slavery that pitted one against the other to maintain disagreement.

In later years, they revised the name of the chapter to posthumously honor one of my adversaries, even though they were aware of his documented history of moral turpitude against another state trooper. While I had personal issues with the decedent, I never challenged their decision because I had estranged myself from the chapter.

Despite being out for an extended period, I had presumed that they would've initiated the investigation into my accusations when I returned. Chief Leader Ralesny's office had concerns regarding which unit would investigate them. I did not expect fairness, so it didn't matter.

I firmly maintained that they unfairly treated minority state troopers when filing complaints. I pointed out that three state troopers filed charges against Warrant Agent Wenyal for improper conduct. The male complainants were respectively African-American, Hispanic, and Caucasian. The Caucasian complainant was the only one whose issues they had addressed. After an investigation, to present an appearance of legitimacy, they transferred Warrant Agent Wenyal. Nevertheless, a short time later, he was rewarded with a promotion to squadron officer in another unit and subsequently selected to attend one of the premier law enforcement schools.

Due to Warrant Agent Wenyal's extraction, Investigative First Officer Midos was promoted to warrant agent and took over the unit. His residual position went to Investigative Officer Nieps.

After I had filed a formal complaint against Warrant Agent Kriecher for giving me a low score in the Work Intervention Unit interview process back in 2001, they promoted him to squadron officer. The insult was that they placed him in command of the Work Intervention Unit, thus controlling whether I received a promotion or not. His transfer made absolutely no sense; but then again, they did whatever they wanted.

Squadron Officer Kriecher was the prototypical minority candidate. He was average in stature, unassuming, but looked impressive in his uniform. Nonetheless, the most appealing non-physical characteristic about him was that he knew his place. They received his uncontested compliance because of his somewhat disturbing disciplinary background record.

Early in his career, when Squadron Officer Kriecher was an inquirer, he pled guilty to "disobeying a direct order, intentionally providing false statements, making misleading statements, carrying unauthorized weapons, and failure to perform a duty." With this type of disciplinary record, I understood why they promoted him and placed him in such an important role; he was the perfect minority to showcase because they controlled him.

In March 2004, after recuperating, I returned to the Work Intervention Unit. Being an "indisputable whistle-blower" would undoubtedly be problematic for my life and career. I had created an emotional drawbridge to protect myself from those whom I suspected wanted to harm me. My presence made the office environment a bit tense and uncomfortable for some of my colleagues.

During my first week, Squadron Officer Kriecher had placed another investigative officer in a promotable position. I subsequently met with him and asked why he didn't consider me. Without thinking, he said, "Francis is a worker bee." When he realized he couldn't walk that comment back, he quickly responded, "I promise, you will get the next promotion." I knew he was trying to appease me, but I wondered why he didn't think much about my abilities or me because we'd never worked together.

Afterward, Warrant Agent Midos and I met regarding case assignments. I had expected screened investigations; however, he assigned me two cases that followed a similar pattern of taking an inordinate amount of time to investigate properly.

In the first case, the complainant claimed the Work Intervention Unit inquirer intentionally stalled his investigation. He, too, provided me with several copies of forty-five-day extension letters sent to him by the Office of Professional Lawyers. Moreover, within the case jacket, I found an incriminating e-mail drafted by an assistant commander solicitor expressing his intention to stall the complainant's investigation by not turning over records to the Federal Work Intervention Commission. This compelling evidence should've proved that they did it deliberately, but they expectedly deemed the investigation unsubstantiated.

The second case epitomized the disparate treatment of minorities. The complainant alleged that another state trooper sexually harassed him and also claimed that his supervisor retaliated against him. I perused the case jacket and noted that concerning the sexual harassment allegation, the complainant and principal were African-American males. The retaliation principal was a white male supervisor.

I met the assistant commander solicitor assigned to the case to discuss a game plan. She said, "Both principals are in the process of being promoted and are being paid for their higher ranks, so you can start the investigation." I thought this was fair.

I then shared my investigative strategies, but she interrupted and said, "The investigative officer's promotion won't be held up due to the investigation, but the state trooper will have to wait for the completion of the investigation before we make a determination."

I interjected, "How can a decision be made regarding who is going to get promoted and who has to wait?"

She decisively said, "It's our decision!"

I sat there dumbfounded before I blurted out, "Shouldn't I be allowed to complete the investigation before you make a decision?"

She responded, "We've decided already."

I retorted, "What message will this send to African-American state troopers?"

I then noticed the stunned look on her face before she advised, "There's nothing I can do about it."

I conducted my investigation and interviewed everyone involved, which was time-consuming, due to the number of witnesses; however, they paid the principals the additional salary, so no one suffered financially.

Several months later, the results of the investigation exonerated both principals, and they backdated the African-American state trooper's promotion. In any event, it set a dangerous precedent. I thought my existence in the Work Intervention Unit was to treat everyone fairly and not to be complicit in the special dispensation given to specific individuals.

There was no doubt that my days in the Work Intervention Unit were going to be numbered by Squadron Officer Kriecher. Over the course of two months, he had promised me three separate promotions, but none materialized. I didn't know if he was stringing me along or if he didn't have the ascribed authority of a squadron officer. I had seen other squadron officers resolve promotional issues without any problems. He should've realized he was just a token—or maybe he did and just accepted it.

Chapter 32

Deprived

Quietude maintains the status quo.

About two weeks following the nonexistent promotions, Squadron Officer Kriecher called me on my cell phone. After a few moments of meaningless conversation, he said, "You are going to be transferred immediately to Assistant Chief Leader Montoya's section—however, without a promotion."

Shocked by his admission, I asked, "Why the change? Is there a problem that I'm unaware of?"

He responded, "Several individuals came forward and alleged that you had badmouthed the Work Intervention Unit."

I thought, *You've got to be kidding me!* I expected they'd conspire against me, but this was ridiculous. Sometimes the person you'd never expect to harm you turns out to be the one doing the damage. I needed to know who started the drama.

A group of African-American state troopers was eating lunch at an in-service training session when someone brought up the issues I had had with the Work Intervention Unit. A few of them were aware of the stalled investigations because they had attempted to get their problems resolved without much success. During their discussion, one state trooper said that the stress from the unit caused my medical problem.

He also said that I should've been promoted instead of Investigative First Officer Nieps.

I wasn't there and had no control over his comments, but a female colleague who sat at the table, Inquirer H. Payasa, reported excerpts of the chatter to her white male supervisor. Private conversations among African-American state troopers were usually privileged and just ways of venting about injustice. Her behavior is reminiscent of freed slaves under the Meritorious Manumission Act of 1710, who were rewarded for snitching on other slaves attempting to run away. I didn't know what I had done to her. Nonetheless, her actions baffled me because we had had many conversations regarding the mistreatment of minority state troopers, and she always portrayed herself to be someone with a good character based on her religious beliefs. I wondered when she had lost her voice and interest in progress. More so, what was it in her upbringing that prepared her to dismiss the ill treatment of minorities?

They eventually assigned my case to the Office of Police Fairness, which was formed as a result of a federal consent decree due to our racial profiling shenanigans. It, too, was staffed with handpicked state troopers and retired law enforcement personnel. The Office of Police Fairness was purportedly autonomous, but they also reported to the Office of Professional Lawyers. Having an agency investigate itself is tantamount to a self-fulfilling prophecy. I knew what was in store for me, and it wasn't right. Ironically, one of the assigned state troopers later sued because he complained about their office not complying with the consent decree.

On the day of my official transfer, which was almost six months after exposing the misconduct, the investigation regarding my allegations against Squadron Officer Drimmer and Squadron Officer Kriecher commenced.

I met with Investigator W. Locus from the Office of Police Fairness—a retired officer from a local police department. While sitting in his office, I observed a cassette tape recorder on his desk, which surprised me. It appeared that the Work Intervention Unit was the only internal investigative unit that didn't audiotape interviews. He afforded me an opportunity to talk about everything that had happened to me. Now it was going to be officially memorialized.

I tried to impress upon him that I was removed from the Work Intervention Unit because I was a whistle-blower. I explained that I was supposed to be transferred as an "acting" investigative first officer, but they rescinded the offer due to the pending internal investigation. Investigator Locus looked puzzled, but I couldn't tell if he was sincere or not. He then asked me, "Is there anyone who'd corroborate your allegations against Squadron Officer Drimmer and Squadron Officer Kriecher?"

I mentioned the luncheon where Squadron Officer Drimmer acted mockingly in an effeminate manner and that several unit members witnessed it. I needed to show that others were aware of his behavior as well. Nonetheless, I told him that the sexual harassment incidents occurred when he (Drimmer) and I were alone. However, I provided him with the names of three impartial individuals who were fully aware of Squadron Officer Drimmer's demeaning behavior.

Regarding Squadron Officer Kriecher, I told him to speak with the board members when I interviewed for the Work Intervention Unit in 2001. After implicating damn near my entire office, I knew there was no turning back.

I then asked Investigator Locus, "What are your intentions regarding my allegations against other members of the NJSP and the Office of Professional Lawyers?"

He replied, "I have only been assigned to investigate your allegations against Squadron Officer Drimmer and Squadron Officer Kriecher." It was evident that they gave him marching orders, so I departed from the interview knowing they determined the outcome.

The following day, I met with Assistant Chief Leader Montoya in his office. At the time, he was the most senior state trooper and the highest-ranking Spanish-speaking Hispanic. Several white colleagues who had Spanish surnames only acknowledged their Hispanic background when it benefitted them, but many didn't even speak Spanish.

He greeted me with his all-too-familiar phrase, "Me casa es su casa." (My house is your house.) Unfortunately, he didn't realize that the house wasn't his and that minorities were just visitors. We then explored his new section facilities. His actions were that of an official tour guide. It was fitting. As we walked, he spoke highly about the outfit, and it almost made me nauseous. I had seen this behavior in other state troopers who had "drank the Kool-Aid." I wouldn't partake in the consumption because I could never share his manufactured enthusiasm with a clear conscience.

Over the years, numerous Hispanic state troopers complained about Assistant Chief Leader Montoya's reluctance to do more to promote them. They were educationally and professionally qualified, but they were often overlooked for promotions while under his command. They claimed that he was a propaganda tool only useful for saying "cheese" while taking staged photos that exploited his minority status.

We later returned to his office, and I told him of the pending allegations against me. He spoke about his previous internal issues, being one of the first Latinos to make it to the commissioned officer rank, and advised me to "keep the faith." His behavior reeked of tokenism. I thought, *Faith, in this outfit? You must be out of your damn mind!*

He then said, "I don't have a position for you, but you can choose any unit under my command."

Disappointed is not a strong enough word to express my feelings when he said this to me. I had known him for more than twenty years and had worked under his command on a few occasions. He could've advocated on my behalf and come up with a better resolution. However, like other impotent minority leaders, they walked back their authority imparted to them via their rank when it came to doing anything substantive. He did nothing for me because I believed he only cared about his career.

When I looked at his pinup board and observed the Opposition Terrorism Unit, where Warrant Agent Chivalric was the company head, I opted to go there. We'd worked well together, and I knew he would treat me fairly. However, I didn't realize that on paper, I'd be "detached" (temporarily assigned) to the unit, which would later be the excuse given to exclude me from the promotional process.

Within days of the meeting, I met with Squadron Officer Nandora and Assistant Commander Solicitor A. Hannel (an African-American who was the top assistant under Commander Solicitor Hamper) to discuss my remaining allegations. My initial reaction to the meeting was that he had requested it to continue the cover-up. I asked him, "Why are my allegations being separated into two investigations?

He replied, "Some of your issues possibly violate the State's policy, and others are internal matters. To alleviate any conflicts of interest, I will be conducting my investigation."

I thought, *Yeah, okay. Do I look that stupid?* He was a part of the festering problem, and I didn't expect anything from him. For me, he was just another black face that made me even more suspicious of minorities chosen as their representatives.

The sexual harassment and racial discrimination allegations were going to be difficult to prove. However, the stalled investigations would've been easy to substantiate if they merely conducted an audit; but they already knew the results. Nevertheless, I knew that by running the inquiry from their office, they could control the outcome of my complaint.

Assistant Commander Solicitor Hannel went on to say, "You should choose your battles."

His comment was a veiled threat. I would've respected him more if he had told me to just shut my mouth and stop attempting to open Pandora's box. Regardless, I wasn't going to back down.

Chapter 33

Coalition of Dishonesty

Be the cause of action that initiates the evolution.

After being transferred from the Work Intervention Unit, it was just a matter of time before I expected the payback to commence. The premise for moving me was because I had "badmouthed" the unit. *How can you badmouth something by telling the truth?* The most compelling part of their little scheme was that they left a trail of damaging evidence that would surface years later.

In April 2004, as per protocol, before being considered for a promotion, a disciplinary background check had to be conducted. Someone from the Work Intervention Unit contacted the Office of Official Police Ethics and inquired if I had any pending investigations. They sent an official e-mail and reported that I didn't, which meant they could've promoted me. *I am truly appreciative that we at least kept good records, because this fact spoke volumes regarding what they did to me afterward.*

However, two days later, Investigative First Officer Nieps sent an internal memorandum to Chief Leader Ralesny regarding a complaint he had filed against me for official misconduct. In it, he suggested that I'd been trying to receive a promotion by extortion. His actions were personal because he should've reported it directly to the Office of Official Police Ethics, but it didn't surprise me since I had implicated him in my complaints against Squadron Officer Drimmer. Nonetheless, all his allegations were based on hearsay, and they shouldn't have entertained them.

Subsequently, and unbeknownst to me at the time, several days after Investigative First Officer Nieps's memo, (now) Vice Marshal Ribbon, on behalf of Chief Leader Ralesny, sent a memo to the commander solicitor seeking professional advice. It claimed that, in essence, I was attempting to undermine the Work Intervention Unit process. He stated that Acting Vice Marshal G. Nandora had advised him that Assistant Commander Solicitor Hannel was actively and personally addressing concerns raised by me, which may touch upon Work Intervention Unit issues, as well as comments allegedly made by me concerning the Office of Professional Lawyers and the entire Work Intervention Unit process.

He then expressed concern about my health due to my perceived stress and mistreatment from working in my office and claimed I was creating a work environment that was not conducive to achieving the critical goals of the division. He cited the fact that I had sought legal advice from an attorney who had filed several lawsuits against the NJSP explicitly concerning the Work Intervention Unit process.

Based on the allegations, he suggested that I not be placed in a promotable position. Instead, he said I needed to be transferred out of the Work Intervention Unit without the promise of promotion until I could prove myself worthy.

It appeared that I had upset them, and he tried to create a factual scenario, based on lies, to remove me. However, if my actions were so egregious and warranted taking me out of a promotable position, then why didn't they immediately suspend me? Also, it was apparent that Vice Marshal Ribbon had no clue about my medical condition. Ulcerative colitis is an autoimmune disease and is not caused by stress. I guess he wanted to paint a sympathetic picture that he cared about me.

My time in the unit proved that a substantial percentage of those who filed a complaint would never have their concerns addressed. Many of the civil lawsuits filed by complainants criticized the Work Intervention Unit for either improperly investigating complaints or intentionally stalling investigations. Neither Chief Leader Ralesny nor

Vice Marshal Ribbon had the "backbone" to challenge me personally. There was no doubt in my mind that they had crushed the souls of other minorities and retaliated against me to send a message because I wouldn't shut my mouth and go away.

Although I didn't get my hands on the document mentioned above until years later—upon reading it, there was no doubt they had targeted me. However, and more importantly, a revelation made me realize race may have played a determining factor in this matter.

Around the same time frame, a white investigative first officer—who had worked in another office that investigated similar controversial issues—filed a lawsuit against Chief Leader Ralesny and Vice Marshal Ribbon. The investigative first officer had a postgraduate degree and graduated from a prestigious law enforcement school. In his case, however, they promoted him three times to the rank of vice marshal after he had filed his lawsuit.

Chapter 34

Fraudulent Supremacy

Respect the rank, but challenge the person.

My first couple of weeks in the Opposition Terrorism Unit was routine. I eventually met with the department manager and received my procedural "welcome aboard" speech. He told me that he had heard about my internal problems, but it was his understanding that my promotion was forthcoming because his supervisor had a position for me as a section data manager. However, Vice Marshal Ribbon advised him that Chief Leader Ralesny wouldn't consider it until they had completed my investigation. I thought it was fair but questioned why I wasn't afforded the same exception as my white colleagues. Their two-tiered system of justice kept me on the bottom rung.

In the coming months, the department manager and his supervisor were promoted to vice marshal and assistant chief leader respectively. With their promotions, a new department manager, Squadron Officer S. Sauhund, transferred to the section. I was familiar with him, but we had never worked together. Nevertheless, while assigned to the Work Intervention Unit, I crossed paths with his younger brother, Inquirer J. Sauhund.

One afternoon, I went to Inquirer Sauhund's unit in response to an investigation that involved him harassing his office colleague. As I walked by the kitchen, where he was sitting with other inquirers, he made a snide comment about my presence. I didn't confront him because I didn't know him; instead, I reported him to his supervisor, who later gave him a verbal reprimand.

Before becoming the department manager, Squadron Officer Sauhund had been assigned to Chief Leader Ralesny's office and was aware of my intention of filing a lawsuit. When he transferred into the bureau, he immediately denied me supervisory duties. I inquired why, and he said it was because I was detached and not permanently assigned to the unit. It made absolutely no sense because I was the most senior investigative officer under his command. He also went out of his way to undermine my credibility.

As an example, a supermarket manager contacted our office and claimed that a distributor delivered a suspected bottle of a contaminated liquid to his store. He noted the container had some cryptic writing on it and believed someone might have tampered with it. There was a concern because other cases of product tampering had surfaced, and they thought it was terrorism-related.

I made the required notifications and interviewed all the witnesses. The bottle's contents ultimately tested negative for any contamination. I reported the results to my immediate supervisor and closed the case. However, a colleague told me that while in a unit meeting, Squadron Officer Sauhund questioned my decision-making and disparaged me in front of others. He had every right to doubt my investigative measures, but if he had had a problem with me, he should've brought it to the attention of my direct supervisor. However, he, too, was a minority and may have been less respected than me. Unfortunately, I allowed this to get to me, which exacerbated my ulcerative colitis.

My warrant agent said that he observed dark circles underneath my eyes and noticed that I had lost weight. He recommended I seek assistance from the Member Help Group to help deal with the stress. I told him that I had a bacterial colon infection lest I'd appear incapable of dealing with my issues. I had kept my sessions with my counselor private but had secretly met with her to reconcile other stressors.

In one of our sessions, she told me that she met with Chief Leader Ralesny and Vice Marshal Ribbon for monthly progress reports. She said, "Chief Leader Ralesny believes you're disloyal to him because of a rumor that you're going to sue him." In essence, he wanted some relationship to test my loyalty. He wanted me to shut up and maintain the status quo.

I told her, "Loyalty goes both ways." In the back of my mind, I never thought when I took the oath in 1986 that I'd face this issue. Afterward, I asked her to mention my name at the next meeting and see what they said.

While in the Opposition Terrorism Unit, the wrath of Squadron Officer Sauhund didn't end with me. Warrant Agent Chivalric didn't get along with him either because he questioned Squadron Officer Sauhund's disparate treatment of the unit's minority supervisors. My direct supervisor was a Hispanic male with twenty-three years of experience and was a practicing attorney. The other supervisor was a white female with twenty-plus years and a master's degree, and she had spent three and a half years investigating war crimes in several European countries. No one questioned Squadron Officer Sauhund's intelligence and exceptional analytical skills, but I believed he felt intimidated. Everyone in the bureau had at least a bachelor's degree, and he didn't. He also had been previously found guilty of violating the Work Intervention Unit policy, which may have been part of the reason why he disliked me.

Another afternoon, Warrant Agent Chivalric called me at home and told me that Squadron Officer Sauhund had placed another supervisor into a promotable position. I couldn't question the supervisor's qualifications, but he hadn't even completed his full term in the investigative officer rank. I was senior to this individual and had more terrorism experience based on my time working on the Anti Radical Team, so I wasn't going to let this go unchallenged.

I immediately called Squadron Officer Sauhund to determine why he didn't consider me. He said, "Due to you not being permanently assigned to the unit, you are ineligible."

Without getting into a debate, I accepted his position because I had no other choice. He then told me that I would get the next promotion. I had heard this before. Shortly after that, they promoted the supervisor, and I formally transferred to the unit.

During this period, I still hadn't received any response to the formal charges lodged against me. It had been almost four months since they told me about the allegations. I placed a call to the Office of Official Police Ethics, and they said that no charges were pending, so I expected the promise of a promotion to be fulfilled.

In mid-2004, I met with Warrant Agent Midos to sign my performance evaluation from my time in the Work Intervention Unit. The meeting should've been a simple encounter, but he brought along another warrant agent as a witness, so I knew something was about to happen. He told me that someone accused me of violating three separate rules and regulations. Really?

The first allegation was that I had badmouthed the unit. I thought he was disingenuous because we both knew that the Work Intervention Unit policy was ineffective. Not this again! He then brought up the names of two state troopers who alleged I had disparaged the unit.

I remembered the conversations that I had with both of them because I expressed that their respective cases were going to be difficult to prove. It was my experience that many potential witnesses deny seeing or hearing anything because they ran the risk of affecting their future promotions. My honesty probably caught them off guard.

The second allegation claimed that I had lied about my reason for having a case transferred to a different investigator. I had been assigned to investigate a complaint of a hostile work environment filed by a white male first officer against an African-American male squadron officer who was an associate of mine. The complainant was upset because the squadron officer didn't promote him. His notion was that it was reverse discrimination. *I guess he didn't realize that minorities have no real power in the NJSP—so he was grasping for anything to justify his complaint.*

When they gave me the case, I perused the file and noted that he had sought legal advice from an attorney, W. Chuman, who had won a few civil lawsuits against the NJSP. I, too, had previously met with the attorney to discuss my rights as a potential whistle-blower. Even though neither one of us retained him, he had received assistance in filing a pro-se lawsuit against the NJSP.

When I realized that my prior consultation could be viewed as a conflict of interest, I went to Warrant Agent Midos. I told him the case should be given to someone else because the complainant was uncomfortable with my friendship with the squadron officer, which was the truth and should've been understandable. I didn't want my involvement with the attorney to be an issue if the investigation was unsubstantiated.

As an aside, Mr. Chuman committed suicide several years later. I will always remember our meeting, when he called me courageous for becoming a whistle-blower. He was indeed a champion of justice.

My actions should've put an end to this matter, but when they transferred the case to another investigator, oddly, the complainant reported a different story.

He told the new investigator that I suggested a female investigator take the case. I didn't care who received it, but why he said that caused me to question his motivation. Nonetheless, it wasn't a secret that the complainant, Investigative First Officer Nieps, and Vice Marshal Ribbon were academy classmates. In my periodic psychosis, I questioned whether there was a conspiracy to attack me. By way of confirmation, they promoted the complainant to warrant agent shortly after that. This wasn't the only time I had a case transferred in the best interest of the unit.

Another time, they accused my former warrant agent in the Middle Protection Unit of violating the State's workplace environment policy and assigned his case to me. In this instance, I knew that I couldn't be objective because I had never worked with a more two-faced and backstabbing person. On several occasions when we worked together, he allowed one of his subordinates to disrespect me and did nothing about it. I was also fully aware of his inappropriate behavior toward female civilians. While it was none of my business, he was married and tried his best to have sexual relations with many of the women that worked in the office or within the same building.

I immediately told my superiors about my concerns, and they reassigned the case. Again, I thought I had done the right thing.

The third allegation claimed that I had released confidential information about an ongoing investigation. They kept throwing everything at me, trying to see what was going to stick. I told Warrant Agent Midos that I didn't speak with anyone and welcomed him producing the person(s) that claimed that I had—of course, he couldn't. It was my understanding that because they had counseled me, it should've been the end of their probe.

In August 2004, I e-mailed Vice Marshal Nandora to advise her that I would be on vacation for most of the month. I kindly informed her, "Ma'am, if they don't resolve my issues upon my return, I will be serving the NJSP with a notice of intent to file a civil lawsuit."

She said, "I understand, but I think that everything will be okay."

My frustration level was getting to me, and this was my last attempt to get them to leave me alone.

In September 2004, I received a letter from the Office of Professional Lawyers reporting that my complaint against Squadron Officer Kriecher and Squadron Officer Drimmer was unsubstantiated. They shocked me by how uncharacteristically fast they had completed their investigation, but I wasn't surprised by its results.

Investigator Locus, who conducted the investigation, had interviewed several individuals in the Work Intervention Unit, some of whom knew nothing about my allegations. Disturbingly, he didn't question my three disinterested witnesses, who could've corroborated my complaints against Squadron Officer Drimmer and show a broader pattern of his inappropriate behavior.

Regarding my allegations against Squadron Officer Kriecher, I told Investigator Locus that it was my perception—based on what Squadron Officer Rivers and Squadron Officer Drimmer said to me—that the sole reason for him (Kriecher) giving me a low score could've been because I was a black male. I went on to say that the Work Intervention Unit had accepted one person, which was (then) Inquirer Nieps. I noted that most, if not all, of the black applicants had a minimum of a four-year college degree. Inquirer Nieps, although experienced, only had an associate's degree. I guess that meant nothing to him because he was doing what they told him to do, which was to investigate for the sake of appearances. For the record, he also never officially interviewed Squadron Officer Rivers or Squadron Officer Drimmer.

On September 8, 2004, I met with Assistant Commander Solicitor Hannel to discuss the remainder of my allegations. I knew that I'd be the face attempting to force them into transparency, so I wasn't too optimistic about any substantive change. He had covered up everything regarding the Work Intervention Unit corrupt process. In particular, he said that he had interviewed SACS Esel regarding the "special report" I had submitted. He claimed it was her position that we met as colleagues and not as a superior to a subordinate. She maintained authority over the entire office, and we were never on the same level. As expected, at no time did he address her statement about the report being "discoverable." My disrespect of black and brown faces in token display cases mounted.

Later that day, they served me with an official internal complaint charging me with several violations of our rules and regulations. The timing of the charges came on the heels of the e-mail I had sent to Vice Marshal Nandora in the latter part of 2004, referencing my notice of intent to sue.

Within a week of being served, Investigator P. English (from the Office of Police Fairness) contacted me and advised that because of a potential conflict of interest, she and Investigator Locus were going to conduct my investigation. About a week later, I met with them in a conference room in the Office of Official Police Ethics. I brought along an investigative officer's union representative as a witness.

FYI, this was only one of two times in a period of seven years that the union—which I faithfully paid my dues to every month—actually assisted me. While they didn't throw me to the wolves, they never provided me with any viable life preservers to save my career.

The investigators presented me with the exact charges that Warrant Agent Midos counseled me for two months earlier. They appeared unaware of the prior counseling session. The right hand didn't know what the left hand was doing. I told them that they should construe the meeting as "double jeopardy" (prosecuted twice for the same charges).

After I had shown them a copy of the performance evaluation that reflected my counseling, they seemed dumbstruck but continued with their interview. I then presented them with the same information that I had provided to Warrant Agent Midos and waited a few months for their results. Unfortunately, I had more significant issues to address.

Chapter 35

Medical Awakening

Confirm that the image you portray is genuine.

In early 2005, my ulcerative colitis flared up again—but this time, with a vengeance. I went to the bathroom more than fifteen times per day, and my stool made the toilet bowl look like a red mosaic. I had lost a significant amount of weight, and when I looked in the mirror, my sunken eye sockets shocked me. Who was that person?

I was subsequently hospitalized and received intravenous medication. The protruding plastic tubes hindered my movements and frustrated me when I had to go to the restroom. I stayed in the hospital for about a week, and they eventually released me after my symptoms subsided. My doctor placed me on complete bed rest for several weeks, but the outfit made me submit to a "fit for duty" evaluation at a mental health facility. This session was their attempt at trying to get me to retire on a medical disability.

When I met with the attendant, she had me fill out a very lengthy questionnaire, which centered on my state of mind. Even though I was agitated at what had happened to me, I made sure to place all the blame on the system and not a particular person. After I finished, the attendant expressed that my responses were reasonable and sent me on my way with no questions regarding my mental health.

My time at home gave me an opportunity to decrease the job-related stress; but foolishly, I looked forward to getting back to work. The NJSP has an unlimited sick policy—unlike most jobs that affix a certain number of days that someone can be out of work and still get paid—but I never abused it.

A week before returning in mid-2005, I received a telephone call from Warrant Agent Chivalric regarding a disparaging remark made against me by Squadron Officer Sauhund. He said that Squadron Officer Sauhund, while in a meeting with non-State police personnel, referred to me as "a zero as a supervisor and a zero as an investigator." Some parts of me wished that he had not told me, but I appreciated his loyalty to our friendship.

Upon my return to the office, I filed an internal complaint against Squadron Officer Sauhund. I had had enough of his nonsense. Warrant Agent Chivalric and I discussed my concerns, and then he shared some of the issues that he, too, had with him. Afterward, he said that they transferred him. He was happy because he said he could no longer work for such an ignorant person. I didn't want him to leave because he always had my back.

Sadly, years later, after retiring, he passed away. I had an opportunity to speak with him just before his transition, and little did I know that when he told me "Thanks for being a good friend," he was saying goodbye. While studies show a weak correlation between stress and his cause of death, it is my firm belief that Squadron Officer Sauhund's actions were a contributing factor.

Warrant Agent J. Cabell, the new company head, subsequently transferred to the Opposition Terrorism Unit; and as he became acclimated, my problems with Squadron Officer Sauhund continued. They posted the promotional tier rankings, and I noticed that he dropped me after I had filed the complaint against him. Moreover, a few colleagues told me about other negative comments he made about me. I brought it to the attention of Warrant Agent Cabell, and he filed another internal complaint against Squadron Officer Sauhund on my behalf.

After a while, the walls appeared to be crumbling around Squadron Officer Sauhund. Rumor had it that Chief Leader Ralesny wasn't pleased with all the negative attention, so he elevated Warrant Agent Cabell to the assistant department manager's position to keep tabs on him. Chief Leader Ralesny, instead of transferring his friend, made things difficult for everyone else.

Following Warrant Agent Cabell's elevation, they transferred two individuals into the unit. The first person was Investigative Officer J. Rilde (another friend of Chief Leader Ralesny), who, three years earlier, had worked for me while we were assigned to the Anti Radical Team. He was seven years junior to me and was promoted to investigative first officer and became my direct supervisor. The role reversal would've stressed out most, and I was no exception.

The second person was my classmate, Investigative First Officer A. Battle. I didn't know him that well, but we had similar educational credentials. To my knowledge, he didn't have any experience in terrorism investigations, but he possessed NJSP ancestry, which caused me to be suspicious of him. Their presence in the office didn't sit well with me, but I had to accept it because of our paramilitary background. We don't ask questions.

In a short period, Investigative First Officer Battle made it a point to diminish my authority by assigning cases to those that I supervised without my knowledge. I had never worked with him and couldn't understand why another one of my academy classmates would also be involved in attacking me, but I suspected Squadron Officer Sauhund because his antics never stopped.

During a meeting, while in the presence of our colleagues, he made light of the fact that some of the supervisors under his command had filed complaints against him. As the only supervisor at the meeting, he intentionally directed his comments at me. I sat seething because I couldn't do anything, and he knew it. He was too arrogant to realize that this had everything to do with his poor leadership. More so, his passive-aggressive stance was indicative of his insecurity and cowardice. I wondered why because most superior officers loved to flaunt their rank. It appeared that his idiocy wasn't going to cease, so I had to change tactics.

Previously, while in a meeting, I recalled the (new) deputy of investigations, Assistant Chief Leader F. Riddle, telling everyone that we could receive a copy of our promotional rankings. I did my due diligence and typed a report requesting a copy of all my rankings before and including those authored by Squadron Officer Sauhund. I wanted to read the rationale for why he had dropped me.

In late 2005, due to the persistent harassment, I officially filed my lawsuit. As a way of trying to mitigate some of the damage, they transferred me to the Methodical Crime North Unit. A new start would be refreshing, but the constant struggles with Squadron Officer Sauhund had reaggravated my medical condition; but this time, it was more severe.

One evening, while at home, I had been going to the bathroom an inordinate number of times. My colon bled profusely, and the vise grip–like pain in my stomach doubled me over. The only relief was taking warm baths; but after a while, that didn't help. Dehydration and malnourishment took control, lest I would have to use the toilet. I walked around in a delusional state and kept asking myself, "Why the hell are you allowing them to do this to you?" I was in a dark place mentally, and the solitude wasn't helping.

Some scary thoughts took up residency in my mind because I wanted to take the air out of someone's lungs permanently. None of my imaginary actions would've been justified, but faced with a "fight or flight" position, I was going to fight to the end regardless of how things would've turned out. Fatal ruminations caused me to consider checking out and being with family members who had passed before me. Luckily, they were only fleeting thoughts.

I needed to go to the emergency room, but on a few occasions, I couldn't get up off the floor. My forecasting demise seemed imminent; I would go out alone like I had spent most of my life.

After a while, I mustered up the strength and attempted to gather myself and drive to the emergency room. However, I didn't want to risk getting into an accident, so I called a colleague that lived nearby.

When he arrived, I noticed the surprised look on his face as I opened the door. I gathered my things, and he assisted me with getting into his truck. While driving to the hospital, he asked me why I took so long to seek help. Truthfully, I didn't want my condition to get back to those who retaliated against me. I wouldn't allow them to get any pleasure out of my discomfort. I had hit rock bottom and needed to find my way back. My family wasn't fully aware of my issues either. I didn't want to burden them with my problems because I was the "disciplined one." In hindsight, I knew my behavior was selfish.

We sat in the emergency room for several hours, waiting for me to see a doctor. When my turn came, my colleague stood up and hugged me. I watched as he walked away and wished I was leaving as well.

A hospital attendant then placed me in a wheelchair and pushed me into a back room. I removed my clothes and put on a light-blue gown. A nurse arrived and took my vital signs. My blood pressure was high, which became my routine due to years of confronting many superiors. She then inserted a needle into my right arm, which facilitated the intravenous saline solution to offset my dehydration.

The attending physician arrived and explained that he had to examine me digitally. WHAT! He could've just taken my word that there was a problem. I noticed the size of his hands and winced.

Subsequently, two gastroenterological specialists determined that my ulcerative colitis had gotten worse. I had also developed a bacterial infection and lost a tremendous amount of blood, which resulted in two blood transfusions. Afterward, I was placed on a liquid protein diet and prescribed antibiotics.

Weeks had passed, and I became aggravated because I wanted to go home. A few of my friends stopped by unexpectedly and were shocked by my appearance. I hadn't shaved and looked emaciated because I had lost about fifty pounds. Some of them pleaded with me to quit and find another job. I wished it were that easy.

Eventually, the symptoms subsided, and they released me. I recuperated for several weeks, but I wasn't out of trouble. My self-imposed hermitic lifestyle was probably doing more bad than good because I reverted to my in-depth internal conversations. My doctors cautioned that any relapses could significantly increase my chances of either having my colon removed and wearing a colostomy bag or getting colon cancer. The news devastated me, but I realized it would be something I'd live with for the rest of my life—or what would be left of it if the latter occurred.

Chapter 36

Under Siege

Ignorance is bliss until it affects you.

I had been on administrative leave for approximately five months. My body's immune system kept me in an uncertain state of health. As per the rules for being off duty, I had to be home Monday through Friday between 9:00 a.m. and 5:00 p.m. There were numerous unannounced visits from investigative officers assigned to the Duty Consent Unit. Whenever someone rang my doorbell, I invited him or her in with a smile on my face. A few of them took me up on my offer, but some just made sure that I was home and departed with little to no conversation.

During this time, I maintained my therapy sessions with Ms. Polly. Innocently, I believed we had developed a good relationship. In my angst, I didn't socialize, and distrustful colleagues made me question their motives because they were all potential enemies. She referred me to a female psychiatrist because she thought I was suffering from a mild case of depression. It never dawned on me that my reclusiveness was the onset of my so-called mental health issues; but now I knew why and could own it.

We met in her office, which appeared staged for initial patient screenings. After a brief conversation about trivial matters, we got down to the crux of my issues. I told her that sleep was no longer my friend, and closing my eyes wasn't guaranteed. Paranoia had hijacked my thoughts and parked itself in a continuous spin cycle. I had to step outside of myself to make sure I saw things correctly or if it had been a figment of my imagination. Also, some days, I stayed in bed staring at the ceiling. I questioned why the sun rose most mornings because it wasn't worth going to work.

She immediately recognized what was going on with me and said, "Once your brain's serotonin level became unbalanced, more than likely, this was the beginning of your depression."

Wow, an official diagnosis. I just thought I was in a funk from dealing with a massive load of NJSP crap. She prescribed an antidepressant, Lexapro, and recommended that I take it for a couple of months. Departing from her office made me more depressed. I still had a few years remaining before I could retire, and I didn't want to spend them taking pills.

The medication helped because it made me numb to my surroundings, but it also had side effects that lessened my otherwise voracious libido and increased my level of seclusion. Fortunately, my girlfriend at the time was very understanding and supportive.

I had a follow-up session with Ms. Polly and asked about her monthly meetings with Chief Leader Ralesny. She nonchalantly told me that he said, "Tell Vincent that his career is over and that he should think about retiring due to his medical condition." I should've known that I'd be throwing my career away by challenging him. However, it was her cavalier disposition that shone a new light on our relationship. The connection she had with Chief Leader Ralesny had developed into a conflict of interest, but I knew that I had to formally document her comments regarding what he said because my contemporaneous notes could add credibility to who told the truth at a later date.

In her official position, she appeared to be an undercover operative. Other state troopers complained that she hadn't acted in their best interest when she spoke with Chief Leader Ralesny. There needed to be a safe place where we could get things off our chest without having comments come back to haunt us. After she relayed his message, I severed all contact with her. Moreover, I adamantly apprised other state troopers to avoid the Member Help Group office. Years later, during a deposition, she denied that she told me that Chief Leader Ralesny said my career was over. My suspicions about her were correct.

Shortly after that, I went to a new therapist referred to me by another state trooper. As I walked into her office, something told me that I was going to be all right. A featured colorful elongated couch appeared more for lounging than sitting. Dim lights and burning incense permeated the room, which made the atmosphere very soothing. She sat in a slightly elevated chair, so I needed to look up at her when she spoke, but I was cool with it. Surprisingly, we clicked, and she always kept a sympathetic smile.

She didn't take long to familiarize herself with my issues. Our sessions revealed a lot about why things had bothered me so much, but what I couldn't understand was the anger I had toward Squadron Officer Drimmer's behavior. She had me talk about the time when he attempted to touch my leg. I remembered that although I was physically bigger than him, he had rather large hands. At that moment, I immediately flashed back to when Sandy had molested me when I was eleven years old. Then it all made sense. He, too, had huge hands—which was why I became so angry with Squadron Officer Drimmer.

After a few sessions, she diagnosed me as suffering from post-traumatic stress disorder (PTSD). Great, here we go again, another official diagnosis. I never thought I had suppressed any of the job-related traumatic events throughout my career, but she explained that the retaliation could be construed as a traumatic event as well. After realizing it wasn't just me being abnormally sad, I had a different perspective on my mental status, and trying to handle stressful situations took precedence. I needed to have post-traumatic growth be a part of my future healing.

Believing that my job status was going to get worse, I contacted the Federal Work Intervention Commission and filed a complaint against Chief Leader Ralesny for discrimination based on my medical condition. Due to what Ms. Polly had told me, it was clear that he had used my medical condition against me when he suggested that I retire. He wasn't a physician, and it wasn't his place to discuss my health issues with anyone.

Internally, I knew that Chief Leader Ralesny had the support of the Office of Professional Lawyers, but I didn't think he had any pull at the federal level. I had no clue what the feds were going to do, but I had to report him to every available agency to get him and his cronies to leave me alone.

After looking at the facts of the case, the Federal Work Intervention Commission informed me that I met their standards regarding a violation and issued me a "right to sue" letter, which would later be crucial.

I returned to work in February 2006 and reported to the Methodical Crime North Unit. My new office was closer to home, but it had a different set of issues. I had been clueless about crime bosses and crime families, but I looked forward to the challenge. Nevertheless, I still needed to resolve my performance evaluation issue from the Opposition Terrorism Unit, so I made a formal request to meet with my classmate Investigative First Officer Battle.

The NJSP uses their performance evaluations to promote whomever they wanted. I *hated* this system because it was unfair to anyone that was not in the good graces of the command staff.

We met in my new office, but I wasn't looking to have any small talk. There was no doubt that my grimace made him uncomfortable as he tentatively sat down, handed me the document, and asked me to share my thoughts. I reviewed it and noted that he listed me as average in seven of the eleven benchmarks, where I previously had been rated above average or exceptional. Why did I drop off in my performance? Proper procedure dictated counseling to correct any deficiencies before he made any changes.

We had worked together for only three months, and he observed me interact with those I supervised only once. On that one occasion, he gave me a positive written appraisal, so none of his actions made any sense.

Maintaining as much civility as possible, I looked him straight in his eyes and said, "This is the worst performance evaluation I've received since becoming an inquirer!" Afterward, I mentally shut down, didn't say another word, and stared at him like I was crazy. He left my office looking scared and confused.

His exploits were an extension of the ongoing punishment for speaking out. I speculated that someone from Chief Leader Ralesny's inner circle put him up to it. Within days, I also filed a complaint against him with the Department of Workforce. I didn't expect my complaint to go anywhere because he, too, was a part of their system.

The transfer to the Methodical Crime North Unit was well needed. My new supervisors were colleagues whom I respected, and I looked forward to working with them. They gave me supervisory duties afforded most investigative officers and had two inquirers assigned to my squad. I had been on a light duty status, which meant I stayed in the office and transcribed wiretap cassettes because I didn't have much else to do. However, I didn't mind because it gave me a chance to regain my health.

After two months, I returned to full duty status and conducted investigations and assisted those I supervised with their cases. Targeting contemporary organized crime figures was exciting because most of them got their script from watching the HBO series *The Sopranos*.

As the weeks went by, I followed up on a previous request to receive a copy of my promotional rankings. I asked my warrant agent about the whereabouts of the documents. He told me that no one had contacted him, which led me to believe that someone intentionally stalled the paperwork from getting to me, so I submitted another report and waited.

Three months passed, and I still hadn't received any information. Frustration made me do something unconventional, which had the potential to get me reprimanded. I sent an e-mail directly to Assistant Chief Leader Riddle requesting his assistance.

In the e-mail, I reminded him of what he had said about having access to our promotional rankings. He could've issued me a written reprimand or a more severe punishment for not following the proper protocol, but I didn't care.

Within two days, I had the paperwork in my hands. I had upset someone, but I didn't know whom—and frankly, at that point, it didn't matter. Shortly after that, my warrant agent verbally counseled me for not following the proper communication procedure.

My rankings showed that every time I filed a complaint against Squadron Officer Sauhund, he dropped me in the tier and never provided any specific reasons why. The documents that I needed for my lawsuit didn't mitigate my problems because it became more personal.

One day, I received an official NJSP envelope mailed to my home. As I slowly opened it and pulled out the contents, I noticed that one of the documents had the words "HE IS A PUSSY" handwritten on it. Another paper was a court decision regarding freedom of speech, and the last was a personnel order noting the promotion of Squadron Officer Drimmer to the rank of vice marshal. I couldn't imagine who was responsible, but I knew it came from someone intimately involved. The sender wrote the name of a male African-American state trooper on the envelope to make it appear that he had sent it to me. I immediately called him, and he denied any knowledge of the letter.

I reported the incident to the Office of Official Police Ethics, but I thought trying to track down the person responsible would've been impossible. However, during the investigation, the letter was examined for DNA evidence, and they determined that more than likely, a Caucasian male sent the documents. The investigator then confirmed who had accessed the NJSP Human Resources database that stored our telephone numbers and mailing addresses.

Over a period of two months, two Caucasian individuals had accessed my information. The first person was my supervisor, who had a legitimate reason. The second person was First Officer H. Mofeta, another one of my academy classmates who had worked in the Work Intervention Unit. I didn't have any pending matters with his unit, so I speculated that he was responsible. I assumed proving he sent it was going to be easy. Nevertheless, they said there was insufficient evidence to substantiate the investigation. Again, I had no pending matters with his office; and to me, this was just another example of how I could never receive any justice from their internal system.

Chapter 37

Unsympathetic

During difficult times, don't be afraid to stand alone.

In October 2006, as part of the revolving door of leadership, Warrant Agent D. Vanrus transferred to the Methodical Crime North Unit as the new company head. Coincidentally, I was temporarily assigned to a task force in Unamon County and relegated to a roving surveillance team, which meant that I wouldn't have immediate access to a bathroom. Sadly, though, my ulcerative colitis flared up again.

My superiors were more than aware of my medical condition, but they either didn't understand its troubling side effects or didn't care. I asked Warrant Agent Vanrus, who selected me for the surveillance detail. He told me that it was the department manager, Squadron Officer M. Drecksack. There were other investigative officers assigned to the wiretap, but they could've selected a junior inquirer from my office.

I scheduled a meeting with Squadron Officer Drecksack to discuss this matter. I had never worked with him but soon learned he, too, was a classmate of Vice Marshal Ribbon and Investigative First Officer Nieps and had a family member who had been a state trooper. Again, I'm not claiming a conspiracy against me—just stating facts.

Around this time, I had fired my attorney because he wasn't as aggressive as I would've liked. I made a straightforward request: contact the news media because I wanted to shed some light on what was going on in the New Jersey State Police. He kept telling me that it was going to happen, but it never did, so he had to go. *(Unfortunately, about seven years later, he committed suicide. He was a very soft-spoken and gentle giant. May he rest in peace.)*

My new attorney, M. Jaidem, had also represented other state troopers. He had scheduled a meeting with a newspaper reporter to discuss all of our cases. The reporter painstakingly outlined pending lawsuits that had been filed against the NJSP for exposing their corruption. I assumed the timing of the article, published in a local newspaper in October 2006, had something to do with the ongoing retribution. However, surprisingly, many of my colleagues viewed me as a stand-up person and wished me well in my lawsuit.

About a month later, I forwarded a memo to Assistant Chief Leader Riddle because I didn't want anyone else to suffer similar consequences. In the memo, I mentioned that I had documented my allegation of a pattern and practice of how high-ranking officers found guilty of violating the State's policy regarding the workplace were allowed to retire without being punished. I also claimed that as a result, numerous lawsuits had been filed, which cost taxpayers millions in out-of-court settlements.

I waited for something on the order of a letter noting that he had received my special report and an official apology for what had happened to me. What the hell was I thinking? For me, there would never be an admission on their part.

I knew I hadn't endeared myself to him because he was now required to do something, but I wasn't going to go away until someone had addressed this issue. In the interim, I received a response from the Department of Workforce denying the complaints I had filed against Squadron Officer Sauhund and Investigative First Officer Battle.

Again, I had expected the results of their investigation. However, they failed to acknowledge that while assigned to the Anti Radical Team, (then) Inquirer Rilde was my subordinate. Due to this promotion, he became my immediate supervisor.

Investigative First Officer Rilde was competent and qualified, but I believed, based on my credentials, seniority, and experience, that I, too, should've been considered for the promotion. What is even more suspect was that according to the report, Assistant Chief Leader Riddle "placed" Investigative First Officer Rilde in that position. We had a selection process, so how can someone be placed in a position?

In the coming months, a warrant agent who was in charge of an investigation unit alleged that Investigative First Officer Battle had violated our rules and regulations. As a result, Investigative First Officer Battle received his comeuppance because they removed him from his company head position, transferred him, and took him out of contention for future promotions.

While his misfortune appeared appropriate, it seemed like the New Jersey walls of injustice had collapsed around me. A couple of months after I received the Department of Workforce letter, my attorney told me that my lawsuit was dismissed. At that moment, I believed that they had won. Nonetheless, I instructed my attorney to file an appeal.

In January 2007, after conducting surveillance for three months, I met with Squadron Officer Drecksack in his office. I explained to him that I had difficulty being on the surveillance detail; and on two occasions, due to being stuck in bumper-to-bumper traffic in New York, I soiled myself. I wasn't looking for any sympathy, but a little consideration would've been helpful. I didn't know what type of response I was going to receive, but I placed him on notice that my disability was problematic.

Three months after my meeting, I remained on the detail. There was nothing that I could do and no one else to tell. All the proper channels were aware of my medical condition, but they intentionally ignored me. A few of my squadmates, who were from different police departments, covered for me on several occasions while I made emergency restroom stops.

In April 2007, I delivered a package to our headquarters, and by accident, I ran into Squadron Officer Drecksack in the hallway. "How's it going on the wiretap?" he asked.

His deceitful attempt at making small talk annoyed me, but I played along. "It is going great, sir. We are getting a lot of useful information that we can use later." I thought this was a good time to bring up my difficulties with the surveillance detail again. "Sir, I also wanted you to know that my ulcerative colitis has been acting up, and it is difficult because I don't have access to a bathroom."

He quickly remarked, "I can sympathize because my brother suffers from a similar affliction, and I see what a poor quality of life he has regarding his illness."

His response left no doubt that he knew what stress does to those of us who are afflicted with this disease.

He went on to say, "I will see if there is an administrative position for you."

As a squadron officer, he didn't need to look for anything; he could've just assigned me to that role because it wasn't a selection process.

As expected, I remained on the detail until its completion at the beginning of June 2007. I subsequently submitted two separate requests to transfer to a different unit to get away from him.

Chapter 38

The Redeemer

Leave a legacy so that your deeds will be revered.

A few months after submitting my request for a transfer, the Political Misconduct Unit solicited new inquirers. In response, Squadron Officer Drecksack sent out a mass e-mail to his respective company heads, which stated, "Canvass our personnel to see if any of them want to transfer to Political Misconduct. If they do, they are dead to me." Who says stuff like this? To my knowledge, I had been the only one who had requested a transfer.

How could a commissioned officer be so uncharacteristically irresponsible and childish? Even if it was a joke, the mere fact that he sent it questioned his competency. I subsequently filed an internal complaint against him with the Department of Workforce, but they declined to investigate it. They wanted it resolved internally and returned it to the NJSP.

A short time later, Vice Marshal J. Falem, the (new) commanding officer, called me regarding the complaint. He said that my case wasn't going to be a full-fledged internal investigation. Instead, he'd conduct a performance incident inquiry, which carried no discipline. When he told me this, I knew the fix was in, and I'd have to continue to play their game.

We met in my office, and I told him that I accepted there'd be no discipline meted out. Vice Marshal Falem berated Squadron Officer Drecksack's behavior and politely apologized for his actions. I was satisfied they addressed the issue even though I knew he was sent to appease me. Ironically, I learned Vice Marshal Falem was also a classmate of (now) Assistant Chief Leader Ribbon, Squadron Officer Drecksack, and Investigative First Officer Nieps. Again, just stating a fact. I didn't expect this to go over well with them and waited for what was to occur next. As predicted, I didn't have to wait long.

My third quarterly performance evaluation was due, which should've been prepared by my direct supervisor. However, because I was detached, the task force supervisor, Investigative First Officer W. Koverm, completed it.

Investigative First Officer Koverm was an assistant company head in the Methodical Crime Central Unit. He was junior to me by about a year and a half but outranked me. We met on the first day of the wiretap and exchanged a short greeting. The next time we spoke was about six months later, just before the completion of the wiretap, and that conversation was as brief.

I received my performance evaluation about a month after we completed the wiretap. One afternoon, I came to my office and observed a large manila envelope lying on my desk. I opened it and looked at the benchmarks. Again, I had been dropped and given average ratings in several categories. Once more, for the record, he should've scheduled a meeting with me to discuss any shortcomings and then give me an opportunity to make improvements before dropping me. Even though the performance evaluations are subjective, I often wondered what criteria my supervisors used to evaluate me. As usual, I contested it and requested a meeting with him and his supervisor. The chances of getting it changed would be almost impossible because it would make the initial evaluator look incompetent.

On the day of the meeting, I brought along an investigative officer's union representative as a witness. I paid my union dues, so I might as well take advantage of them. When Investigative First Officer Koverm and his supervisor arrived, I greeted them, and the meeting commenced.

I explained to his supervisor that it was my belief I was unfairly rated. I told him that I purchased a digital camera and used my digital video recorder to assist in the collection of video surveillance footage. I pointed out that on several occasions, my prior experience conducting surveillance, while on the Anti Radical Team, saved the detail when the targets almost got away. Also, I revealed I had only spoken with Investigative First Officer Koverm on two separate occasions, and at no time did he supervise me. Moreover, I told him that even though my medical condition flared up, I had remained on the detail. After presenting my case, it was Investigative First Officer Koverm's turn.

He confirmed our two speaking occasions and that he was unaware of my affliction. He went on to say that he didn't feel he needed to be "hands-on" because I was a senior investigative officer. He admitted speaking with the Unamon County squad supervisor and told me that they commended me for my expertise and participation.

Then why are we here? I thought. His supervisor said he would consider the evidence and get back to me.

Attempting to get my evaluation changed would be troublesome because it rarely happened. That said, two weeks later, we reconvened, and they presented me with a revised assessment that pleased me. However, more fittingly, a few months later, a female state trooper sued Investigative First Officer Koverm and his supervisor for subjecting her to a hostile work environment, gender discrimination, and retaliation.

Toward the middle of 2007, I formally requested to speak with the assistant chief leader in command of the Investigation Branch. Prior demands were either rescheduled or never happened. The meeting was an attempt to be reconsidered for a promotion. Being that we didn't have a fair promotional system, I wasn't going to wait around for them to bestow it upon me. I was going to fight for what I believed I deserved.

In the intervening years, Squadron Officer Nandora—who, years earlier, sat in on my meeting with Chief Leader Ralesny—was promoted to assistant chief leader and agreed to meet with me.

We met in a little secluded office at our headquarters. Typically, an assistant accompanies a high-ranking officer, but she came alone. I thought the setting was strange, but I couldn't complain—at least she decided to see me. I respected her and thought she'd be fair. However, her superior was Chief Leader Ralesny, and he had made it known that he had no use for me.

I presented her with the same documents that I provided to the Office of Official Police Ethics and the Department of Workforce, where I hadn't received a favorable resolution. I watched as she skimmed through my paperwork, and her facial demeanor changed. Her professionalism always appeared front and center, which put to ease my concerns of being ignored again.

I told her, "I'd appreciate if you'd investigate what happened to me and decide who's telling the truth."

She responded, "I can assure you I will conduct an independent investigation and inform you of my results."

I knew she cared about the NJSP but ran into numerous obstacles during her career with some of the cemented old guard philosophy: "We can do whatever we want to do."

Over the next couple of months, my optimism grew slightly.

I didn't want my issues to affect my judgment, so I said as little as possible, even though most of my colleagues knew what was happening to me.

In the fall of 2007, Assistant Chief Leader Nandora called me and said, "Vincent, my investigation is completed, and I want to apologize for what they did to you. I know that it's no consolation, and unfortunately, those responsible have retired."

My heart sank.

She continued, "Although no one can be disciplined, the right thing to do is to transfer you to the Industrial Trash Unit and place you in an acting investigative first officer position."

Finally, someone believed me! The recognition was long overdue, but I knew it would ease a lot of the stress I had endured.

In the coming months, Assistant Chief Leader Nandora retired, so the timing of her promise of promotion had been paramount. She was the only person with the courage to resurrect my career. I can't thank her enough because, at any point, she could've toed the company line and ignored my concerns. My good fortunes didn't stop with her.

In late 2007, I won my lawsuit appeal, and they reinstated my case. Over the course of my last months in the Methodical Crime North Unit, my medical condition became more manageable, and they adjusted my work status and assigned me to two more wiretaps. I monitored calls from suspected mobsters and didn't have to endure the stress of conducting roving surveillance anymore. I looked forward to my new assignment and pending promotion.

Chapter 39

Tested Supervision

Stand beyond the collective norm.

As the New Year rolled in, things began to get better. The New Jersey Legislature finally admitted the State's role in the history of slavery. While it was long overdue, I recognize it took resolve to document it officially. Moreover, in early 2008, I transferred to the Industrial Trash Unit as the acting assistant company head. (The promotional posting came once a year, so my actual elevation wouldn't happen until sometime later.) My new supervisory duties had seemingly provided me with a seat at the table, where we made unit decisions. I had longed for this spot because I wanted to make a difference.

My direct supervisor was the company head, Investigative First Officer W. Shutz, whom I had known since the mid-1990s; however, my transfer negated his cousin (another investigative officer in the unit) from being promoted. Over the years, his cousin and I always had a very cordial relationship because we were academy classmates. He had worked in the unit since 1993 and should've been promoted instead of me based on his institutional knowledge.

After a week, I called him into my office and explained the situation that had necessitated my transfer. I asked him to be patient until I got promoted, and I would then seek a transfer to the academy to help him.

My disclosure appeared to have appeased him, and our relationship remained professional.

The Industrial Trash Unit conducts background investigations on individuals and businesses seeking a license. Historically, mobsters had infiltrated the industry by controlling the labor unions. With my background in organized crime, this was going to be a good transition.

Although my daily functions were administrative, I learned quickly, which allowed me to spend some time in the field with the investigators. I welcomed the opportunity to observe and familiarize myself with their duties.

After several months, our supervisors told us that we had to take on ancillary responsibilities. The Executive Integrity Office, which had disbanded due to fiscal issues, came under our control. They investigated companies applying for school construction contracts. We had received a little reprieve with the addition of three enlisted personnel.

The new inquirers arrived at our office to set up their cubicles. The new squad supervisor was the younger brother of one of the defendants in my lawsuit. My transfer also affected him because he was positioned higher than me in the promotional tier ranking system. Again, I knew this might cause some tension because he, too, should've been promoted before me. Nonetheless, I decided the best way to address this precarious situation was to speak with him immediately.

Once he settled in, we met in my office and talked about our respective career paths. The conversation then turned to when his brother was my supervisor. I made it very clear that on the advice of my attorney, I included several individuals in the lawsuit because of their involvement. I never had a problem with his brother. Reversing the roles, I would've appreciated him letting me know. He said that he understood and looked forward to working with me. I had no reason to believe that he wasn't sincere.

Chapter 40

Manipulated Outcomes

Your view of others may not always be what it seems.

After spending fifteen months in the Industrial Trash Unit, I thought all my troubles were behind me. I got along with everyone in my office and couldn't have been happier. It was as if my equilibrium had returned.

In January 2009, as predicted by African-American novelist James Baldwin in 1963, the first African-American (Barack H. Obama) was sworn in as the forty-fourth president of the United States. While I had a hard time trusting people of color in state government, I gave our president the benefit of the doubt. Yes, we can! Even better, on May 9, 2009, after being denied since 2004, I was officially promoted to investigative first officer. Five damn years! I was overjoyed!

Wait! Pump the brakes! The celebration didn't last long because, within a month of my promotion, the commanding officer decided to transfer me.

Previously, I had told Warrant Agent Shutz, who had been promoted with me, that I had agreed to transfer to the academy because of my academic experience. Someone started a rumor that my next assignment would be the Background Check Unit, which conducted investigations on incoming recruits. The disliked often landed there before retiring. I knew I wasn't their favorite, but I still had a lot to offer.

Once I became aware of the gossip, I met with the new department manager, Squadron Officer Rowlem, to discuss my status. I didn't expect much from her because just like a few of my adversaries, she had NJSP ancestry and would never advocate on my behalf. Why should she? We didn't know each other, but I worked for her, and that is what good leaders should do. Sorry, I digress.

Walking into her office was like going back in time. She had state police memorabilia positioned on her walls, desk, and bookshelves. From all the smiling pictures with other state police personnel, it was evident that they liked her. I asked about the identities of the people in the photos; and as I thought, they were close friends and family members.

I then took a seat, and we discussed my assignment. I questioned my pending removal. She told me not to believe any of the stories, but her hollow response told me otherwise.

We discussed my unsolicited transfers and continuous positioning at the bottom of the promotional tier ranks. I then told her about my expectation of being promoted to warrant agent and figured she'd pass it along to her boss. Instead, she said, "You are still on probation for your recent promotion." Technically, she was right, but there were others who circumvented that rule. I knew she didn't have any authority to promote me, but she said she'd forward my concerns to Vice Marshal T. Falsch—mission accomplished.

In no time, I met with Vice Marshal Falsch and his assistant, Squadron Officer M. Depp. Vice Marshal Falsch and I had worked together at the Greenville Station in the early 1990s. He was also formerly in charge of the Office of Official Police Ethics and had been personally aware of my prior allegations against several high-ranking members. I was anxious to hear his justification for transferring me.

Like any other meeting I had had with someone I had worked with, we reminisced about our past. Back then, Inquirer Falsch requested my presence to help him lock up a notorious carjacker from Elkanda. I knew he probably felt more comfortable working with me because I was black and from Elkanda. Due to our work history, I had expected a lot from him regarding resolving some of my concerns.

When we eventually got down to business, I explained my reason for requesting the meeting. Vice Marshal Falsch said, "Your supervisor speaks very highly of you." He then said, "Warrant Agent Shutz told me you'd be amenable to transfer once your promotion became official."

I reiterated my position. "Sir, I am pleased where I am because it is a reasonable accommodation. Also, I agreed to transfer, but only to the academy."

He then said, "When I made the recommendation, there were no specifics regarding your wishes."

I couldn't fight the transfer because it was a lateral move, and I wouldn't be affected financially or as a supervisor. At that point, I knew anything I said would be counterproductive because his word was final. He then said, "You have been highly recommended for your administrative skills, and based on my operational needs, I could use you in the Neutron Surveillance Unit."

Additionally, I explained (retired) Assistant Chief Leader Nandora's reason for promoting me and why another one was warranted. He looked a bit perplexed because he, too, said I was still on promotional probation. My dissatisfaction with all the cookie-cutter leaders was mounting. However, what he said next stunned me. He proclaimed, "When I was in the Office of Official Police Ethics, I read the official report regarding your retaliation allegation. And while it was unsubstantiated, I still had many unanswered questions as to why your promotional rankings dropped without a legitimate reason."

Now, I don't proclaim to be the smartest inquirer of the bunch, but if I had read an investigation report and still had questions about its findings, I'd deem it incomplete.

Vice Marshal Falsch was about to retire and had provided Squadron Officer Depp, who would be his replacement, with options for resolving this matter. He recommended that I prepare a report outlining my concerns to the Advancement Criteria Unit and have them support any possible redress. I had hoped that he would suggest a more realistic alternative, but maybe he didn't know any better.

The Advancement Criteria Unit is responsible for making sure that each unit followed the "promotion" policy. However, its concept is oxymoronic because there has never been a bona fide system to promote anyone objectively. I submitted the report anyway but knew I was jumping through hoops to make them address the inherent inequities.

The promotional process entailed a few first officers and warrant agents sitting in a room and advocating for the person(s) they want to get promoted. There is a consensus regarding the top picks for promotion, but they had to go through the motions of a meeting and officially document that an actual process took place. A list is then generated and presented to the squadron officers, vice marshal, and assistant chief leaders before being sent to the chief leader for validation. The chief leader then submits the final list to the Office of Professional Lawyers for their approval. Those not selected are then ranked concerning who would be next in line to get promoted. It is purely subjective, which makes it more controversial. The most disturbing thing about this process is that everyone knows it's a sham—even the unions.

Within a month, I received the Advancement Criteria Unit's official response. According to them, everything was forthright, and my situation wasn't going to change. To make it even worse, their patron saint of bad news was an African-American messenger. So predictable.

In mid-2009, I transferred into the Neutron Surveillance Unit, which was probably the most specialized technical unit in the NJSP. Fortunately, I was there for my administrative abilities and didn't need to get involved in the day-to-day operations. I met with my new company head, Warrant Agent J. Sahila, who had been in the unit for more than twenty-three years and was an expert in the field of electronic surveillance. He showed me around and introduced me to my new colleagues.

I quickly settled in and learned my duties. I reconciled telephone and cable accounts, which amounted to a yearly expenditure of approximately $500,000. Any mistakes on my part could potentially jeopardize ongoing criminal investigations, wiretaps, or surveillance operations that utilized our services. I did what they required, but I wasn't going to allow my concerns to fade.

My last-ditch effort to get my past issues resolved would be at the discretion of Assistant Chief Leader Andrist, who had replaced Assistant

Chief Leader Nandora. The rotating door at the higher ranks made it challenging to build a relationship with those who cared about our future.

Assistant Chief Leader Andrist had worked closely with Assistant Chief Leader Nandora and had been aware of the reason for her promoting me. I also learned that he was a doctoral student and an adjunct professor, which made us academic colleagues. I believed he was a decent person based on things that I had heard about him.

A few weeks had passed, and I met with Assistant Chief Leader Andrist and the recently promoted Vice Marshal Depp in our Central Headquarters. I didn't have a game plan because I wanted to speak freely and let the dialogue dictate the direction of our discussion.

Initially, we discussed my productivity in the Industrial Trash Unit, and then we talked about my transfer to the Neutron Surveillance Unit. I told him that I didn't think that Warrant Agent Sahila was mentoring me, and I asked to be moved somewhere else. He interrupted me and said he was familiar with Warrant Agent Sahila's management style and would be making some changes. He then asked, "Do you think you're capable of taking over the Neutron Surveillance Unit?"

I thought briefly and responded, "From a technical standpoint, I don't think I have the skill set."

He rebutted, "I understand. But with your education and leadership ability, I believe you're a perfect candidate."

I smiled and said, "I'd appreciate the opportunity."

After several minutes of small talk, we said our obligatory goodbyes.

It was refreshing to interact with someone who cared about standards. Based on our meeting, I believed things were going to get better. However, the drama from the Civil Servant Council (formerly the Department of Workforce) continued.

After approximately two years, I received the results of my complaint against Squadron Officer Drecksack. Again, I wasn't shocked by their anticipated unsubstantiated findings. They claimed that after a thorough review of all the documents, they found no evidence that I complained to anyone that being on a roving surveillance detail was difficult due to my medical condition. They also claimed that they believed that I was content with my assignment and didn't need a reasonable accommodation.

Their response was utterly ridiculous. How can conducting surveillance be a light duty assignment if I required access to a bathroom? Within two weeks of receiving their findings, I was back in their office to resolve other stalled investigations because I had to go through the motions.

I had previously submitted a special report to (retired) Assistant Chief Leader Riddle regarding corruption within the Office of Professional Lawyers and had hoped to get some updated information.

I met with an all-too-familiar person: Ms. J. Vider, director of the Civil Servant Council. At one point, she had been in charge of the Work Intervention Unit, which had also stalled my prior investigations. I paused and waited for her to rattle off something nonsensical.

Predictably, she said they hadn't started it. Almost three years had passed since I had filed the complaint. Ironically, they were in the process of investigating my allegations against the Office of Professional Lawyers for intentionally stalling an investigation. I can't make this crap up. She went on to say, "Vincent, I must also apologize because the complaint you filed against Chief Leader Ralesny in 2004—for a violation of your reasonable accommodation claim—wasn't addressed in our prior investigation."

We were in 2009!

At every level, when I reported internal corruption, they retaliated against me. I thought the Civil Servant Council was an independent agency, but it became apparent that all State agencies perpetuated the charade. Of all the cases that I had filed with them, the average time it took to complete their investigation was about two and a half years. Their "Model Procedures for Internal Complaints Alleging Discrimination in the Workplace" only allocated a total of 180 days, including extenuating circumstances, to complete an investigation. I knew what they were doing, so I sat back and waited for their inevitable unsubstantiated findings. However, they threw me a curve ball by having my pending case assigned to another State agency.

At first, I was upset; but I realized that this, too, was a part of their diversion. I needed to carry on fighting the internal factions within state government; but I knew that if I didn't continue to do my job, they'd have ammunition against me. Nonetheless, they hobbled my career again.

Chapter 41

Rendered Invisible

Struggling is as gratifying as prospering.

As time progressed, my assignment in the Neutron Surveillance Unit had gotten better. Warrant Agent Sahila's attitude changed, and he taught me the unit's inner workings. We had developed an exceptional relationship and understanding with each other.

The most thrilling part of my job was watching the inquirers conduct their daily tasks. They were the real artisans and did exceptional work. Climbing telephone poles and installing covert surveillance cameras was just part of their day-to-day activities. It brought back memories of my days in the military. Their most unusual feat was designing contraptions to fit into awkward areas to gather either video or audio recordings.

After a few months, and with the retirement of Assistant Chief Leader Andrist, a new department manager, Squadron Officer D. Samen, transferred in and took command. He was the former administrative officer for Assistant Chief Leader Andrist and had graduated from the NJSP academy two classes after me. With his inclusion, my former Industrial Trash Unit supervisor, Warrant Agent Shutz, was elevated as his assistant department manager.

Within weeks, Squadron Officer Samen met with everyone under his command to discuss career development. During our meeting, he spoke about his management philosophy, while I provided him with my expectations of the promises made to me regarding advancement. He replied, "Based on your recent promotion, you're still on probation and in the bottom tier of the rankings." I got tired of hearing this response. Their rationale is that once you get promoted, you automatically go to the bottom tier for the promotion to the next rank.

Ironically, they promoted both Squadron Officer Samen and Warrant Agent Shutz when I received my promotion, but they were still in line for their next promotion. Regardless, I believed the plans had already been put in place, and I presumed the unit would be turned over to me once Warrant Agent Sahila had retired.

Several weeks later, Warrant Agent Sahila and I attended an administrative meeting with other company heads and their assistants. My expectations were high because this was going to be my opportunity to interact with my peers so they could get to know me.

A lot of technical and administrative dialogue was discussed, but I spoke up when it pertained to the Neutron Surveillance Unit. At the end of the assembly, Squadron Officer Samen went around the room and asked for everyone's thoughts. Sitting directly to his left, I should've been the first person to express an opinion. However, he deliberately skipped past me and started with the person sitting to my left. I looked down at my hands to make sure I wasn't dreaming and that I was actually at the table. There was no way he could've missed the only African-American in the room. I waited while he went around the table and my colleagues spoke. In fairness, I thought he would've given me the final word, but it didn't happen. Being at the table meant nothing because they didn't acknowledge my presence. When the last person finished, he thanked everyone and quickly walked out. His deliberate snubbing crushed my spirit as I departed.

When I returned to my office, Warrant Agent Sahila pulled me to the side and said, "I saw what happened. I could understand how you feel."

I replied, "I am used to it." What else could I have said?

Within two days, I met with Warrant Agent Shutz because Warrant Agent Sahila told him about my apparent brush-off. He attempted to appease me and maintained that Squadron Officer Samen didn't do it intentionally. However, I questioned why I met with him and not the squadron officer. Nonetheless, I let it go.

In the coming weeks, as things settled down, I got involved with the day-to-day operations. I didn't know when Warrant Agent Sahila was going to retire, but I had no problem remaining in the unit. However, one morning, while in my office, I received a telephone call from Warrant Agent Shutz requesting a meeting with him and the squadron officer. I wondered what they could've wanted because I hadn't filed any complaints against anyone. To the contrary, I was quite happy and got along with all my new colleagues.

When we met, I immediately knew something wasn't right. Squadron Officer Samen's typical phony smile was gone and replaced with a look of concern. We shook hands, and his weak grasp was different from the firm one that I had previously noticed. Wasting no time, he said, "I want you to know that I think you are doing a great job." He went on to say that Vice Marshal Depp asked him to present me with a potential transfer option to the Transportation North Unit as a zone supervisor. He then said, "If you accept the offer, it will look favorably upon you, and I could see a promotion for you to warrant agent in eighteen months to two years."

He should've just extended his hand so I could kneel down and kiss his ring for being so kind. We discussed the reason for the transfer, and I instantly knew that I was being asked to step aside so others could get promoted.

Squadron Officer Samen then said, "You can change your mind if you aren't happy."

Frustrated and tired of being undervalued, I reluctantly agreed.

I returned to my office and told everyone of the probable transfer. Most were shocked that I accepted the offer, but I was just exhausted from all the years of fighting. The transfer would, in fact, be a downgrade in the title and supervisory responsibility. They had no justification for moving me other than that they can do whatever they want.

Later that evening, I made a few telephone calls to get the advice of a few trusted colleagues. They said I'd be foolish if I accepted it. I respected their opinions and subsequently sent them an e-mail to advise them that I had changed my mind.

The next morning, while on my way to work, Warrant Agent Shutz called me on my cell phone and said he had received my e-mail and wanted to speak with me. We met in his office, and I told him that I believed Squadron Officer Samen's comments were a veiled threat. He attempted to defend his boss, but I interrupted him and said that I would willingly accept a transfer, but only if given an assistant company head's position. He stated that he would schedule a meeting with Vice Marshal Depp to discuss my concerns. As a result of my transfer, I learned that they would promote three white males and demote me. The sliding scale for promotions never seemed directed toward my benefit.

In early 2010, Warrant Agent Sahila and I met with Vice Marshal Depp. Warrant Agent Sahila attended the meeting because he wanted to advocate on my behalf. We walked into his office and were about to take a seat when Vice Marshal Depp said, "Who invited you motherfuckers?"

I didn't think he was talking to us, so I turned around and saw Squadron Officer T. Macal (an executive officer) and Squadron Officer Samen standing behind me. I wasn't expecting them to be there for his backup, but he could've at least been more professional.

We all sat down, and he started the conversation by telling me that he was pleased with my performance and that everyone spoke highly of my interpersonal skills. Blah, blah, blah—my fine-tuned bullshit detector immediately tuned him out. We then discussed why he needed to move me. We agreed that a seasoned squad investigative officer, whom I supervised, needed to remain in the unit instead of getting transferred. With my expectation of taking over the unit, I had advocated on the investigative officer's behalf and looked forward to him being my assistant.

However, Vice Marshal Depp then smugly said, "I thought I was doing you a favor because the new office is close to your home."

I interjected and asked him, "What happened to Assistant Chief Leader Andrist's offer of placing me in charge?"

He quickly replied, "You misunderstood what he said."

From his comeback, I knew the situation would go nowhere.

He then said, "No one predicted Warrant Agent Sahila would retire so soon, and I can't move you from the bottom of the tier rankings." He went on to say, "If I promote you, I would be facing litigation for years."

I knew he didn't care about being sued because it wasn't coming out of his pocket.

I expressed my apprehension with being downgraded and stripped of supervisory duties. I said, "Not only would it be embarrassing, but it would also signal to the white inquirers that I wasn't to be respected."

He claimed it wasn't a demotion. I was unaware of anyone else that previously served as an assistant company head and then demoted to a zone supervisor position.

As the conversation continued, he then told me that I would also be "operational" and placed back on the streets to lock up criminals. He surprised me with this statement because he was well aware of my medical condition and reasonable accommodation.

We bandied back and forth until he became noticeably upset by my stiff posture and responded, "I didn't have to have this meeting with you. The only reason I am doing it is that I like you!"

I was so lucky for his generosity. His unprofessionalism caused the conversation to come to a head when he commented on my pending lawsuit and how it would possibly resolve any past retaliatory issues. He was out of line because it had nothing to do with him. I told him, "It seems like you've made up your mind, but just know that you're advocating for someone to be promoted to investigative first officer at fourteen years, which took me almost twenty-four years to achieve!"

After everything was said, I couldn't continue to hide behind a fake smile to keep from showing my true feelings. I then stood up, shook his hand, and departed from the meeting. Consistently meeting with the likes of these men, whom I knew had no intention of supporting me, made me realize that I needed to have my head checked. I kept telling myself to deal with the nonsense because I would be retiring within the coming year.

I'd seen them attempt a similar bait-and-switch move before, so my immediate thought was to challenge the subjective transfer; but I knew that he would prevail. I then looked into his premise that I was still on promotional probation. It seemed rather strange because they promoted a few of my colleagues who were in a similar situation. I also needed an official answer about the difference between an assistant company head and a zone supervisor.

I contacted the director of the Personnel Document Unit, who was responsible for maintaining information regarding rank and job descriptions. She confirmed my suspicions that a zone supervisor was indeed a step down from an assistant company head and a decrease in supervisory responsibility. I waited two days before the official transfer before filing a complaint against Vice Marshal Depp and Squadron Officer Samen.

As the days passed, my looming transfer date became closer. I tried to wrap my head around the enduring blatant disrespect and racial discrimination. I went to my office looking like a walking zombie. The dark circles under my eyes made them appear puffier. My body was there, but I was mentally a beaten man.

One afternoon, while driving home from work, an unexpected deep thumping in my chest caused me to pull over. My breathing instantly became labored, and my heart started beating faster: I couldn't slow it down. Was this the beginning stage of a heart attack? I gathered myself and immediately drove to the emergency room, where they performed a battery of tests.

Soon after, I met with the attending physician, a soft-spoken middle-aged black man who had a calming bedside manner. We talked briefly about my negative results for any heart condition, but he suspected that I had suffered an anxiety attack. When he said this, I looked away because this should've been something that I could control. He then questioned me about what was causing the anguish, and I went off on a tangent about damn near everything that had happened to me since being transferred to the Work Intervention Unit. Afterward, he strongly suggested that I find a better way of coping or the next incident might be cardiac arrest. Everything in my life had spiraled downhill.

The day of my transfer, I met with my new supervisor, who a day before I outranked. Due to the build-up to the inevitable, I mentally couldn't accept the ongoing retaliation. I advised him that I didn't feel well and went home. An impromptu visit to their official doctor caused me to be placed on sick leave—again.

While out recuperating, as expected, they promoted the three white males I had mentioned. Upon my return a few months later, they placed me back in an assistant company head position in the Transportation North Unit.

Chapter 42

Deconstructing the Hype

Test the waters of change or drown in a sea of inertia.

For nearly two decades, they programmed me to believe in the New Jersey State Police "we are all family" rhetoric. If that was the case, I couldn't explain why some of my colleagues, whom I thought were friends, became distant. The lifeline I needed for survival always failed me.

The continuous retaliation became equivalent to getting a root canal; they kept drilling and drilling until they could get to the base of their problems—me. I didn't want to appear incapable of handling pressure, so I remained in the game because I had a duty to protect future state troopers from the callousness of the corrupt leaders. My participation also provided information for others to follow should they consider becoming a whistle-blower.

Reporting internal misconduct doesn't come without consequences. Retaliation is a bedrock tactic used by many agencies as a useful tool to intimidate and dissuade those daring to challenge them. In any event, whistle-blowers need to document everything that happened to them. I can't overemphasize this enough. A legal way to accomplish this is to request as many internal records that you can obtain. Gathering these files is typically achieved by petitioning the State's Open Public Records Act, which houses all government records. More importantly, if you secure documents outside of the normal process, they most definitely will come after you for releasing confidential information, which has the potential to get you suspended—so be careful.

The whistle-blower must also exhaust all internal mechanisms regarding their allegations. The State of New Jersey requires that you report your complaint to an investigative unit. In my case, every time I believed they retaliated against me, I filed a complaint. When my complaints were internally investigated or pursued by another State agency, they were all predictably found to be unsubstantiated. As a result, I filed several appeals.

Even though they denied all my appeals, I did everything they required to move forward. It also left a trail of additional evidence—if the lawsuit ever made it to court.

On several occasions, I tried to resolve or settle this matter. After I had filed my lawsuit, I attended a "court-ordered" arbitration meeting along with an attorney from an outside law firm hired by the State. This type of firm handles a significant number of civil lawsuits filed against the State of New Jersey because of political patronage, but how they are selected is anyone's guess.

The court-appointed arbitrator recommended a promotion to warrant agent without any back pay. Several state troopers had settled their lawsuits with a promotion instead of monetary gain, and mine should've been a no-brainer. After consulting with my attorney, we agreed to the proposed settlement. I just wanted what I believed I had earned and hoped the corruption would cease. Unexpectedly, they didn't accept and reneged. At that point, I knew that this matter was personal for someone. The arbitration hearing cost me thirteen hundred dollars, and the State (or taxpayer) paid a similar fee. I believe their position was to send a clear and unequivocal message that I'd never be promoted to the commissioned officer ranks, no matter how much it would cost.

In another attempt to shed light on taxpayer abuse, I reported my suspicions of the outside law firms to the Office of Financial Affairs—another State agency. I met with an investigator whom I knew from my days of working on the Anti Radical Team. He told me that I wasn't the only person who had come forward. He said, "We have open source documents, which confirmed that for the calendar year 2008, the State of New Jersey paid more than forty-five million dollars to these law firms." He went on to say, "Our office is investigating how certain law firms got on this list to conduct business."

I told him, "If I can be of any assistance, please give me a call." I left their office knowing they, too, were full of it. For the record, no one called.

Also, I highly recommend that future whistle-blowers avoid divulging confidential information to any in-house employee assistance counselor. They are not your friends. Their job is to protect the State. Conversely and more importantly, I strongly advise consulting with a private mental health professional because of patient-client confidentiality. My therapists did a fantastic job helping me reconcile many unresolved issues. In the end, however, the most significant decision that the whistle-blower must make is whether they are going to subject their family to the extreme amount of stress that will inevitably follow. The toll can be insurmountable, and some aren't mentally capable of dealing with it. Numerous whistle-blowers have committed suicide and this reality hasn't escaped law enforcement as well.

Initially, I thought my problems were manageable; but the adverse effects and lack of organizational support were, at times, more than I could bear. The counseling sessions lessened my stress, and working out at the gym at 5:00 a.m. helped even more. Several times, I stood in front of a punching bag contemplating how much damage I was going to inflict upon it. It wasn't enough just to sweat. I needed to experience the stinging pain vibrate throughout my fists, wrists, and arms. My shoulder joints ached from the relentless pounding, but I was in destruction mode and didn't care if I hurt myself. I had damaged my hands and often walked away with torn and bloody skin on my knuckles—but it made things better.

Lastly, in spite of my health issues, I knew I did the right thing by exposing the truth. However, the most disturbing aspect of my ordeal was the dreadfully unexpected behavior of some two-faced colleagues.

Chapter 43

Decolorized Gatekeepers

Don't let complicity be your new opiate.

Over the years, many people proclaimed that everyone must challenge themselves and step outside of their comfort zone to find their true meaning. As I wrote this chapter, William Shakespeare's quote rang out: "To thine own self be true." These words have guided my actions throughout my adult life, and I had to take responsibility for all the decisions I had made.

In 1903, Dr. W. E. B Du Bois—a noted black intellectual and civil rights activist—wrote that the "talented tenth" or the "exceptional men" of the black race would teach and lead while bringing about social change. His bold prediction fell well short of its stated objective because of some compromising black folks who didn't live up to their responsibility. A lot of work still needs to be done.

Writing this chapter was a struggle because reading it might tarnish someone's image of the outfit. However, it is essential because many minority state troopers believe that an implicit internal Jim Crow-ism still exists. They promoted some black and Hispanic state troopers to the command staff and seemingly essential positions within the organization but routinely segregated them from actual power. A new doctrine—"included but still unequal"—became an unofficial policy.

The NJSP claims to utilize objective criteria to select its leaders, but you'll never find any document that would pass the scrutiny test of its validity.

In a paramilitary organization, a person's earned rank garners respect. Many local and county police departments incorporate a test or interview for their promotion process. In most cases, the best-qualified person is probably chosen—unlike the NJSP, where someone's character and integrity could prevent them from advancement. Reprehensibly, the NJSP replicates leaders who are routinely called stab in backs. Similar to going to a restaurant and needing to take a seat facing the door to see who's coming in, I never trusted the shady individuals with real or perceived power. The list of these people is inexhaustive because once one retires, others are already waiting in line.

It is my opinion that our entire promotional system has been historically subjective and inherently defective; it needs immediate revamping. There are too many storylines to follow when it comes to promotions. Who are friends with whom? Will favors be called in? Will you pledge undying loyalty to my command staff and me? To say the least, it is an ass-kissing and a "good ole boy" network. I subscribe to the theory that they should promote someone based on a total person concept (i.e., seniority, merit, education, disciplinary record, emotional intelligence, and performance evaluations). The only good thing that I will say about the promotional system is that everyone must pass a physical agility test before being considered. This requirement does not get prorated over the course of someone's career.

Chief Leader Ralesny made two failed attempts at instituting a written promotional test. Each one was based on our internal standard operating procedures and had no component to measure anyone's potential. His figurative kicking the can of a promised promotional exam throughout his administration frustrated most. Taxpayers doled out hundreds of thousands of dollars to a politically connected vendor, only to later have it scrapped. However, I—like many of my colleagues—passed both exams.

There had been rumors that some of his inner circle didn't meet the educational requirements for promotion. He disregarded the entire process to promote more of his cronies to the higher ranks. In the late 1980s, there were only two assistant chief leaders and five vice marshals. During Chief Leader Ralesny's term, he increased the number of assistant chief leaders to six and the number of vice marshals to twenty, which allowed him to build his fiefdom.

Trickle-down leadership is ineffective, especially when the chosen ones didn't have to go through a formal and fair process. Moreover, I believe Chief Leader Ralesny did it to maintain a splattering of minority contestants strategically placed in his command staff so that he could showcase diversity on the official NJSP website. As a learned man, Chief Leader Ralesny failed to realize that he perpetuated this delusion and never empowered the chosen minorities based on the offices he had assigned them.

To date, New Jersey and Rhode Island are the only state police agencies that don't require an objective promotional test. As a result, it is preposterous for anyone to believe that we have developed the most qualified. Our record of highly publicized internal scandals is endless. If they don't implement a legitimate process, we will continue to be criticized and ridiculed in the media. Some of his command staff personnel were like dandelions, which, on the surface, appeared acceptable; but behind the scenes, they were destroying an otherwise professional garden. We had the talent, but he continually surrounded himself with some who were also corrupted by their rank.

In his book *Highest Duty: My Search for What Really Matters*, Captain Chesney "Sully" Sullenberger wrote, "To get promoted, you had to be a good politician. You needed to develop alliances and find a well-connected mentor. Yes, certain people . . . I didn't put the effort into it. I felt I could get by on my own merits . . ."

Captain Sullenberger is the airline pilot who saved all the passengers on Flight 1549, which crashed into the Hudson River in January 2009. Like him, I prepared myself so that I didn't have to play any political games or be a part of the secret social handshake clubs. I didn't have the time or energy to go through the whole fake male bonding. I couldn't see myself befriending people whom I knew were dishonest and devoid of plain decency. Self-determination chartered my course to rid me of any vestiges of the "special favors" progression.

In the grand scheme, I couldn't begrudge anyone who sought personal advancement; however, I took exception when it came at the expense of compromised morals. I will never prop up those who don't come correct. *Some* of the minorities chosen to lead the Work Intervention Unit may have closed their eyes to the brazen racial and gender discriminatory practices. They also alienated and discounted the complaints of non-favored white state troopers. Based on the individuals that I knew, there was no doubt in my mind that they were intentionally placed in charge to make it appear that they'd take minority complaints seriously. Their silent consent and blind loyalty are character flaws; but in the world of the NJSP, it equates to promotional advancement. Nevertheless, unlike them, I couldn't shut up, and I didn't know my place. I wasn't conditioned to be a lemming that marched in lockstep over a cliff and not question suspect authority. I understood that they didn't have the courage or conviction to speak out. As a result, organizationally, we have been at the mercy of men and women who follow amoral orders that have curbed our progress.

Certain minorities, quite naturally believed that they were a part of the "A-Team." They felt entitled because some of them had been the only face of color in the decision-making meetings. As the cup runneth over, they probably didn't realize that the "Kool-Aid" they drank caused them to overlook having their strings pulled by the "puppeteers" (Chief Leader Ralesny and Assistant Chief Leader Ribbon). These misguided folks used their faux power as a hustle and became the deal brokers for the establishment. Surprisingly, many of them complained early in their careers that, for a myriad of reasons, they were overlooked for a promotion. Interestingly, I often heard some of them say that they couldn't help other minorities because they'd be viewed as playing favorites.

The game has always been unfair; now they think that by doing it the right way, things would change. Sadly, they hid their ignorance in plain sight. The systematic poor state of minorities in the NJSP is due, in part, to selfish individuals who only cared about their paths.

Remnants of Stockholm syndrome fester in many of their psyches because their opinions favored the hierarchy who continually screwed us. We've never marched in a synchronized fashion because something or someone always derailed our cadence.

To those African-American individuals chosen as the perfect minority, who've dependably been absent from doing more to bring attention to the glaring discrimination, "You should all be ashamed of yourselves!" You were supposed to be our Tuskegee Airmen and set the standard for our greatness, but some of you were the low-hanging fruit that they quickly picked and co-opted. Perhaps this cowardice dates back to when some of our ancestors were enslaved and didn't want to upset their "master." While slavery allegedly ended on June 19, 1865, some of you continued to have a slave mentality. Your self-hatred appears fringed on a mental pathology, which needs to be professionally treated.

Dr. Joy DeGruy, a renowned social researcher, wrote in her book *Post-Traumatic Slave Syndrome: America's Legacy of Enduring Injury and Healing,* "As a result of centuries of slavery and oppression, most White Americans in their thoughts, as well as actions, believe themselves superior to blacks. Of greater import, too many African-Americans unconsciously share this belief." I think this theory partially explains why many of us looked to our white counterparts for acceptance.

Foolishly, I expected a few of the credible minorities to vouch for my character with their upper-echelon peers; but the range of the black experience is vast, and I couldn't presume many of them to be down for any cause other than their own. To some of them, I was the infamous persona non grata, and they didn't want to be in my company. When they observed me approaching, they'd nervously walk away.

We needed to close ranks to curtail the constant internal problems. However, they, too, showed their true colors because I eventually found myself battling against their "black wall of collusion." To add insult to injury, a select few, over the years, subserviently testified in court that there was absolutely no racial discrimination within the New Jersey State Police. Really? Undoubtedly, my depiction will upset some, but it only applies to those if the shoe fits.

Now don't get me wrong; I understand that "double marginality" is prevalent among minority groups in law enforcement. Nevertheless, I wasn't going to diminish my racial identity just to be accepted as some of my colleagues did so well. Working for a predominately white male organization can be very conflicting, but there are times when you must upset the boss man to make him realize that he is wrong. While I know the NJSP didn't corner the market on the game of discrimination, the hierarchy played it so well and kept the conversation relevant. For African-Americans and other minorities to combat it, we must continually debunk the social order, which assumes that any person of color is inferior.

Disgracefully, some of my self-centered associates maintained the prevailing system of corruption and were rewarded with an enhanced pension for their conspiracy of silence. Still and all, I wonder how they will feel when they have retired and are referred to by the generic prefix, Mr. or Ms. To them, I ask, "Do any of you remember the forty years of our exclusion and what the first African-American state trooper sacrificed for us in the 1960s?

For those Hispanic individuals who are similarly guilty of not doing more, I say, "Get off the bench and get into the damn game." For years, the image of race in the NJSP had, for the most part, been a binary of black and white. However, Hispanics have surpassed African-Americans as the most significant minority group, but their increased numbers didn't always translate into contiguous promotions.

The Deployment Control Section housed a significant number of Hispanic state troopers, and at one time, it was headed by a bona fide Spanish-speaking assistant chief leader. In conferring with some of my colleagues, the consensus was that the assistant chief leader didn't advocate on their behalf. All the same, what also perplexed me was that Chief Leader Ralesny, a non–Spanish-speaking half-Hispanic, had sanctioned this conspicuous rebuffing as well. Ironically, several years earlier, I recall a conversation with (then) Investigative Officer Ralesny, where he complained that he wasn't getting promoted because he was Hispanic.

For those former Hispanic colleagues who were placed in command positions and did absolutely nothing, I say, "Your silence hurts you more than you know." Don't forget about the numerous undercover details that they recruited you for because of your specific language skills, only to give the promotion to your well-connected white colleague. Do any of you remember the forty-plus years of your exclusion and what the first Hispanic state trooper sacrificed for you in the late 1960s?

Finally, for those female individuals who reaped the benefits of trailblazers that fought against inequity, I ask, "When will it be your turn?" Being subjected to sexual harassment and gender discrimination should've caused a lot of you to be outraged. However, except for a select few, most of the females who privately acknowledged the despicable behavior never publically alleged it. You had a chance to expose the contemptible culture, but you failed. I guess some wanted it to remain a well-kept secret, but their tacit compliance will probably subject future female state troopers to similar conduct. Do any of you remember the fifty-plus years of your exclusion and what the first female state trooper sacrificed for you in the 1970s?

Undoubtedly, a few of my former colleagues will claim that I am displeased because of my stymied promotional trajectory. This sentiment is partially correct. I, too, had lofty goals of ascension like most. Nonetheless, my lack of promotions was solely due to a few vindictive individuals who were given the green light by Chief Leader Ralesny and Assistant Chief Leader Ribbon to deliberately sabotage my career.

As for Chief Leader Ralesny, he may have been in charge of the outfit, but he was never the overseer of my convictions. He didn't have enough self-awareness to leave at the appropriate moment and must have had some secret files on a few politicians for him to survive several administrations. However, similar to the governor, his stint at the helm should've had a term limit of no more than eight years as well. Expectedly, he squandered several opportunities to make institutional changes. He targeted the rank and file for their offenses but came up woefully short by not punishing his command staff personnel who were culpable for more egregious acts. At some point, I had hoped that he would come to his senses and reveal that he had a shred of common decency. Let's say I am still waiting.

In the latter part of my career, I was often referred to as a malcontent by some commissioned officers. I couldn't care less about their impression of me. They couldn't bully me, and I'd be damned if I became their all-too-familiar company man or that turn-the-other-cheek type of person.

New Jersey's political corruption pollutes every aspect of government, and more individuals needed to stand up and represent the voiceless. I am glad that I dared to provoke them while I was still employed because "my integrity matters!" To my naysayers, I must impart a relevant quote by Marcus Garvey: "Men who are in earnest are not afraid of consequences."

Chapter 44

Resilience

Let a storied past be your new beginning.

I am what I am, and nothing more. When you see me, see me and not what you want to see, because I can only be who I am and what I am. Just me.

Well, that is my story. In retrospect, some of the negative things that happened to me have framed the person I am today. Reporting the internal corruption weighed on my conscience because I had to do it. I often wondered why more state troopers didn't because they didn't need permission to do the right thing. Moreover, in writing this book, I intended to share my thoughts regarding why I became a whistle-blower and to provide a blueprint for others to follow.

My ulcerative colitis mentally took me to some dark places. Visions of having my colon removed tormented my daily process of reflection. As I continued writing, however, I derived significant meaning from my struggles.

In navigating forward, the NJSP, under the auspices of the Office of Professional Lawyers, needs to implement a fair disciplinary and promotional system. Nonetheless, I've done my part to call attention to the issues that existed for me. However, regarding any authentic reform, the conversation continues to travel in a circular motion with absolutely nothing getting resolved. Just ask those that suffered under Chief Leader Ralesny's tenure.

Any optimism regarding the Office of Professional Lawyers becoming a respectable law enforcement entity waned over the years. Most of the assistant commander solicitors that I dealt with had no compunction about lying even though they were officers of the court and had taken an oath. In spite of my delusion, I realized that our system of state government is—and, for a very long time, has been—inept and unprincipled.

As for the NJSP, even though there have been two minority leaders, it is my firm belief that based on a documented history, they continue the legacy of being an intolerant organization. Their discrimination is tantamount to a herpes virus that you usually don't see until it blisters. As expected, it made periodic appearances over the course of my career and brought negative media backlash along the way. We needed a self-check litmus test to address the systemic structural discrimination. Hopefully, one day, white male state troopers will recognize the power of their privilege and confront the internal problems. They need to share a few of the private conversations they've had with other white state troopers concerning racial and gender discrimination to push this issue to the forefront.

In addressing the historical discrimination, the New Jersey State Police needs to set up a public forum, similar to the former apartheid South Africa's Truth and Reconciliation Commission, which granted immunity to those who committed atrocities and confessed their involvement. A comparable day of reckoning would allow past and present leaders an opportunity to tell the truth about how they mistreated those who challenged them.

The repetitive chant of positive change was marginal at best. For the NJSP to evolve, they need to select a leader who will abolish nepotism, cronyism, racism, homophobia, sexism, and all other established internal corrupt principles. Until then, we will remain in a collective denial of the problems. I realize this is an excellent benchmark to attain, but we must attempt it because the citizens of New Jersey have high expectations.

Whistle-blowing presents an ethical dilemma for the law enforcement profession. Thus, it is critically important that whistle-blowers are provided sanctuary under the New Jersey Personnel Oversight Decree, a State policy that must be taken more seriously for it to become active. Despite the negative repercussions, however, if professional standards are improved and corruption ceases, then the practice of whistle-blowing justifies its means.

There have been more than eight thousand members who have earned the right to don our uniform. Serving side by side with a significant number of them has been an honor. Luckily, the majority of them didn't succumb to the learned behavior of the internal dysfunction.

In many organizations, there are some who believe that the governing rules don't apply to them. Much of the institutional change that we were forced to adopt (i.e., video cameras and documentation of the race and gender of occupants in motor vehicles) was undertaken as a result of two cosmetic federal consent decrees, the last of which came during my career. Each should've served as an autopsy to figure out what has factually injured us, but they only placed a gauze pad on the infected wound.

Pathetically, though, we will go through harder times because of a cohort of close-minded command officers who—like in Machiavelli's *The Prince*—became intoxicated with power. I neither feared nor respected them because similar to the cowardly character in the *Wizard of Oz*, they, too, stayed behind a protective curtain (their rank).

Leadership is like threading a needle. You don't always get it right the first time; but with earnest practice, your chances get better. However, I compared our bad organizational syndrome to the arcade game *Whac-A-Mole*. You knock down one incompetent leader and another one pops up in its place. In echoing the words of the late defense attorney Johnnie Cochran, "We don't paint all policemen with the same brush, but we have to change the culture so that the bad police fear the good police." Embarrassingly, the opposite is the status quo in the NJSP.

They promoted some of the state trooper defendants in my civil lawsuit at least twice. They elevated Squadron Officer Drimmer to the rank of vice marshal just before he unexpectedly passed away.

I have mixed emotions about his untimely death because he had badmouthed me to others. I'm quite sure he was trying to save face, but he should've told the truth. At one point in my career, I considered him an associate. Before his transition, he could've reached out to me and cleared his conscience about the sexual harassment because they swept my accusations under the rug. Disappointingly, he chose to take it to his grave. I hope he didn't destroy anyone else's career.

Countless memories have filled my employment—mostly good and a few that were bad. Lamentably, however, throughout my hardships, it was Chief Leader Ralesny's fringe involvement in the misconduct that ruined the latter years of my career. He allowed many of his cronies to attack my character, and his unconscionable reactionary responses to the never-ending problems only aggravated matters. At times, I wondered if there was anyone in charge or if the outfit was operating on autopilot. His lack of proper guidance kept us on the road down a cul-de-sac and never allowed the organization to progress. Numerous state troopers filed lawsuits against him—one of which, according to the news media, was for retaliation because of an allegation that he fathered a child out of wedlock. Whether it is true or not is none of my business, but it goes to show the trouble he attracted. He often dismissed the lawsuits because he claimed that in any large organization, you are bound to have some people who are dissatisfied.

The millions of dollars paid to settle civil lawsuits during his tenure should've been an indication that something was wrong. In my opinion, he is a disingenuous person and a shameless liar, which was confirmed by a vote of no confidence given to him by the rank and file in the latter part of 2011. The continued scandals and the crisis with some of his command staff who lacked credibility boggled my mind.

Our system was imperfect, and as the idiom "to act as the canary in the coal mine" came to mind, I had to challenge the entire disciplinary reporting process to prove that it was irresponsive. Foreseeably, I paid more than my share of physical and mental dues. Over the years, several friends asked me why I didn't just quit. I can only say that it was my psychological programming that conned me into thinking that things would eventually get better.

When I became a state trooper in 1985, I expected to stay for a maximum of thirty years as long as I was healthy and enjoyed working. As it became unmistakably apparent that our system of justice had been undermined and ignored at every level, it cemented the fact that I needed to leave ASAP. No way was I going to live in the shadow of what could have been. I didn't want to be the braggart who proclaimed to be the most senior state trooper in the outfit and hang around for an "attrition promotion."

During the months leading up to my retirement, I talked to a few of my academy classmates regarding our respective careers. Most believed that the NJSP provided a great opportunity, but the novelty of the job had worn off. As time passed, some of us started to experience the unfavorable effects of a system that didn't recognize individual talents. Many retired at the twenty-five-year mark, a few stayed to pay off their kids' college tuition, and some remained a bit longer to maximize their pensions.

As my last days wound down, I made a conscious decision to mentally divorce myself from the organization. I could no longer shoulder the daunting responsibility of being one of the few who tried to fix our dysfunctional family. Many of my colleagues whom they promoted to the commissioned officer rank often displayed the same dictatorial traits of former superiors that they complained about years earlier. The "Dr. Jekyll and Mr. Hyde" personalities I had observed over time became too exhausting to decipher.

However, I owe the outfit a debt of gratitude because they've made me the disciplined and professional man that I am today. I want to think I was an ambassador in and out of uniform and will mourn the end of my career. My departure was bittersweet because I will miss a lot of my former colleagues. We shared something special, but I eagerly look forward to life as a civilian with a new identity.

The day I turned in my uniforms and duty weapon to the state trooper assigned to the logistics unit, he had asked me if I wanted anything as a keepsake. I momentarily paused because I had previously thought about what I would say if asked. I told him, "No, just take it all." The bewildered look on his face didn't bother me because he had no idea about my conflicted journey.

At the beginning of 2011, I officially retired as an investigative first officer. However, I didn't allow my retirement to halt my resolve to rid the outfit of its discriminatory practices. As a result, I opened a pro bono consulting business to assist others. I have spoken with numerous state troopers, local police officers, and corrections officers who had heard about my lawsuit and reached out to me for guidance. My reward is that they continue the fight.

Chapter 45

Day of Reckoning

A corrupt system cannot remain intact if truth perseveres.

In the fall of 2011, I accepted a full-time tenure-track professor's position. My health had gotten significantly better, and things were going well. At times, I had completely forgotten that my lawsuit was still pending. However, the old emotions surfaced when my court date arrived a year later.

The day of the trial made me realize that my state police journey was going to end where it all started—in the City of Elkanda. Returning home was a compelling irony.

Walking up to the front doors of the courthouse was a somber moment. The halls of justice never interested me because it appeared that they only served those who could afford it. I wanted my cynicism to be wrong.

Over the years, I didn't divulge many of my issues to anyone; but my mom knew everything. Sadly, she had seen a lot of the physical stress that the lawsuit had caused me, but I wanted her to witness me telling my story to the jury. Although we were always extremely close, we became inseparable after I started to see she was growing a little forgetful. I moved back home because my siblings lived in another state, and I wanted to care for her properly. Ultimately, my life revolved around her when she developed bladder cancer and began to deteriorate before my eyes. Nonetheless, it was an honor chauffeuring her to all her doctor's appointments because it gave us more quality time together.

With an inability to predict the future, I focused on having her tell me about her life, much of which I never knew. While the talks were numerous, the one that stood out was when I questioned why she had a picture of a "white Jesus" on her bedroom wall. Her response was contentious. I should've known not to challenge someone raised in the South. My attempt at giving a funny retort almost caused me to get smacked. In the end, I'm glad she had a strong faith that eased her concerns about life. Just sitting next to her and listening to her stories was an extraordinary experience.

Unfortunately, the bladder cancer was too much for her to overcome. Death knocked on her door and stole my beacon of light. Mom passed away approximately six months after her diagnosis and just days after Mother's Day and her seventy-fifth birthday. She embodied everything that was good in life. Our last few months together will forever be memorable. While I understand dying is natural and inevitable, I am at peace. I know her positive spirit will be there to get me through the trial.

The sheriff's officer situated at the front entrance to the courthouse made me empty my pockets and walk through a metal detector. After twenty-five years in law enforcement, it felt weird being a civilian.

Once cleared to proceed, I noticed my attorney standing off to the side. He appeared confident because he had tried cases in this building for almost forty years. We took the elevator to the third floor to meet my fate. The butterflies in my stomach fluttered continuously, and I had to breathe deeply to calm myself.

The building's interior decor was immaculate, which made me wonder why the rest of the city wasn't as well. Polished beige marble floors and redwood benches accentuated the hallway's ambiance. There was also an unexplained calmness, which seemed contradictory to a criminal court system that I had dealt with for many years. Then it dawned on me. This courthouse resolved civil trials that catered to those seeking monetary damages. My issues were about principles, but the New Jersey State Police made it about taxpayer's money.

I believed the judicial system set me up to fail because the presiding judge dismissed my case back in 2006. My attorney attempted to get her to remove herself because we didn't think she would be fair, but she denied our motion—another reason for my skepticism.

Walking into the courtroom didn't sit well with me knowing my case was close to being decided. Positioned in front of the room was a long brown table with four red leather chairs placed underneath. Slightly ahead of it was a similar desk that accommodated the court clerk and the assigned sheriff's officer. The judge's bench sat elevated, giving it an air of judicial superiority. To the left was the jury box where eight perfectly aligned chairs sat empty. Filling those seats with fair-minded peers was paramount for my trial.

Judge David entered from her chamber's door in the standard black robe. She was a rather attractive middle-aged woman with streaks of gray hair, which gave her a regal appearance. Everyone stood to afford her the respect that accompanied her position. Even though I was displeased with her previously throwing out my case, her soft voice and gracious smile kept me sidetracked. Once she settled in, we all took our respective seats.

One of her duties was to lead the jury selection process. Her expertise was evident as she waded through the approximately one hundred unfortunate citizens selected for the pool. In all of my years, I never found one person who wanted to sit on a jury. After apprising them that the trial would take about three to four weeks, more than half the potential jurors raised their hand to be excused based on a hardship. You see, I told you.

As I looked out into the courtroom, I wondered how many people I might know. Sitting in the back row was a family member I hadn't seen in a while. I knew that I had to tell the judge because if he was selected, it was going to cause a problem. I leaned over to my attorney and told him about my situation, and they sent my cousin home. I had a sense of fair play because I wanted everything to be aboveboard regardless of the conclusion.

Following a somewhat heated downsizing and several peremptory challenges, the final jury comprised of four African-American women, two white women, one Hispanic woman, and one white male. Only six of the eight jurors would decide the case, and the remaining two would be the alternates. The white male juror and one white female juror were relegated to a separate room, while the remaining six took their places. The judge's instructions were very succinct; the defendants would start, and we'd follow.

The defense attorney stood about 6'3" tall and looked dapper in his blue designer suit. He brought along an office associate, an attractive young woman who appeared fresh out of law school. Her pubescent facade had later annoyed me because it didn't coincide with her brilliant performance before the judge. However, over the course of several years of interaction, I developed a level of respect for them because they always acted professionally; it wasn't personal.

The defense attorney stood up and slowly walked toward the jury box and presented his opening remarks. He looked at them and said, "Discrimination is not so bad." Puzzled looks were evident on some of the juror's faces. He went on to say, "We discriminate in our everyday life."

I thought, *Where is he going with this?*

He continued, "We discriminate in the television shows that we watch and even in the soda flavors that we drink."

I couldn't believe that he was being paid a sizable hourly rate to come up with such malarkey. He then stumbled over his remaining scripted comments, which only took about five minutes. I looked at my attorney, and he had a look of disbelief on his face. He quietly leaned over and whispered in my ear, "My opening will be about an hour."

When the defense rested, my attorney smugly stood up, faced the jury, paused momentarily, and then told them, "You are not going to hear about or see a smoking gun. However, you will have to view all the evidence in its proper context."

For the next hour, as promised, he systematically described every aspect of my allegations and poignantly explained how I became a de facto enemy of the New Jersey State Police. After he finished and returned to our side of the table, I whispered in his ear, "Excellent job."

After the introductory comments had concluded, we took a break. The defense attorney motioned my attorney to the side and pompously offered us twenty thousand dollars to settle. They believed that they were going to get the case dismissed. He had no clue that I was going to fight them to the marrow of my bones.

When my attorney presented me with their offer, I told him, "This isn't about money. I want my day in court." He then looked at the defense attorney and shook his head to indicate no deal.

In the interim, the defense submitted several briefs to exclude some aspects of the case. We adamantly challenged their motions, but they succeeded based on a two-year statute of limitation. The judge disallowed the sexual harassment complaint, racial discrimination allegation, and everything against the Office of Professional Lawyers. It was a bastardization of the legal process because justice was supposed to be blind—instead, deceit had shackled its legitimacy.

My whistle-blowing and reasonable accommodation claims survived the judge's chopping block. The only individual being held responsible was Chief Leader Ralesny, and the single entity on trial was the New Jersey State Police. With the stage set, my attorney called me to testify.

I walked toward the stand while trying to remain as composed as possible. Still mourning the passing of my mother, I had lost weight from not eating correctly, and my usually fitted blue suit loosely sagged and may have given off a different perception. I then took the stand, raised my right hand, and affirmed that I'd tell the truth.

For approximately seven years, I had waited for this day to arrive. Like most events in my life, I was going to do it alone. I looked out into the courtroom and only saw my adversaries' sullen facial expressions. The occasional ominous stare was comical. I never let my fears survive; so if I wasn't afraid to challenge them before, what made them think they could rattle me now?

Recounting my law enforcement background established my credibility. My attorney gave me enough leeway to tell the jury about all my assigned units. Afterward, he asked me about my formative years. When I spoke, my eyes locked on to the jurors' so they could gauge my sincerity.

My descriptions of my employment at the pizzeria and car wash garnered slight smiles from three of the African-American jurors. Their subtle nods kept me optimistic that they were paying attention. The trial was going to be a long competing narrative, but I wanted them to remember my plight.

I testified for a day and a half before the defense had their opportunity to ask questions on cross-examination. It didn't make a difference what he'd ask me because the truth never changed. I had expected an elaborate question-and-answer session, but he only wanted to know one thing: "Have you ever asked someone to retire before completing an investigation?"

Unsure of what he was attempting to glean from me, I indulged him. "Yes, but I was told to do so by SACS Esel." Similar to his opening, his cross-examination was just as brief.

At the end of my testimony, the jurors had an opportunity to ask questions for clarification. The keenness of their inquiry sent a strong message to the defense that they had a vested interest in getting to the truth. The judge eventually excused me, and I returned to our side of the table. I looked at my attorney and noticed a bewildered expression on his face. He then asked, "What is their defense?"

The next witness that we called was Warrant Agent K. Nieps. We had already gotten a glimpse of his testimony because we deposed him about two years earlier. We expected him to be their weakest link. All his hearsay allegations against me came from my academy classmate Investigative Officer Payasa. The jury was now going to hear what caused me to have my promotion to investigative first officer stalled for five years.

Warrant Agent Nieps recounted the numerous conversations and communications he had exchanged with Investigative Officer Payasa. As a well-seasoned inquirer, he should've known better than to take someone's word without adequately vetting the source or at least confronting me. Of the six complaints that he had filed, none had anything to do with what I said or did. His feelings were hurt because he believed I had been talking about him behind his back. As he sat giving testimony, I wondered if he felt foolish because when asked if he had heard me say anything disparagingly about him, he replied, "No." After we had discredited him, the defense attorney tried to salvage his testimony to no avail.

Next up was Squadron Officer Kriecher. Here again, we already knew what he would say. He had been disciplined early in his career for lying and falsifying reports in an internal affairs investigation. Our strategy was to compare his career to mine because he was a year younger but had six months more on the job. It didn't take long for my attorney to smear his reputation.

On the stand, even though he was my adversary, he did an excellent job. I appreciated him because he was very thorough. His stellar military background added to his professionalism, and he had a command of our internal policies. The fact that he was well-spoken gave him more credibility. However, another problem, aside from his disciplinary issues, was that he didn't have a college degree. Unlike most of our colleagues, they promoted him four times within five years. The jurors looked confused about his upward mobility compared to the fact that I had to fight for a single promotion within that same time frame. A separate issue I believed he faced was that he was the only enlisted African-American witness and may have appeared suspect to the African-American female jurors. After a half day of testimony, we discarded him, and there was no significant rebuttal. The first two days went exceedingly well.

The following days were even better. The first witness was Ms. Polly. Our only concern was that she claimed Chief Leader Ralesny said my career was over due to my medical condition. Of course, she denied any knowledge of him saying it; but we exposed her as being a stooge for the NJSP, which would be documented in the official transcripts for other state troopers to read.

Next, we summoned Chief Leader Ralesny to testify. He didn't come in his state police uniform, which I had expected because that was his identity. He did, however, bring along a contingent of yes-men. I had not seen him since we deposed him two years prior, and his face looked weathered. It seemed that the stress of actually being the first sitting chief leader to have to testify in a whistle-blower lawsuit might have caught up to him. His appearance was monumental because I knew that he wasn't going to stray from his deposition testimony, which meant he had to lie—again.

Chief Leader Ralesny walked toward the stand, and I immediately noticed that he looked like he couldn't be bothered. As customary, when he raised his hand, he swore that he'd tell the truth, so I couldn't wait to hear his responses.

My attorney subtly lured him into a sense of calm by asking him questions about his state police and educational background. He was appointed chief leader in a hotly contested challenge from an authentic Spanish-speaking Latino candidate.

The selection process for his chief leader's position was unique. The Office of Professional Lawyers allowed interested candidates to submit their résumés online for prescreening. I forwarded my résumé, and unfortunately, I never received a follow-up e-mail. But at least I tried.

Chief Leader Ralesny was the first chief leader who had attained an advanced degree and attended a prestigious business school. His pedigree should've impressed any jury. My attorney then seized the moment and asked him what he thought about my credentials. He claimed that he believed that I was competent and knew I had a doctorate and had graduated from the Federal Training Academy.

We then threw him softballs, and I sensed that he was comfortable testifying. In fact, as the head of the NJSP, there shouldn't have been much that could have rattled him—if he was telling the truth.

After softening him up, my attorney went for a body blow and asked him the first of many accusatory questions, which caused the jury and the judge to doubt his testimony. "Chief Leader Ralesny, do you recall having a meeting with Mr. Martin and (then) Squadron Officer Nandora in which he apprised you of his allegations?"

I knew that he had lied at his deposition, but I was unsure of what he was going to say in court. He said, "No, I don't recall that meeting."

His answer reminded me of Los Angeles Police Department, Detective Mark Fuhrman saying that he didn't recall calling black people "niggers" in the O. J. Simpson trial.

Three of us were at that meeting, and there was no way he could have forgotten it. There could only be one reason for his response. The power that he believed he had over the years had gotten to him and made him think he was untouchable. I looked at the incredulous facial expressions of the jurors, and my optimism grew slightly.

The grilling continued as my attorney followed up with a memo authored by Squadron Officer Nandora that documented the meeting. For added emphasis, we had him read it aloud to the jury. After finishing, he said that he still didn't recall it. I guess it's not perjury if you tell a lie long enough and you start to believe it. He should've known that jurors are unforgiving if you lie to them. We had peeled back his lack of character and exposed him.

During his testimony, my attorney asked him several questions about my reasonable accommodation claim. His response probably did as much damage as he confirmed that he knew about my condition, but he denied saying that my career was over because of it. As our questioning wound down, the looks on the jurors' faces revived my faith in the judicial system. When Chief Leader Ralesny walked off the stand, his body language was very telling. He didn't have the swagger as the head of the state police; instead, he looked indefensible.

The remaining defendants—Squadron Officer Sauhund, Squadron Officer Samen, Investigative Officer Battle, SACS Esel, and Assistant Chief Leader Ribbon—all took the stand toward the end of the trial but couldn't say anything to dishonor my career. However, SACS Esel flat-out lied about never suggesting that I not submit my "special report" outlining my concerns about internal corruption. This bothered me because she was an officer of the court—and if she lied, who else would follow suit? Overall, they only tried to justify that their actions against me were warranted.

As a rebuttal witness, we brought in a female supervisor that Squadron Officer Sauhund had discriminated against while we were under his command. She detailed all the unfair treatment by Squadron Officer Sauhund against her, another minority supervisor, and me. I gave her my ultimate respect because she testified while still working for them.

The last non–state police defendant, Investigator Locus, probably did the most damage to their case. He had investigated Warrant Agent Nieps's allegations against me. When asked what he thought about them, he said that they were all based on a "bitching session" among some state troopers. For a moment, I thought he was intentionally trying to sabotage them. Afterward, we told the judge that we didn't need to explore it any further.

With the whistle-blowing testimony completed, Squadron Officer Drecksack testified regarding my reasonable accommodation complaint. He had already stated that he was aware of my medical condition in his deposition, so we didn't need to drill down any further into his testimony. His claim that he thought I had been assigned to an office listening to wiretaps didn't fly with the jurors. When told that I remained on the roving surveillance detail until its completion seven months later, he stuttered and stammered over his explanation of why it happened. For me, it was a wrap.

The defense attorney then recalled some of the defendants for clarity. As each one of them retook the stand, I observed a sense of arrogance from their body language. I sat and waited for them to attack me.

Most people have an image of themselves that may be in stark contrast with how others view them. I knew I wasn't immune to this self-perception, so I wanted to hear why they believed I might have been incompetent. However, they didn't present any evidence to justify their beliefs.

After they finished, my attorney's rebuttal, again, made them look suspect. I questioned whether they had a Plan B. I believed they thought my case was going to be thrown out.

My heart fluttered as both sides finally rested. After a drawn-out three-week trial, my case was on the verge of being resolved. The judge instructed the jury regarding what they were to consider in rendering their decision. Afterward, they asked pointed questions about damages. I wondered what the other side was thinking.

The jurors were eventually sent to the deliberation room and required to answer eight specific questions. The first seven related to me being a whistle-blower, and the remaining question pertained to my reasonable accommodation claim. The waiting game had begun.

They had so much information to digest, and as we neared the end of the first day of deliberation, my attorney turned to me and said, "No doubt this will be held over until tomorrow." I had seen this scenario on numerous court television programs and had to decompress.

Around half past four, the jurors sent a question to the judge asking for clarification on one of the charges. The judge advised that they had already been given specific instructions and told them to keep deliberating. Moments later, the jurors notified the court officer that they had reached a verdict.

That was quick, I thought to myself.

A small cadre of attorneys that had been observing the court proceedings walked up and wished us luck. My attorney turned to me and shook my hand. I looked him in the eyes and told him, "Regardless of the verdict, I am proud of the job you did."

Just as the female jurors walked back into the courtroom, we stood as they took their respective seats. The top of my stomach cramped, but I kept my composure. When the foreperson read the verdict, I knew all eyes were going to be on me. I didn't know if they would prevail or if I'd become the victor.

The judge then asked, "Madam Foreperson, have you reached a verdict?"

My knees quivered, and my upper body tensed as she stood up and said, "Yes, we have, Your Honor."

A repetitive drumroll rang out in my head as the judge read the first question. "Has plaintiff Vincent Martin proved by a preponderance of the evidence that they retaliated against him in violation of his whistle-blowing claim?"

The jury foreperson answered, "Yes."

The judge then asked, "Has plaintiff Vincent Martin proved by a preponderance of the evidence that they retaliated against him in violation of his reasonable accommodation claim?"

Again the jury foreperson answered, "Yes."

At that moment, I knew I had won.

After the judge had released the jury from their duty, she addressed both sides and thanked the attorneys for their professionalism throughout the court proceeding. She went on to say that it was going to be her last trial, and she was retiring from the bench.

My attorney told me that the governor probably punished her for allowing the case to proceed. Strangely, his disclosure troubled me because I remembered the stress that I had endured when she initially threw my case out in 2006. All the same, I appreciated her pleasant disposition.

The thought of winning also made me realize that the State would find a way to overturn the jury verdict. Regardless, my saving grace is that I am free from their retaliatory grasp.

Chapter 46

The Final Judgment

Wake up early before it's too late to be great.

Politics and corruption are predictable bedfellows in New Jersey. After the verdict, they wouldn't leave well enough alone and couldn't care less how much it would cost; their goal was to exhaust me financially. Something needs to be done about this because they are playing with house money, and the deck is stacked against all litigants.

They appealed the verdict, and the Appellate Court found that the trial judge gave fatally flawed instructions to the jury, and they remanded the whistle-blowing portion of the case back to the trial court. As for my reasonable accommodation claim, the judges sided with them in that they had not waived their "sovereign immunity" when it came to their defense. What that meant was because they are a State entity, I couldn't sue them, and they dismissed my claim. Nevertheless, we appealed to the New Jersey Supreme Court, which only selected a few cases every year to examine. Fortunately, we prevailed, and the fight continued.

At the beginning of 2017, after hearing oral arguments from both sides, the New Jersey Supreme Court rendered its findings. In a stunning decision, they reinstated my initial claims of discrimination, which were similar to my reasonable accommodation claim, and they entered a judgment in my favor and awarded me substantial monetary damages. They also left the door open to pursue a trial for my whistle-blowing allegations.

I expressed to my attorney that I was satisfied with the results and didn't want to pursue a new trial. However, after negotiations with representatives of the Office of Professional Lawyers, we settled the pending matter, including interest and attorney's fees. Coupled with the monies paid to the outside law firms and salaries paid to staff, the taxpayers of New Jersey were forced to dole out more than two million dollars for the incompetence and arrogance of a select group of State employees that didn't care about telling the truth. And to think that this matter could've been resolved ten years earlier with a single promotion to warrant agent without any back pay.

Litigation should never last this long. After more than thirteen years, the drama was finally over. I will be eternally grateful to our New Jersey Supreme Court for rekindling my shaken belief in the criminal justice system.

The result of the jury's verdict and the New Jersey Supreme Court's decision shed some light on the internal issues and ended any questions regarding Chief Leader Ralesny's actions and complicity throughout my lawsuit. His legacy of numerous lawsuits filed against him and individual members of his command staff is a reflection of the climate he created. The internet has recorded his transgressions and chronicled a trail of careers he ruined. Nonetheless, he wasn't the only guilty party. The Office of Professional Lawyers is the most noteworthy culprit because they allowed him to go forward with his retaliatory exploits. They must dissolve their relationship with the outfit because they cannot defend and prosecute state troopers and still serve in the best interest of the taxpayers.

In due time, I know I will forgive my nemeses. The dates of their retirement staggered and my soured feelings diminished slightly as each left the outfit.

As I finally put this ordeal behind me, history will evaluate whether my actions were beyond reproach. Only time will tell.